STEP·BY·STEP

Gourmet Cookbook

STEP·BY·STEP

Gourmet Cookbook

—

Creative cooking made simple

Wordsworth Editions

Step-by-Step Gourmet Cookbook

If you have ever hesitated over the idea of inviting friends to a dinner party and announcing *Petit Sauté de Poulet aux Girolles*, then the *Step-by-Step Gourmet Cookbook* is for you.

Cooking in the very best classic tradition need not necessarily mean years of apprenticeship to some master *chef de cuisine*. Many famous recipes, though their very names may *sound* complicated at first, are really quite straightforward once they are explained and laid out in a straightforward way. The *Step-by-Step Gourmet Cookbook*, whilst not for the beginner, makes excellent classic cooking as straightforward as it can be.

The recipes are graded according to their required skills into three categories, using a star system: 'Very simple', 'Simple' and 'Challenging'. The full preparation and cooking times are given as an added guide, and each recipe's instructions are presented in numbered stages, with suggestions for garnishing and decoration. Many of the pages also have additional footnote paragraphs with yet more advice and information, side-dish recipes and handy tips.

The *Step-by-Step Gourmet Cookbook* tells you how to make everything from *canapés* and *terrines* to *Jambonneaux de Poulet aux Cèpes* (Stuffed Chicken Legs with Mushrooms), from seafood salads to *Châteaubriands Béarnaise* (Porterhouse Steaks with Béarnaise Sauce). Hors d'oeuvre, fish, vegetable dishes, exotic desserts – and there is a guide at the back to help you choose the most suitable wines for each part of the meal. The contents listing gives all the recipes in their English names, and these appear beneath the French at the head of each recipe. The *Step-by-Step Gourmet Cookbook* puts gourmet cooking right at your fingertips.

You will find *Petit Sauté de Poulet aux Girolles* on page 89. It takes just 45 minutes. *Bon appetit, et bonne chance!*

Table of Contents

Each dish is followed by its total preparation and cooking time. (See note 1 at the end of this Table.)

The star (★) system used throughout the book, indicating the degree of simplicity or difficulty of each recipe, is as follows:

★ *Very simple*   ★★ *Simple*   ★★★ *Challenging*

Notes: Getting the Best out of this Book

1. The preparation times given in the Table of Contents and with each recipe are minimum times: they will vary according to the cook's ability and the equipment available. Certain of the recipes require periods for macerating or chilling. These have not been taken into account in the times given in the table, but are indicated in the recipes.

2. It is best to use double cream for most recipes – it is the nearest equivalent to French cream. Remember also that the French use unsalted butter, and this is assumed in the recipes unless otherwise stated.

3. Certain of the recipes require cooking *au bain-marie*. This consists of placing whatever is to be cooked in a saucepan inside a larger saucepan filled with almost-boiling water. This method is ideal for cooking certain delicate sauces or other dishes which would react badly if exposed to a direct heat.

4. It is always best to use red or white wine vinegar in the recipes where vinegar is required; the result will not be the same if you use malt vinegar. In the same way, freshly ground black pepper should always be used in preference to ready-ground pepper.

5. Oven Temperatures. The following are Gas, Fahrenheit and Centigrade equivalents:

Gas	¼	½	1	2	3	4	5	6	7	8	9
°F	225	250	275	300	325	350	375	400	425	450	475
°C	110	120	140	160	170	180	190	200	220	230	250

6. It is important when using these recipes to follow the exact proportions. A set of kitchen scales, measuring jug, glass and spoons are essential. Follow either metric *or* avoirdupois measurements in each recipe.

7. To help you choose the right wine for your meal, see page 160.

Artichauts aux Bouquets

Serves 4. Preparation: 15 min Cooking: 35 min

Artichokes with Prawns

★ ★

- ○ **4 artichokes**
- ○ **juice of 3 lemons**
- ○ **200g (7 oz) prawns**
- ○ **15 sprigs chervil**
- ○ **200ml (7 fl oz) double cream**
- ○ **20g (¾ oz) butter**
- ○ **salt and pepper**

1. Cut off the stalks of the artichokes. Trim about 1cm (less than ½ in) off the ends of leaves. Wash well under cold running water, spreading the leaves slightly.
2. Bring to the boil a large saucepan of water and the juice of 2 lemons. Add the artichokes and cook for 30 minutes. Drain and leave to cool.
3. Meanwhile, shell the prawns. Put aside. Squeeze the juice from the remaining lemon. Wash the chervil and chop finely.
4. When the artichokes have cooled, spread the top leaves, pull the inside leaves out and, using a teaspoon, scrape away the hairy choke. Put aside.
5. Melt the butter in a frying pan. Add the cream and stir until it starts to boil. Add the remaining lemon juice. This should result in a frothy sauce. Then add the prawns and chopped chervil. Season with salt and pepper. Leave to cook for a further 2 minutes.
6. Fill each artichoke with the mixture and serve at once.

For a heartier dish, serve this over boiled white rice.

Concombres Farcis

Serves 4. Preparation: 10 min Cooking: 35 min

Stuffed Cucumbers

★ ★

- ○ **2 cucumbers**
- ○ **½ head fennel**
- ○ **1 small green pepper**
- ○ **3 stalks chard**
- ○ **1 mozzarella cheese (about 175g/6 oz)**
- ○ **50g (2 oz) flaked almonds**
- ○ **5 sprigs fresh mint**
- ○ **coarse salt**
- ○ **juice of 1 lemon**
- ○ **30g (1¼ oz) butter**
- ○ **salt and pepper**

1. Peel the cucumbers, cut off the ends, and halve lengthways. Scoop out the seeds and discard.
2. Prepare the vegetables: wash the chard and fennel; wash the pepper and discard the seeds. Cut the vegetables into pieces and steam them for 20 minutes (10 minutes if using a pressure cooker).
3. Melt 20g (¾ oz) butter in a frying pan over a medium heat. Brown the chard, fennel and green pepper for 5 minutes. Reduce the heat. Add the remaining butter to the frying pan and sprinkle in the almonds. Fry gently until they are beginning to brown. Then add the finely chopped mint leaves. Season with salt and pepper and mix well.
4. On chopping board roughly chop the contents of the frying pan. Meanwhile, bring to the boil a large saucepan of water, and add 2 pinches of coarse salt.
5. Blanch the cucumbers in boiling water for 5 minutes. Drain and leave to cool.
6. Stuff each cucumber with the vegetable mixture. Press the stuffing down and leave to cool. Arrange the cucumbers on a serving dish. Surround with the remaining stuffing and pour over the lemon juice. Garnish with strips of mozzarella.

Poivrons Farcis

Serves 5-10. Preparation and cooking: 1 hr 30 min

Stuffed Peppers

★★

○ **10 medium-sized green peppers**
○ **1 onion**
○ **1 clove garlic, chopped**
○ **700g (1½ lb) minced steak**
○ **100g (4 oz) rice**
○ **6 tomatoes**
○ **15ml (1 tbls) olive oil**
○ **30g (1¼ oz) breadcrumbs**
○ **30g (1¼ oz) butter**
○ **1 bunch parsley, finely chopped**
○ **salt and pepper**

1. Preheat the oven to 170°C (325°F; gas mark 3).
2. Bring some salted water to the boil in a large saucepan. Cut the tops off the peppers (these will be used as lids), remove the seeds and core, and wash. Blanch the peppers and lids in boiling water for 5 minutes. Remove and drain, but leave the water on the heat.
3. Plunge the tomatoes into the water for 10 seconds. Drain, peel and remove the seeds. Put aside 2 tomatoes.
4. Heat the olive oil in a frying pan. Add 4 tomatoes and mash them with a fork. Season. When the liquid from the tomatoes has evaporated, reduce the heat and simmer for 15 minutes, until the sauce thickens.
5. Peel the onion and slice thinly. In another frying pan melt 20g (¾ oz) butter over a medium heat. Sauté the onion slices for 10 minutes. Add the garlic and minced steak. With a fork, mix in the rice, chopped parsley and the 2 remaining tomatoes, chopped. Season and simmer for 5 minutes.
6. Spoon the stuffing into the peppers and cover with the lids. Place in an ovenproof dish.
7. Soften the remaining butter and combine with the breadcrumbs. Spread over the peppers. Surround the peppers with the tomato sauce. Place in the oven and cook for about 1 hour, or until tender.

Feuilles de Vigne Farcies

Serves 6. Preparation: 30 min Cooking: 1 hr 20 min

Stuffed Vine Leaves

★★★

○ **1 tin (500g/18 oz) vine leaves**
○ **150ml (10 tbls) olive oil**
○ **500g (18 oz) onions**
○ **200g (7 oz) rice**
○ **50g (2 oz) currants**
○ **30ml (2 tbls) pine nuts**
○ **3 lemons**
○ **salt and pepper**
○ **15 mint leaves**

1. Peel the onions and slice thinly. Heat 60ml (4 tbls) olive oil in a frying pan and brown the onions over a low heat for 10 minutes. Add the rice and cook for 5 minutes.
2. Squeeze the juice from 1 lemon. Wash and chop the mint leaves. Add the mint, lemon juice, pine nuts, currants and 45ml (3 tbls) olive oil to the rice in the frying pan. Season. Simmer for 5 minutes, then leave to cool.
3. Wash the vine leaves in cold water. (If you have been able to obtain fresh vine leaves, blanch them for 3 minutes, then drain.)
4. Spread out a leaf, shiny side downwards, and place a tablespoon of stuffing into the centre. Fold the stem end over the filling, then fold the sides towards the middle and roll up. Squeeze the rolled vine leaf lightly in your hand. Continue with the rest of the leaves in the same way.
5. Layer the stuffed leaves tightly in a flameproof casserole. Squeeze the juice from 1 lemon and pour over the vine leaves. Add 45ml (3 tbls) olive oil and 30ml (2 tbls) hot water. Put a plate over the stuffed vine leaves to prevent them from opening while cooking. Cover with a lid and simmer for 1 hour. Leave to cool in the casserole. Serve cold, garnished with the remaining lemon, sliced.

To make a mayonnaise: in a bowl, dissolve 3 pinches of salt with 5ml (1 tsp) vinegar. Add 1 egg yolk and 5ml (1 tsp) French mustard. Mix with a wooden spoon. Leave to stand for 1 to 2 minutes. Then add 100ml (3½ fl oz) of oil, a little at a time, beating continuously with a wooden spoon. Finish beating with a whisk.

Canapés à la Tapenade

Serves 5-10. Preparation and cooking: 20 min

Anchovy Paste Canapés

★

- ○ **10 slices bread (from a cottage loaf), crusts removed**
- ○ **1 small green pepper**
- ○ **200g (7 oz) large black olives**
- ○ **100g (4 oz) anchovy fillets in oil**
- ○ **30ml (2 tbls) capers**
- ○ **60ml (4 tbls) olive oil**
- ○ **juice of 1 lemon**
- ○ **pepper**

1. Stone the olives.
2. Mash the olives, anchovy fillets and capers. Add the olive oil, a little at a time, along with the lemon juice, until you have a thick sauce. Season with pepper to taste and refrigerate.
3. Cut the pepper in half, discard the seeds and cut into thin strips.
4. Toast the bread on both sides. Spread the sauce on the hot toast and garnish with the strips of pepper.

Canapés aux Anchois

Serves 4. Preparation and cooking: 15 min

Anchovy Canapés

★

- ○ **4 slices white bread, crusts removed**
- ○ **2 small tins anchovies in oil (50g/2 oz each)**
- ○ **10 radishes**
- ○ **3 sprigs parsley, roughly chopped**
- ○ **3 hard-boiled eggs**
- ○ **pepper**

1. Cut each slice of bread into 2 triangles.
2. Shell and slice the eggs. Wash, trim and slice the radishes.
3. Put the anchovies with their oil in a saucepan. Leave them to melt over a low heat, stirring with a wooden spoon, until they take on the consistency of a paste. Remove from the heat and season lightly with pepper.
4. Toast the bread on both sides and spread with anchovy paste. Garnish with the slices of egg and radish and sprinkle with parsley. Serve at once.

Canapés à l'Ail et aux Oeufs

Serves 2-4. Preparation and cooking: 15 min

Egg and Garlic Canapés

★

- ○ **4 slices wholemeal bread, crusts removed**
- ○ **4 eggs**
- ○ **1 clove garlic**
- ○ **15ml (1 tbls) olive oil**
- ○ **20 black olives**
- ○ **salt and pepper**

1. Stone the olives and mince them as finely as possible. Peel the garlic, cut in half and rub on each slice of bread. Fry the bread in oil for 2 minutes on each side.
2. Prepare a *bain-marie*. In the small saucepan break the eggs and stir with a wooden spoon (as if making scrambled eggs). (This method, *au bain-marie*, is used so that the mixture remains smooth.) Season with salt and pepper. Top each slice of fried bread with the egg mixture and place the minced olives on top.

Canapés aux Pointes d'Asperges

Serves 5-10. Preparation and cooking: 10 min

Asparagus Canapés

★

- ○ **10 slices rye bread, crusts removed**
- ○ **100g (4 oz) tin asparagus tips**
- ○ **50g (2 oz) butter**
- ○ **100g (4 oz) grated Gruyère cheese**

1. Open the tin of asparagus tips and drain. Toast the slices of bread on both sides and butter them while still hot.
2. Garnish each slice with asparagus tips. Sprinkle with the grated cheese. Put the slices of bread under the grill until the cheese starts to melt. Serve at once.

Fenouils en Marinade

Serves 4. Preparation: 15 min Marinade: 24 hr

Marinated Fennel

★

○ **2 heads fennel**

For the marinade:
○ **2 lemons**
○ **45ml (3 tbls) olive oil**
○ **15ml (1 tbls) wine vinegar**
○ **15ml (1 tbls) capers**
○ **3 sprigs tarragon**
○ **salt and pepper**

1. Trim off the bases and stems of the fennel. Wash, halve them and cut into strips. Place in a shallow dish.
2. Prepare the marinade: peel and slice the lemons. Remove the stalks of the tarragon. In a bowl, place the oil, vinegar, capers, tarragon leaves, salt and pepper. Add the slices of lemon and mix.
3. Pour the marinade over the fennel and refrigerate for 24 hours. Drain and serve.

Other vegetables, such as onions, diced carrots, white or red cabbage, peppers, cucumbers, black radishes or celery, can be marinated in the same way. This marinade may also be used for poached fish: cod, anglerfish, tuna.

Try serving an assortment of marinated vegetables, accompanied by gherkins, olives and marinated mozzarella cheese, which you prepare in the following way: cover slices of cheese with olive oil, garnish each slice with an anchovy and sprinkle with oregano or thyme.

Salade de Foies et de Pommes de Terre

Serves 4-6. Preparation: 20 min Cooking: 20 min

Chicken Liver and Potato Salad

★ ★

○ **10 potatoes**
○ **3 eggs**
○ **300g (10 oz) chicken liver**
○ **50g (2 oz) tin anchovies in oil**
○ **30ml (2 tbls) olive oil**
○ **juice of 1½ lemons**
○ **30g (1¼ oz) butter**
○ **5ml (1 tsp) parsley, coarsely chopped**
○ **salt and pepper**

1. Wash the potatoes. Cook them in their jackets for 20 minutes in boiling salted water. Meanwhile, hard boil the eggs.
2. Cut the chicken livers into pieces. Melt the butter in a frying pan and fry the livers for a few minutes, until they become tender. Put aside. Open the tin of anchovies. Pour away the oil and fry the anchovies in a small saucepan, until they become a paste.
3. Remove the eggs from the water and drain the potatoes.
4. In a large bowl, dissolve a pinch of salt in the lemon juice. Add the anchovy paste and olive oil. Season with pepper.
5. Skin the potatoes while still warm. Slice them and place in the salad bowl. Mix with the sauce. Add the chicken livers. Mix again. Top the salad with the sliced hard-boiled eggs and sprinkle with parsley. Serve still warm.

Choose boiling potatoes which will not flake after cooking. The potatoes must still be warm when dressed with the sauce, so that they will absorb it properly.

Why not excite your guests' appetite with something different? Try serving raw vegetables à la croque au sel *(with buttered bread and salt). Serve broad beans, small green peppers or small artichokes.*

Tarama

Taramasalata

Serves 4. Preparation: 10 min

★

○ **200g (7 oz) smoked cod's roe**
○ **juice of 1 lemon**
○ **1 slice white bread**
○ **30ml (2 tbls) milk**
○ **30ml (2 tbls) oil**
○ **12 black olives**

1. Bring some water to the boil in a saucepan. Place the cod's roe in the boiling water for a few seconds. Drain and remove the skin.
2. Soak the bread in the milk. In a bowl, mash the roe with the bread. Add the lemon juice and stir with a fork, adding the oil a little at a time. Serve with black olives.

You can use a vegetable mill for this recipe. The bread and milk can be replaced with 45ml (3 tbls) double cream.

Salade de Crustacés

Shellfish Salad

Serves 4. Preparation: 30 min

★★

○ **1 tin (200g/7 oz) crabmeat**
○ **150g (5 oz) prawns**
○ **1 litre (2½ lb) cockles**
○ **12 oysters**
○ **1 tin (50g/2 oz) anchovy fillets in oil**
○ **30ml (2 tbls) capers**
○ **30ml (2 tbls) French mustard**
○ **45ml (3 tbls) oil**
○ **juice of 1 lemon**
○ **1 bunch watercress**
○ **5ml (1 tsp) chervil, coarsely chopped**
○ **salt and pepper**

1. Wash the cockles. Cook over a high heat until they open. Drain and remove from their shells.
2. Open the oysters. Pour their juice into a saucepan, and bring to the boil. Poach the oysters in this juice for 1 minute and drain.
3. Drain the crabmeat and anchovy fillets. Remove any cartilage from the crabmeat. Shell the prawns. Cut off the stalks of the watercress, wash the leaves and drain.
4. Place the mustard in a bowl, and add the oil a little at a time, stirring continuously. Season, with salt and pepper, and add the capers, lemon juice and chervil. Mix all ingredients well.
5. In a bowl, mix together the watercress, oysters, cockles and sauce; place the crabmeat in the centre, surrounded with prawns and anchovy fillets. Serve.

Salade de Maquereaux

Mackerel Salad

Serves 4. Preparation: 20 min Cooking: 20 min

★

○ **2 mackerel**
○ **4 potatoes**
○ **15ml (1 tbls) vinegar**
○ **30ml (2 tbls) oil**
○ **4 chives, finely chopped**
○ **60ml (2 fl oz) white wine**
○ **salt and pepper**

1. Cook the potatoes in salted water for 20 minutes. Bring some water to the boil in another saucepan. Clean the mackerel and cut off their heads. Poach in boiling water for 10 minutes. Drain and remove the bones and skin. Cut the flesh into pieces.
2. Place the pieces of mackerel in a salad bowl and pour over the wine, then add the vinegar and oil. Season with salt and pepper. Add the chives. Peel and slice the potatoes while still warm, and add to the salad. Mix well and serve at once.

Fish can be the basis of a good sauce. A few examples: anchovy fillets and garlic which you pound together and to which you add some olive oil; purée of smoked herring to which you add some oil, lemon juice and herbs; fish leftovers (such as tuna or cod) reduced to a purée with onion and tarragon leaves. You can also mix these leftovers with lemon butter and parsley.

These sauces may be served with poached or grilled fish. They are also delicious with potato, tomato or other salads.

Moules à l' Ailloli

Mussels in Aioli

Serves 4. Preparation: 20 min Cooking: 10 min

★★

○ **2 litres (4½ lb) mussels**

For the aioli:
○ **3 cloves garlic**
○ **1 egg yolk**
○ **juice of 1 lemon**
○ **240ml (9 fl oz) olive oil**
○ **salt and pepper**

1. Scrub the mussels, scrape away their beards, and wash well under running water. Place in a saucepan, uncovered, over a high heat, shaking from time to time. Remove from the heat when they have opened. Drain.
2. To prepare the aioli: peel and crush the garlic. Place the egg yolk and garlic in a bowl; stir well and leave to stand for 1 hour. Then, stirring all the time with a wooden spoon, add the oil a little at a time, as if you were making mayonnaise. Finish with a whisk. The aioli must be almost solid. Add the lemon juice and salt and pepper.
3. Remove the mussels from their shells. In a shallow dish, mix the mussels and aioli. Serve at once.

You can serve this dish with hot croûtons. It is also good with finely chopped herbs added to the aioli.

Salade de Poulpe

Octopus Salad

Serves 4. Preparation: 15 min Cooking: 1 hr

★★

○ **1 octopus weighing approx 1kg (2¼ lb)**
○ **4 cloves garlic**
○ **45ml (3 tbls) olive oil**
○ **juice of 1 lemon**
○ **5 sprigs fresh basil, coarsely chopped**
○ **pepper**

1. Clean the octopus, remove its ink sac and rinse well under running water. Place in a saucepan and cook, without water, over a low heat until red and tender. Drain, cut into small pieces and place in a salad bowl.
2. Peel and crush the garlic. In a small bowl, mix the garlic, lemon juice and oil. Season with pepper. Pour the sauce over the chopped octopus, and leave in the refrigerator for ½ hour. Before serving, sprinkle with chopped fresh basil leaves.

You can garnish this dish with sliced tomatoes and lemon wedges.

Cocktail de Crabe

Crab Cocktail

Serves 4. Preparation: 15 min Cooking: 10 min

★

○ **1 tin (200g/7 oz) crabmeat**
○ **4 eggs**
○ **90ml (6 tbls) mayonnaise**
○ **15ml (1 tbls) tomato purée or ketchup**
○ **salt and pepper**

1. Place the eggs in a small saucepan, cover with cold water and cook for 10 minutes.
2. Add tomato purée or ketchup to the mayonnaise, mix well. Season with salt and pepper to taste.
3. Drain the crabmeat, removing any cartilage which might have been left in. Flake the crab.
4. Drain the eggs, cool under running water, shell and dice them.
5. In a bowl, mix the crab with the mayonnaise. Add the diced eggs, mixing gently. Turn the salad into individual bowls. Serve cold.

The aioli from Marseilles is a complete dish in itself. Pound some garlic in a mortar, and bind it with some bread (crusts removed) and an egg yolk. Then add olive oil, a little at a time. Aioli is served with vegetables, poached cod or snails. In Provence, one binds the garlic with the egg yolk only – no bread is used – and it is served as it is, or mixed with saffron and served with shellfish.

Brochettes de Jambon et de Pruneaux

Bacon and Prune Kebabs

Serves 5. Preparation: 15 min Cooking: 5 min

★

○ **20 thin slices smoked bacon**
○ **40 prunes, soaked overnight in cold water**

1. Drain and stone the prunes.
2. Wrap 2 prunes in each slice of bacon. Thread 4 slices of bacon on each skewer.
3. Grill the kebabs for 5 minutes, turning frequently. Serve at once.

These kebabs can be served with a mint sauce: mix 15cl (5 fl oz) yogurt with 30ml (2 tbls) double cream. Add a pinch of paprika, about 20 finely chopped mint leaves and salt and pepper to taste.

Brochettes de Lotte

Monkfish Kebabs

Serves 6. Preparation: 15 min Cooking: 15 min

★ ★

○ **1kg (2¼ lb) monkfish**
○ **30 slices smoked bacon**
○ **20 black olives, stoned**
○ **3 sprigs thyme**
○ **1 lemon**
○ **pepper**

1. Discard bones and skin, and cut the fish into small pieces.
2. Wrap each piece of fish in 1 or 2 slices of bacon, and season with pepper. Thread 4 of these small packets onto each skewer, alternating with black olives. Sprinkle with thyme leaves.
3. Cook under the grill for 10 to 15 minutes. Serve hot with slices of lemon.

Boulettes de Viande

Meatballs

Serves 6. Preparation: 30 min Cooking: 20 min

★ ★

○ **500g (18 oz) minced steak**
○ **2 small onions**
○ **30g (1¼ oz) breadcrumbs**
○ **1 egg**
○ **15ml (1 tbls) parsley, coarsely chopped**
○ **15ml (1 tbls) mint leaves, coarsely chopped**
○ **60ml (4 tbls) white wine**
○ **45ml (3 tbls) oil**
○ **20g (¾ oz) butter**
○ **flour**
○ **salt and pepper**

1. Peel the onions, slice thinly, and sauté in the butter over a low heat for 10 minutes.
2. Using a fork, blend the minced meat with the chopped parsley, mint, egg, breadcrumbs and salt and pepper. Add the onions and mix once again.
3. Make walnut-size meatballs: you should end up with approximately 30. Roll each one in flour.
4. Heat the oil in a frying pan until very hot, then fry the meatballs on all sides.
5. Remove when brown and discard the cooking oil. Put the meatballs back in the frying pan and pour over the wine. Cook for 5 minutes. Serve at once.

These meatballs can be served on skewers, alternating with diced tomatoes and slices of raw onion.

You can make kebabs that are not cooked. Try thin slices of ham (Parma or Bayonne style) or smoked meat, wrapped around fresh or dried fruit (whole or cut into pieces), alternating with diced Gruyère cheese.

Moules à l'Ailloli (p17) ▶

Pain de Thon au Persil

Tuna Loaf with Parsley

Serves 4-6. Preparation: 20 min
Refrigeration: 2 hr
★★

○ **2 tins tuna weighing 400g (14 oz) each**
○ **4g (¼ oz) unflavoured, powdered gelatine**
○ **45ml (3 tbls) mayonnaise**
○ **1 bunch parsley**
○ **15ml (1 tbls) capers**
○ **12 gherkins**
○ **10g (½ oz) butter**
○ **6 lettuce leaves**
○ **10 small pickled onions**

1. Wash and dry the parsley. Finely chop 8 of the gherkins, the capers and parsley.
2. Drain the tuna and flake with a fork.
3. Dissolve the gelatine in a few spoonfuls of warm water.
4. In a large bowl, mix the parsley, gherkins, capers, tuna, mayonnaise and gelatine.
5. Butter a soufflé dish or mould and fill it with the tuna mixture. Refrigerate for 2 hours.
6. To unmould, place the dish or mould in hot water for a few seconds, and turn out onto a plate covered with lettuce leaves. Garnish with 4 gherkins and the pickled onions.

Pain de Cabillaud

Cod Loaf

Serves 4. Preparation: 15 min Cooking: 40 min
★★

○ **500g (18 oz) cooked cod**
○ **4 large potatoes**
○ **2 eggs**
○ **5 tomatoes**
○ **15ml (1 tbls) olive oil**
○ **30g (1¼ oz) butter**
○ **1 clove garlic, finely chopped**
○ **15ml (1 tbls) double cream**
○ **salt and pepper**

1. Preheat the oven to 200°C (400°F; gas mark 6).
2. Bring some water to the boil. Plunge the tomatoes in the water for 10 seconds. Peel them and remove the seeds. Heat the oil in a frying pan over a low heat, add the tomatoes and mash with a fork. Season and simmer for about 20 minutes.
3. Peel the potatoes and cook them in salted water for 20 minutes. Flake the fish into a bowl, add the potatoes and mash together with a fork. Add the beaten eggs and fold in the cream. Season to taste.
4. Butter a deep ovenproof dish. Pour in the ingredients and bake for 20 minutes. Add the garlic to the tomato sauce and serve it with the cod loaf.

Sardines Farcies

Stuffed Sardines

Serves 6. Preparation: 20 min Cooking: 15 min
★★★

○ **1kg (2¼ lb) medium-sized sardines**
○ **4 onions**
○ **4 shallots**
○ **4 cloves garlic**
○ **half a French stick**
○ **cayenne pepper**
○ **1 egg yolk**
○ **50g (2 oz) flour**
○ **1 bunch parsley, stalks removed**
○ **240ml (9 fl oz) oil**
○ **240ml (9 fl oz) milk**
○ **salt and pepper**

1. Cut off the heads of the sardines, clean and scrape them. With a sharp knife, cut the bellies lengthways and pull out the backbones. Leave them opened.
2. To prepare the stuffing: discard the crust of the bread, crumb the inside and soak in the milk. Peel the onions, shallots and garlic, chop finely and place in a bowl. Add the parsley; drain the bread and add to the ingredients in the bowl. Mix well, season with salt and pepper and 1 or 2 pinches of cayenne pepper, according to taste. Bind with the egg yolk.
3. Place the flour on a plate. Fill the sardines with the stuffing, close up and roll them in the flour.
4. Heat the oil in a frying pan. Fry the sardines for 2 minutes on each side in the hot oil and serve at once.

Oeufs Brouillés à l'Oseille

Serves 4-6. Preparation: 10 min Cooking: 20 min

Scrambled Eggs with Sorrel

★★

○ **8 eggs**
○ **40 sorrel leaves**
○ **15ml (1 tbls) double cream**
○ **20g (¾ oz) butter**
○ **a few fresh tarragon leaves**
○ **salt and pepper**

1. Wash the sorrel leaves thoroughly under running water. Remove the stalks.
2. Melt the butter in a small saucepan over a medium heat. When it starts to froth, add the sorrel leaves. Cook, stirring occasionally, for 10 minutes.
3. Remove the saucepan from the heat and add the eggs. Place this into a larger saucepan filled with water and cook for a further 10 minutes, scrambling the eggs with the sorrel. When the mixture is cooked, remove from heat.
4. Season with 3 pinches of salt and some pepper. Bind with the cream, which reduces the bitterness of the sorrel. Add the finely chopped tarragon.

Serve with slices of toasted white or rye bread.

Pâté d'Oeufs

Serves 4-6. Preparation: 15 min Cooking: 25 min

Egg and Potato Purée

★

○ **8 potatoes**
○ **4 eggs**
○ **15ml (1 tbls) groundnut oil**
○ **15 sprigs parsley, coarsely chopped**
○ **salt and pepper**

1. Wash the potatoes. Cook unpeeled in salted water for 25 minutes.
2. Meanwhile, hard boil the eggs, drain and shell them.
3. In a bowl, mash the eggs thoroughly with a fork.
4. Drain and peel the cooked potatoes. Add to the eggs, and continue mashing, blending in the oil and chopped parsley. Season. Form the mixture into a round 2 to 3cm (about 1 inch) thick. Serve cold.

Oeufs Pochés en Sauce

Serves 2-4. Preparation: 10 min Cooking: 25 min

Poached Eggs in Mustard and White Wine Sauce

★★

○ **4 eggs**
○ **30ml (2 tbls) vinegar**

For the sauce:
○ **2 shallots**
○ **30g (1¼ oz) flour**
○ **60ml (2 fl oz) white wine**
○ **15ml (1 tbls) French mustard**
○ **120ml (4 fl oz) chicken stock**
○ **30g (1¼ oz) butter**
○ **salt and pepper**

1. Peel and chop the shallots.
2. Melt the butter in a frying pan. Add the shallots, then the flour. When they start to brown, moisten with the wine and stock. Season with salt and pepper and simmer for 20 minutes.
3. Shortly before the sauce is finished, bring 2 litres (approx 3½ pints) of water and the vinegar to the boil. To poach the eggs, break them over the surface of the water. Reduce the heat and simmer for 4 minutes. Remove the eggs with a skimmer and place on a serving dish.
4. Add mustard to the sauce and mix well. Remove from the heat and pour over the eggs. Serve at once.

Poached eggs are delicious with soups: just break the egg directly into the hot soup.

Coquilles Saint-Jacques à la Portugaise
Scallops Portuguese Style

Serves 4. Preparation: 20 min
Cooking: 45 min
★ ★ ★

○ **8 scallops**
○ **2 carrots**
○ **1 onion**
○ **1 bouquet garni consisting of:**
  1 sprig thyme, 2 bay leaves, 3
  sprigs parsley
○ **4 cloves**
○ **200ml (7 fl oz) white wine**
○ **100g (4 oz) butter**
○ **4 large tomatoes**
○ **100g (4 oz) button mushrooms**
○ **juice of half a lemon**
○ **50g (2 oz) grated Parmesan**
  cheese
○ **coarse salt, peppercorns**
○ **salt and pepper**

1. Place the scallops under the grill until they open. Cut through and remove the hinge muscle with a sharp knife, and detach the shells. Scrape off the beard-like fringe and the black intestinal thread. Keep the white flesh with the coral attached. Rinse well under running water. Put aside 4 shells.
2. Prepare a court-bouillon: peel the carrots and cut in half lengthways. Peel the onion, and stick 4 cloves into it. Put 10ml (2 tsp) coarse salt into a large saucepan filled with water, add the carrots, onion, bouquet garni, 5 ml (1 tsp) peppercorns and the white wine. Simmer for 20 minutes. Strain the stock through a sieve. Bring back to the boil, then plunge the scallops into it and poach for 2 minutes. Remove from heat and drain.
3. Preheat the oven to 200°C (400°F; gas mark 6).
4. In another saucepan, bring some water to the boil. Plunge the tomatoes into the boiling water for 10 seconds. Drain, peel and remove the seeds. Remove the earthy base of the stem from the mushrooms, wash and cut them into strips.
5. Melt the butter in a flameproof casserole, add the tomatoes and mash with a fork, then add the mushrooms and lemon juice. Cook, uncovered, for 10 minutes. Season. Add the white flesh and coral of the scallops. Cook for a further 2 minutes over a low heat.
6. Spoon the mixture into the shells, sprinkle with Parmesan and place in the oven. Cook for 10 minutes, or until lightly browned. Serve at once.

Coquilles Saint-Jacques Gratinées
Scallops in Cream Sauce

Serves 4. Preparation: 15 min
Cooking: 35 min
★ ★

○ **8 scallops**
○ **150g (5 oz) button mushrooms**
○ **200ml (7 fl oz) double cream**
○ **3 shallots**
○ **60ml (2 fl oz) white wine**
○ **60g (2¼ oz) butter**
○ **20g (¾ oz) breadcrumbs**
○ **salt and pepper**

1. Place the scallops under a hot grill until they open. Detach the shells with a sharp knife. Keep 4 shells and clean them. Rinse the white flesh and the coral, cut the white part into large pieces.
2. Preheat the oven to 200°C (400°F; gas mark 6).
3. Peel the shallots, chop finely. Remove the earthy base of the stem from the mushrooms, wash and chop them finely. In 50g (2 oz) butter, brown the shallots, mushrooms, white flesh and coral of the scallops. Stir for 5 minutes, then add the white wine. Season. Cook for 10 minutes, then reduce the heat. Add the cream and cook for a further 10 minutes, but do not allow to boil.
4. Fill the shells with the mixture, sprinkle with breadcrumbs and with knobs of the remaining butter. Bake for 10 minutes, until lightly brown.

The best time for enjoying shellfish is during the autumn and winter months. Shellfish can be cooked in various ways, but some of them have a delicate flavour and are delicious eaten raw, with a squeeze of lemon.

Tourteaux Farcis

Serves 4. Preparation: 35 min Cooking: 40 min

Stuffed Crabs

★★★

- ○ **4 live crabs**
- ○ **10ml (2 tsp) curry powder**
- ○ **6 tomatoes**
- ○ **40g (1¾ oz) butter**
- ○ **salt and pepper**

For the court-bouillion:
- ○ **240ml (9 fl oz) white wine**
- ○ **1 onion, studded with 4 cloves**
- ○ **2 carrots**
- ○ **5ml (1 tsp) peppercorns**
- ○ **5ml (1 tsp) coarse salt**
- ○ **1 bouquet garni consisting of:**
  1 sprig thyme, 2 bay leaves, 3
  sprigs parsley

1. Prepare the stock: in a large saucepan, place 2 litres (3½ pints) water, coarse salt, peppercorns, bouquet garni, onion, white wine and carrots. Bring to the boil, reduce the heat and simmer for 30 minutes.
2. Meanwhile, bring some water to the boil in another saucepan and immerse the tomatoes for 10 seconds. Drain, peel and remove the seeds. Melt 30g (1¼ oz) butter in a frying pan, add the tomatoes and mash them with a fork. Simmer for 20 minutes.
3. Preheat the oven to 250°C (475°F; gas mark 9).
4. Plunge the crabs into the stock. As soon as the stock returns to the boil, let them cook for 5 minutes, then remove from the heat. Leave to cool in the stock. Remove the white meat from the legs and claws, scrape off the brown meat, orange meat (the liver) and eggs (if any). Finely chop the crabmeat. Wash the shells and reserve.
5. Add the crabmeat to the tomatoes, stir well with a fork, add curry powder, season with salt and pepper and stir again. Cook for 1 minute.
6. Spoon the mixture into the shells, top with small knobs of butter and cook for 5 minutes. Serve at once.

Moules au Lard

Serves 6. Preparation: 15 min Cooking: 30 min

Mussels with Bacon

★

- ○ **3 litres (6½ lb) mussels**
- ○ **250g (9 oz) smoked bacon**
- ○ **100ml (3½ fl oz) double cream**
- ○ **1 large onion**
- ○ **2 carrots**
- ○ **2 bay leaves**
- ○ **240ml (9 fl oz) white wine**
- ○ **30g (1¼ oz) butter**
- ○ **pepper**

1. Scrub and wash the mussels and scrape off the beard-like strands and barnacles on the shells. Rinse well under cold running water and drain.
2. Dice the bacon, having removed the rind.
3. Melt the butter in a saucepan over a low heat. Fry the bacon for 15 minutes.
4. Peel the onion and chop finely. Peel and slice the carrots. Add the onion, carrots and bay leaves to the bacon. Season with pepper. Fry for 5 minutes, stirring occasionally.
5. Pour in the white wine. Add the mussels. After they start to open, shake the saucepan a few times. Cook until they have all opened.
6. Place the mussels in a dish, keeping their juice. Strain and blend with the cream. Pour the sauce over the mussels and serve immediately.

Soufflé au Fromage

Cheese Soufflé

Serves 4. Preparation: 20 min Cooking: 40 min

★★

○ **15ml (1 tbls) double cream**
○ **4 eggs**
○ **150g (5 oz) grated Gruyère cheese**
○ **2 pinches grated nutmeg**
○ **10g (½ oz) butter**
○ **salt and pepper**

For the white sauce (béchamel):
○ **50g (2 oz) butter**
○ **30g (1¼ oz) flour**
○ **240ml (9 fl oz) milk**
○ **15ml (1 tbls) double cream**
○ **1 pinch grated nutmeg**
○ **salt and pepper**

1. Preheat the oven to 140°C (275°F; gas mark 1).
2. Prepare the béchamel: melt the butter in a saucepan over a low heat. Blend in the flour, stirring well, but do not let it colour. Add the milk a little at a time, stirring constantly with a wooden spoon, and cook for 15 minutes. Season. Add the nutmeg and cream. Stir well and leave to cool.
3. Separate the eggs. Add the yolks to the béchamel, one at a time. Season and add nutmeg, cheese and cream. Stir well. Beat the egg whites until stiff and fold them gently into the béchamel.
4. Butter a soufflé dish or mould, turn the mixture into the mould and bake for 15 minutes at 140°C. Then turn the heat up to 200°C (400°F; gas mark 6) and cook for a further 10 minutes. Serve at once.

Soufflé de Saumon

Salmon Soufflé

Serves 6. Preparation: 10 min Cooking: 45 min

★★

○ **600g (21 oz) salmon steak**
○ **200ml (7 fl oz) double cream**
○ **6 egg whites**
○ **10g (½ oz) butter**
○ **salt and pepper**

1. Preheat the oven to 140°C (275°F; gas mark 1).
2. Grill the salmon steak for 10 minutes on each side. Remove the bones and flake the flesh. Season and put aside in a bowl.
3. Beat 2 egg whites until stiff, and fold into the salmon a little at a time, using a spatula. Work gently until the mixture is smooth. Beat the remaining 4 egg whites until stiff. Whip the cream lightly.
4. Gently stir the cream into the salmon mixture, then fold in the remaining egg whites as lightly as possible.
5. Butter a soufflé dish or mould, and pour the salmon mixture into the dish. Bake at 140°C for 15 minutes. Then turn the heat up to 200°C (400°F; gas mark 6) and cook for a further 10 minutes. Serve at once.

Soufflé de Morue

Salt Cod Soufflé

Serves 4. Preparation: 20 min Cooking: 50 min

★★

○ **600g (21 oz) filleted salt cod (previously soaked for 24 hrs)**
○ **600g (21 oz) potatoes**
○ **400ml (14 fl oz) double cream**
○ **110g (4¼ oz) butter**
○ **1 pinch cayenne pepper**
○ **1 pinch grated nutmeg**
○ **4 eggs**
○ **pepper**

1. Preheat the oven to 140°C (275°F; gas mark 1).
2. Bring some water to the boil and poach the cod fillets for 5 minutes. Drain and remove bones and skin. Put the meat aside.
3. Peel the potatoes and cook them for 20 minutes in salted water (or for 10 minutes in a pressure cooker).
4. Mash the potatoes and chop the cod as finely as possible, or mince in an electric mincer. Separate the eggs. Mix together the mashed potatoes, minced cod, cream, egg yolks, butter, cayenne pepper and nutmeg. Season lightly with pepper. Mix well.
5. Beat the egg whites until stiff.
6. Fold the egg whites lightly into the soufflé mixture. Butter a soufflé dish and fill it three-quarters full. Cook in the oven at 140°C for 15 minutes, then turn the heat up to 200°C (400°F; gas mark 6) and cook for a further 10 minutes. Serve at once.

Mousse d'Artichauts

Serves 4. Preparation: 15 min

Mousse of Artichoke Hearts

★

○ **1 tin (220g/7¾ oz) artichoke hearts**
○ **200ml (7 fl oz) double cream**
○ **10g (½ oz) pistachio nuts**
○ **1 small green pepper**
○ **salt and pepper**

1. Drain the artichoke hearts and dice. Mix them with 15ml (1 tbls) cream and liquidize or pass them through the fine mesh of a vegetable mill. Pour this mixture into a bowl. Whip the remaining cream and fold delicately into the artichoke mixture. Season.
2. Remove the seeds from the pepper and dice. Shell and skin the pistachios, easing off the skins by pinching each nut between thumb and forefinger.
3. Pour the artichoke mousse into 4 ramekins and garnish with the pistachio nuts and diced pepper. Refrigerate before serving.

Mousse d'Avocats

Serves 4. Preparation: 10 min

Avocado Mousse

★

○ **2 avocados**
○ **45ml (3 tbls) double cream**
○ **5ml (1 tsp) cognac**
○ **juice of 1 lemon**
○ **salt and pepper**

1. Halve the avocados and remove the stones. With a spoon, carefully scoop out the flesh, reserving the skins.
2. In a liquidizer, place the avocado flesh, cream, lemon juice and cognac. Season. Blend until smooth.
3. Fill the avocado skins with the mousse. Refrigerate and serve very cold.

Mousse de Faisan en Aspic

Serves 4. Preparation: 20 min Cooking: 40 min
Refrigeration: 2 hr

Pheasant Mousse in Aspic

★★★

○ **1 pheasant**
○ **45ml (3 tbls) oil**
○ **4 sheets gelatine**
○ **120ml (4 fl oz) Madeira**
○ **200ml (7 fl oz) double cream**
○ **30g (1¼ oz) butter**
○ **salt and pepper**

1. Preheat the oven to 200°C (400°F; gas mark 6). Rub the inside of the pheasant with salt and pepper. Rub the outside with oil and butter. Roast for 40 minutes, basting with the cooking juices from time to time.
2. Remove the skin and bone the pheasant. Chop the flesh, then mince with the cream in an electric mincer or liquidizer. Season to taste, if necessary.
3. In a bowl, soak the sheets of gelatine in ¼ litre (9 fl oz) lukewarm water and the Madeira. Leave to cool.
4. Pour some of this liquid into a terrine or mould, brushing it onto the sides. Place in the freezer until set.
5. Pour the pheasant mousse into the terrine and cover with the remainder of the jellied liquid. Leave to set in the refrigerator for 2 hours. To unmould, dip the terrine into a bowl of hot water for a few seconds.

This mousse may be accompanied by an onion mousse. Peel 500g (18 oz) onions and fry them over a low heat with 100g (4 oz) smoked bacon, cut into strips. Add a glass of water and cover the pan. Cook for 30 minutes. If necessary add a little water to prevent the onions from sticking to the pan. Reduce the onions to a purée in a vegetable mill or liquidizer. Add 45ml (3 tbls) whipped cream to the purée and season. You can serve this onion mousse either hot or cold.

Potage Glacé au Cresson

Iced Watercress Soup

Serves 4. Preparation: 15 min Cooking: 30 min
Refrigeration: 2 hr
★★

○ **1 bunch watercress**
○ **100ml (3½ fl oz) double cream**
○ **10 sprigs chervil, coarsely chopped (if available)**
○ **20g (¾ oz) butter**
○ **half a French stick**
○ **2 small cloves garlic**
○ **15ml (1 tbls) olive oil**
○ **salt and pepper**

1. Cut off and discard the stalks of the watercress, wash and drain the leaves. In a saucepan, melt the butter and cook the watercress for 10 minutes. Add 1 litre (approx 1¾ pints) hot water and cook uncovered for 20 minutes.
2. Meanwhile, peel and halve the garlic cloves; cut the bread lengthways and rub each cut side with the garlic. Cut the bread into small pieces (croûtons). Heat the oil in a frying pan over a medium heat. Cook the croûtons on both sides for 5 minutes until brown. Drain on absorbent paper.
3. When the soup is cooked, liquidize it and season. Add the cream and blend again. Pour the soup into a bowl and refrigerate for 2 hours.
4. Before serving, sprinkle with the chervil. Serve the garlic croûtons separately.

If you can't find fresh chervil, save a few leaves of watercress to garnish the soup.

Potage aux Concombres

Iced Cucumber Soup

Serves 4. Preparation and cooking: 25 min
Refrigeration: 2 hr
★★

○ **2 cucumbers**
○ **1 small clove garlic**
○ **1 red pepper**
○ **15ml (1 tbls) red wine vinegar**
○ **15ml (1 tbls) olive oil**
○ **10 sprigs parsley, coarsely chopped**
○ **salt and pepper**

1. Peel the cucumbers and cut into chunks, removing the seeds with a sharp knife. Peel and chop the garlic. Blend the cucumbers and garlic in a liquidizer.
2. Pour the purée into a hollow dish, add 1 litre (1¾ pints) water, a little at a time (if you prefer a thick soup, use less water). Add the vinegar and oil. Season highly with salt and pepper. Mix well and refrigerate for 2 hours.
3. Meanwhile, wash and dry the pepper. Grill on all sides, leave to cool, then peel. Remove the seeds and cut into thin strips.
4. Before serving, sprinkle the soup with the pepper strips and parsley.

Potage Glacé ' l'Oseille

Iced Sorrel Soup

Serves 4. Preparation: 10 min Cooking: 25 min
Refrigeration: 2 hr
★

○ **500g (18 oz) sorrel**
○ **100ml (3½ fl oz) double cream**
○ **20g (¾ oz) butter**
○ **10 fresh tarragon leaves**
○ **salt and pepper**

1. Discard the sorrel stalks; wash and drain the leaves. In a large saucepan, melt the butter over a low heat and add the sorrel. Cook for 5 minutes.
2. When the sorrel is soft, add 1 litre (1¾ pints) hot water. Season with salt and pepper. Cook, uncovered, over a high heat for 20 minutes.
3. Leave to cool, then add the cream. Mix with a whisk. Pour the soup into a bowl and refrigerate for 2 hours. Before serving, sprinkle with chopped tarragon.

Bouillon Glacé en Pastèque

Iced Consommé in Watermelon

Serves 4. Preparation: 20 min Cooking: 3 hr
Refrigeration: 1 hr
★ ★

- 2 chicken legs
- 2 chicken wings
- 1 chicken neck
- 1 turnip
- 2 carrots
- 2 leeks
- 1 bouquet garni consisting of: 2 sprigs thyme, 2 sprigs parsley, 2 bay leaves
- 1 clove garlic
- 2 egg whites, beaten
- 1 watermelon weighing 2kg (4½ lb)
- 150g (5 oz) chicken breast
- 1 green pepper
- 1 red pepper
- 12 button mushrooms
- 2 tomatoes
- 60ml (2 fl oz) sherry
- 5ml (1 tsp) peppercorns
- 2 pinches coarse salt

1. Refrigerate the watermelon. Singe the wings and legs of the chicken over the flames of the cooker to remove any remaining feathers.
2. Peel the turnip and carrots, and prepare the leeks. Cut the carrots and leeks lengthways. Tie the leeks in a bunch with string. Peel the garlic.
3. In a large saucepan containing 2½ litres (4¼ pints) water, place the carrots, turnip, leeks, garlic, bouquet garni, peppercorns, chicken neck, wings, legs and breast.
4. Bring the stock to the boil, skim and reduce the heat. Simmer for 3 hours. Remove the chicken breast after 30 minutes and put aside.
5. After 3 hours, strain the stock and discard the flavouring ingredients. Replace over the heat, and add the egg whites, stirring all the time, to obtain a clear consommé. Cook over a low heat until it starts to 'shiver'. Remove from the heat and strain again. Leave to cool and refrigerate for 1 hour.
6. Bring some water to the boil and immerse the tomatoes for 10 seconds. Remove, peel, discard the seeds and chop the flesh. Wash the mushrooms and peppers. Seed and dice the peppers. Cut the mushrooms and chicken breast into thin strips.
7. Cut off the top of the watermelon. Remove the seeds and a little of the flesh. Pour the chicken stock into the melon and add the sherry. Garnish with the chicken and mushroom strips, diced peppers and chopped tomatoes.

Mulet aux Concombres

Mullet with Cucumbers

Serves 4. Preparation: 20 min Cooking: 15 min
Refrigeration: 1 hr
★ ★

- 1 gray mullet weighing 1kg (2¼ lb)
- 2 cucumbers
- juice of 1 lemon
- 90ml (6 tbls) mayonnaise
- 12 black olives
- 5 lettuce leaves
- 5ml (1 tsp) fennel seeds
- salt and pepper

1. Preheat the oven to 230°C (450°F; gas mark 8).
2. Clean, scale and wash the mullet. Keep it whole.
3. Scatter the fennel seeds inside the fish and place in an ovenproof dish. Season with salt and pepper. Pour into the dish 15ml (1 tbls) water, and cover with foil. Bake for 15 minutes.
4. Meanwhile, peel the cucumbers, remove the seeds with a sharp knife, and cut into slices. Place the slices in a bowl.
5. Stone the olives, and mince them as finely as possible. Add the lemon juice to the mayonnaise with the minced olives; season with pepper. Mix well. Pour the sauce over the cucumbers.
6. Remove the fish from the oven and discard the fennel seeds. Leave to cool, then refrigerate for 1 hour.
7. Place the lettuce leaves on a serving dish, top with the fish, and cover with the cucumber sauce.

You can also use red mullet or mackerel for this recipe, and chicory may replace the cucumbers.

Aspics d'Huîtres

Oysters in Aspic

Serves 4. Preparation: 25 min
Refrigeration: 4 hr
★★★

○ **4 dozen oysters**
○ **120ml (8 tbls) mayonnaise**
○ **2 packets fish gelatine (or substitute 2 packets unflavoured gelatine and use fish stock instead of water)**

1. Dissolve the gelatine in lukewarm water. Pour a thin layer of jelly at the bottom of 4 ramekins and place in the freezer for a few minutes.
2. Open the oysters and discard the shells. Pour their juices into a saucepan, bring to the boil, and plunge the oysters in the liquid for 30 seconds.
3. Prepare some mustardy mayonnaise.
4. Place a layer of oysters at the bottom of the moulds, cover with a layer of mayonnaise and then a layer of aspic jelly. Place in the refrigerator. Repeat this operation until the moulds are filled. Cover with the rest of the aspic jelly. Leave in the refrigerator for at least 3 hours. To unmould, plunge the moulds in hot water for a few seconds.

Instead of oysters, you can follow this recipe using the white flesh and coral of scallops.

Aspics de Colin

Hake in Aspic

Serves 4. Preparation: 25 min Cooking: 35 min
Refrigeration: 3 hr
★★

○ **6 courgettes**
○ **2 red peppers**
○ **500g (18 oz) hake**
○ **1 egg**
○ **45ml (3 tbls) oil**
○ **juice of 1 lemon**
○ **1 clove garlic**
○ **1 handful chives**
○ **1 packet aspic jelly powder**
○ **salt and pepper**

For the court-bouillon:
○ **2 carrots**
○ **1 onion, studded with 4 cloves**
○ **1 bouquet garni consisting of: 1 sprig thyme, 2 sprigs parsley, 1 bay leaf**
○ **120ml (4 fl oz) white wine**
○ **coarse salt, peppercorns**

1. Prepare a court-bouillon: peel the carrots and cut them lengthways. In a saucepan filled with salted water, place the carrots, onion, bouquet garni, white wine and peppercorns. Simmer for 20 minutes. Place a savarin or similar mould in the freezer for a few minutes.
2. Slice the courgettes (1cm/½ inch thick). Trim the peppers, remove the seeds and cut into strips. Bring some water to the boil. Cook the courgettes and peppers in boiling water for 15 minutes. Drain. Prepare a sauce: peel and crush the garlic. In a bowl, dissolve the salt in the lemon juice. Add the oil and garlic, season with pepper and stir well. Add the courgettes and peppers and mix well. Place the bowl in the refrigerator.
3. Plunge the hake in the court-bouillon. When it starts to boil, turn off the heat and leave to cool for 10 minutes. Remove the fish with a skimmer. Strain the court-bouillon through a fine sieve and dissolve the aspic jelly powder in the stock. Pour a little of the jellied stock into the bottom of the mould. Leave to set in the freezer. Remove the skin from the hake and cut into pieces.
4. Place a layer of peppers and courgettes at the bottom of the mould, putting aside 15 slices of courgette. Top with a layer of hake, with another layer of peppers and courgettes on top. Pour on the rest of the jellied stock, filling the mould to the top. Leave in the refrigerator for 3 hours.
5. Before unmoulding, hard boil 1 egg for 10 minutes. Shell and mash with a fork.
6. Unmould the aspic onto a serving dish. Garnish with the remaining slices of courgettes, and sprinkle with chopped chives and mashed egg. Serve at once.

Hake can be replaced by saithe, cod, mackerel, salmon, etc. Instead of courgettes, try substituting cauliflower or cabbage or a combination of cucumbers and tomatoes, all cut into shreds.

Croquettes de Crevettes (p33) ▶

Terrine de Foies de Volaille

Serves 6-8. Preparation: 20 min Cooking: 2 hr

Chicken Liver Terrine

★★★

○ **1kg (2¼ lb) chicken livers**
○ **350g (12 oz) fresh pork belly**
○ **300g (10 oz) pig's liver**
○ **500g (18 oz) boneless pork loin**
○ **30ml (1 fl oz) cognac**
○ **2 eggs**
○ **150g (5 oz) thin rashers unsmoked, streaky bacon**
○ **3 bay leaves**
○ **30ml (2 tbls) powdered gelatine**
○ **2 pinches mixed spice**
○ **salt and pepper**

To seal the terrine:
○ **flour and water**

1. Mince the chicken livers, pork, pig's liver and loin as finely as possible. Dissolve the gelatine in ½ litre (18 fl oz) lukewarm water.
2. Mix all ingredients well and season highly.
3. Preheat the oven to 200°C (400°F; gas mark 6).
4. Fill a terrine with the mixture, place the bacon rashers on top and garnish with bay leaves. Cover with the lid and seal with a strip of flour and water paste.
5. Place the terrine in an ovenproof dish filled with water. Bake for 2 hours. Leave to cool in the oven and keep for 24 hours before serving.

Pâté de Foie de Porc

Serves 6-8. Preparation: 20 min Cooking: 2 hr

Pig's Liver Pâté

★★★

○ **1kg (2¼ lb) pig's liver**
○ **500g (18 oz) fresh pork belly**
○ **2 eggs**
○ **15ml (1 tbls) flour**
○ **50g (2 oz) caul fat**
○ **150g (5 oz) barding fat**
○ **150g (5 oz) fresh bacon, unsalted and unsmoked**
○ **2 pinches mixed spice**
○ **salt and pepper**

To seal the terrine:
○ **flour and water**

1. Remove any hard membranes or nerves from the liver. Finely mince the pork belly, the liver and 3 oz bacon. Add the flour and eggs, season well and add the mixed spice.
2. Cut the remaining bacon into small pieces and season.
3. Preheat the oven to 200°C (400°F; gas mark 6).
4. Spread the caul fat on the bottom of a terrine, cover with a layer of minced mixture, then a few pieces of bacon, then another layer of minced mixture and a few more pieces of bacon. Repeat, finishing with a layer of minced mixture. Place the barding fat on top and cover with the lid. Seal the terrine with a strip of flour and water paste.
5. Place the terrine in a large ovenproof dish filled with water. Bake for 2 hours. Cool and refrigerate for 48 hours before serving.

Pâté de Faisan

Serves 6-8. Marinade: 1 hr
Preparation: 30 min Cooking: 2 hr

Pheasant Pâté

★★★

○ **1 good-sized pheasant**
○ **200g (7 oz) breast of veal**
○ **200g (7 oz) fresh bacon, unsmoked and unsalted**
○ **2 egg yolks**
○ **2 pinches mixed spice**
○ **80ml (3 fl oz) cognac**
○ **salt and pepper**

To seal the terrine:
○ **flour and water**

1. Remove the meat from the pheasant and marinate the flesh in cognac for 1 hour in the refrigerator.
2. Put aside the pheasant breast. Chop the remaining pheasant flesh with the bacon and veal. Season, add the mixed spice and bind with the egg yolks.
3. Preheat the oven to 200°C (400°F; gas mark 6).
4. Place the chopped meat in the terrine, alternating with the slices of pheasant breast. Finish with a layer of chopped meat. Cover the terrine with the lid.
5. Seal the lid with a strip of paste made of flour and water. Bake in the centre of the oven, in a baking tin filled with water, for 2 hours. Let cool and refrigerate for 48 hours before serving.

Croquettes de Crevettes

Serves 4. Preparation: 20 min Cooking: 25 min

Shrimp Croquettes

★ ★

○ **300g (10 oz) shelled shrimps**
○ **4 potatoes**
○ **30g (1¼ oz) butter**
○ **200ml (7 fl oz) milk**
○ **2 eggs**
○ **1 pinch grated nutmeg**
○ **30g (1¼ oz) breadcrumbs**
○ **30g (1¼ oz) flour**
○ **1 lemon**
○ **salt and pepper**
○ **1 litre (1¾ pints) oil for deep frying**

1. Peel the potatoes and cut into large pieces. Cook for 15 to 20 minutes in salted water. Drain and pass through the fine mesh of a vegetable mill. Add the butter, milk, nutmeg, 1 egg and the shrimps to the purée. Season and mix well. If the purée is too liquid, let it dry out over a fierce heat for a few seconds. Leave to stand for 15 minutes.
2. Place the flour in a dish, the breadcrumbs in another, and 1 egg, lightly beaten, in a third. Form the purée into small balls and dip each one in the flour, then in the egg and lastly in the breadcrumbs.
3. Heat the oil. Place the croquettes in a chip basket and plunge into the hot oil for 5 minutes. Drain on absorbent paper and serve with the lemon wedges.

Croquettes de Poulet

Serves 4. Preparation: 20 min Cooking: 10 min

Chicken Croquettes

★ ★

○ **4 cooked chicken breasts, chopped**
○ **200g (7 oz) minced steak**
○ **100g (4 oz) button mushrooms, cut into strips**
○ **1 onion, thinly sliced**
○ **5ml (1 tsp) parsley, coarsely chopped**
○ **30g (1¼ oz) flour**
○ **30g (1¼ oz) breadcrumbs**
○ **1 egg, lightly beaten**
○ **salt and pepper**
○ **240ml (9 fl oz) oil for deep frying**

1. Place the chicken, onion and mushrooms in a bowl. Add the minced steak and parsley. Season and mix well. Form into walnut-sized balls.
2. Place the flour in one dish, the breadcrumbs in another and the beaten egg in a third. Dip each ball in the flour, then in the egg and lastly in the breadcrumbs.
3. Heat the oil in a frying pan. Fry the croquettes in very hot oil for 10 minutes, turning them frequently so that they brown on all sides. Drain on absorbent paper and serve at once.

Croquettes de Gruyère

Serves 6. Preparation: 20 min Cooking: 10 min

Gruyère Croquettes

★ ★

○ **480ml (18 fl oz) milk**
○ **200g (7 oz) flour**
○ **6 eggs**
○ **150g (5 oz) grated Gruyère cheese**
○ **30g (1¼ oz) breadcrumbs**
○ **20g (¾ oz) butter**
○ **salt and pepper**
○ **240ml (9 fl oz) groundnut oil for deep frying**

1. Separate 3 eggs. In a bowl, mix the flour with 3 eggs and 3 egg yolks. Season and stir well until the mixture becomes paste-like.
2. Bring the milk to the boil. Place the paste in a saucepan and add the boiling milk. Cook over a low heat for 5 minutes, stirring constantly. Add the cheese and mix well.
3. Butter a baking sheet and pour the paste onto it, spreading it evenly to a thickness of 1½cm (slightly over ½ inch). Leave to cool.
4. Cut the paste into whatever shapes you choose: round, rectangular, square or triangular.
5. Beat the egg whites, and place the breadcrumbs on a plate. Dip each piece first in the egg whites, then in breadcrumbs.
6. In a frying pan, heat the oil and fry the croquettes for 2 minutes on each side.

Vol-au-Vent aux Rognons

Serves 4. Preparation and cooking: 50 min

Kidney Vol-au-Vent

★★

- ○ **4 individual vol-au-vent**
- ○ **2 pig's kidneys**
- ○ **1 veal kidney**
- ○ **15ml (1 tbls) cognac**
- ○ **15ml (1 tbls) white wine**
- ○ **300g (10 oz) button mushrooms**
- ○ **200ml (7 fl oz) double cream**
- ○ **80g (3¼ oz) butter**
- ○ **salt and pepper**

For the white sauce (béchamel):
- ○ **20g (¾ oz) butter**
- ○ **10g (½ oz) flour**
- ○ **60ml (2 fl oz) milk**
- ○ **salt and pepper**

1. Thaw and bake the vol-au-vent, if frozen. Halve the kidneys, remove the skin and fat. Wipe dry and cut them into slices. Blanch for 5 minutes in boiling water and drain.
2. Cut the earthy base from the mushrooms, wash under running water and cut into strips.
3. Preheat the oven to 230°C (450°F; gas mark 8).
4. Melt 30g (1¼ oz) of butter in a frying pan and fry the kidneys over a high heat. When they have given out all their juices, remove from the heat and drain away the cooking juices. Place the frying pan back on the heat and deglaze with the cognac. Add the cream and white wine, and let reduce over a low heat for 10 minutes.
5. In another frying pan, fry the mushrooms in 50g (2 oz) butter for 10 minutes, stirring with a wooden spatula. Add the mushrooms and kidneys to the cream sauce and cook for a few more minutes.
6. Fill each vol-au-vent with the kidney mixture and bake for 5 minutes.
7. Meanwhile, melt the butter in a saucepan over a low heat. Add the flour and stir well but do not let it brown. Add the cold milk, stirring constantly with a wooden spoon. Season.
8. Take the vol-au-vent from the oven, top each with a spoonful of béchamel, and serve at once.

To deglaze is to add a liquid (cognac, in this recipe) to a pan in which food has previously been cooked, then bring quickly to a boil, scraping up the crusty bits at the bottom of the pan with a wooden spoon.

Bouchées aux Huîtres

Serves 6. Preparation: 25 min Cooking: 40 min

Oyster Vol-au-vent

 ★★★

- ○ **6 individual vol-au-vent**
- ○ **4 dozen oysters**
- ○ **150g (5 oz) butter mushrooms**
- ○ **100g (4 oz) prawns**
- ○ **60ml (4 tbls) double cream**
- ○ **25g (1 oz) flour**
- ○ **juice of 1 lemon**
- ○ **60g (2¼ oz) butter**
- ○ **120ml (4 fl oz) milk**
- ○ **120ml (4 fl oz) white wine**
- ○ **1 onion, peeled**
- ○ **1 bouquet garni consisting of: 1 sprig thyme, 2 bay leaves**

1. Thaw and bake the vol-au-vent, if frozen. Open the oysters, pour their juices into a saucepan, and bring to the boil. Blanch the oysters for 1 minute. Strain the cooking juices through a fine sieve. Put the oysters aside.
2. Preheat the oven to 230°C (450°F; gas mark 8).
3. Shell the prawns and put aside. Put the shells of the prawns and the juice of the oysters in a saucepan, together with the white wine, bouquet garni and onion. Simmer for 15 minutes. Strain through a fine sieve and put aside.
4. Cut the earthy base from the mushrooms and wash under running water. In a saucepan, over a low heat, melt 30g (1¼ oz) butter, add the mushrooms and lemon juice and cook slowly for 15 minutes.
5. In another saucepan, melt the remaining butter, sprinkle in the flour, and stir over a low heat. Then add the milk, a little at a time, together with the reserved stock. Stir with a wooden spoon until it thickens. Remove from the heat and add 60ml (4 tbls) cream. Stir well, add the oysters, prawns and mushrooms, and heat.
6. Fill the vol-au-vent cases with the mixture and bake for 2 minutes. Serve at once.

Vol-au-vent are delicious when filled with scallops, sole fillets, mussels, sweetbreads or brains in a béchamel, to which you can add Madeira or lemon juice.

Anchois Gratinés aux Pommes de Terre
Gratin of Anchovies with Potatoes

Serves 4. Preparation: 30 min
Cooking: 50 min
★★

○ **1kg (2¼ lb) anchovies**
○ **4 large potatoes**
○ **4 ripe tomatoes**
○ **60ml (4 tbls) olive oil**
○ **45ml (3 tbls) parsley, coarsely chopped**
○ **45ml (3 tbls) breadcrumbs**
○ **2 cloves garlic**
○ **salt and pepper**

1. Cut the heads off the anchovies, clean and wash under cold running water and dry on kitchen paper. Divide the fish into fillets, removing the backbone. Peel, wash and cut the potatoes into thin slices.
2. Grease an ovenproof dish, and place in it a layer of anchovies, then one of potatoes; add salt and pepper and sprinkle with oil. Continue adding alternate layers of fish and potatoes, finishing with a layer of fillets.
3. Scald the tomatoes in boiling water for 10 seconds, then refresh in cold water and drain. Skin them, cut in half and remove the seeds. Chop the tomatoes roughly and place on top of the fillets.
4. Set the oven to 220°C (425°F; gas mark 7). Peel the garlic and chop it finely. Add to the tomatoes together with the parsley and the remaining oil, sprinkling the top with breadcrumbs. Bake for 50 minutes.

This dish can also be served cold with a slightly bitter salad, such as endive or dandelion.

Anchois Gratinés aux Aromates
Gratin of Anchovies with Herbs

Serves 4. Preparation: 25 min
Cooking: 25 min
★★

○ **1kg (2¼ lb) anchovies**
○ **4 shallots, finely chopped**
○ **3 cloves garlic**
○ **6 anchovy fillets, canned in oil**
○ **15ml (1 tbls) basil, coarsely chopped**
○ **30ml (2 tbls) parsley, finely chopped**
○ **2.5ml (½ tsp) powdered oregano**
○ **45ml (3 tbls) breadcrumbs**
○ **60g (2 oz) butter**
○ **100ml (3 fl oz) oil**

1. Cut the heads off the anchovies. Clean and wash them under cold running water and dry on kitchen paper. Mash the canned anchovy fillets with a fork.
2. Heat the oil in a saucepan. Add 30g (1 oz) of the butter and then the garlic, shallots, mashed anchovy fillets, parsley and basil. Cook gently for 3 minutes, without letting the mixture brown.
3. Butter an ovenproof dish. Place on it a layer of anchovies and cover with a tablespoon of the mixture. Season with very little salt but plenty of pepper and sprinkle with oregano. Continue with alternate layers, finishing with a layer of anchovies on top.
4. Set the oven to 230°C (450°F; gas mark 8). Melt the remaining butter and pour it over the anchovies. Sprinkle with breadcrumbs and bake for 20 minutes. Serve hot.

Anchois à la Mignonette
Anchovies with Capers and Olives

Serves 4. Preparation: 30 min Cooking: 20 min
★★

○ **1kg (2¼ lb) anchovies**
○ **200ml (7 fl oz) dry white wine**
○ **30ml (2 tbls) capers**
○ **12 black olives, stoned**
○ **45ml (3 tbls) olive oil**
○ **15ml (1 tbls) pepper**
○ **salt**

1. Cut the heads off the anchovies. Clean and wash them under cold running water and dry on kitchen paper. Split the fish open without separating the two fillets and remove the backbone.
2. Finely chop the capers and olives and salt them lightly. Stuff the anchovies with this mixture and reshape them.
3. Set the oven at 230°C (450°F; gas mark 8). Oil an ovenproof dish and place the anchovies on it in a single layer. Add salt, then sprinkle with the pepper, white wine and the remaining oil. Bake for 20 minutes. Serve hot or cold.

Bar au Gingembre

Serves 4. Preparation and cooking: 50 min

Bass in Ginger

★ ★ ★

○ **1.2kg (2 lb) bass**
○ **1 lemon**

For the marinade:
○ **15ml (1 tbls) soya sauce**
○ **15ml (1 tbls) flour**
○ **15ml (1 tbls) sweet white wine**
○ **2.5ml (½ tsp) powdered ginger**
○ **salt and pepper**

For the sauce:
○ **90ml (6 tbls) oil**
○ **30ml (2 tbls) sweet white wine**
○ **5ml (1 tsp) sugar**
○ **2 leeks (white part only)**
○ **100ml (3½ fl oz) hot water**
○ **1 chicken stock cube**
○ **1 root of ginger 3-4cm**
  (1-1½ inch)
○ **salt**

1. Scale the fish, clean, rinse under cold running water and dry. Place in a dish, season with salt and sprinkle with lemon juice; leave for 10 minutes, turning once.
2. Prepare the marinade: whisk the soya sauce and white wine together with the ginger and flour. Season with salt and pepper. Make small cuts along the back of the fish and pour the marinade over it. Leave to marinade for approximately 15 minutes, turning several times.
3. Prepare the sauce: dissolve the stock cube in hot water, add the white wine and sugar; season and put aside.
4. Grate the ginger; wash and cut the leeks into thin slices. Heat the oil in a frying pan and sauté the leeks and ginger gently for 10 minutes, then lift out, reserving the oil to cook the fish.
5. Drain the fish and fry gently over low heat for 3 minutes on each side. Pour the sauce over it and add the ginger and leeks. Cover and allow to simmer for 15 minutes, turning the fish once. Arrange the bass on a serving dish with the ginger and leek sauce and serve immediately.

Thin slices of chinese mushrooms, or button mushrooms can be added to the leeks.

Barbue à la Tomate et à la Crème

Serves 4. Preparation and cooking: 45 min

Brill with Tomato and Cream

★ ★

○ **4 brill fillets, weighing 200g**
  (7 oz) each
○ **100g (4 oz) cream**
○ **500g (1 lb 2 oz) tomatoes**
○ **2 large onions, finely chopped**
○ **100ml (3½ fl oz) sweet white**
  wine
○ **45ml (3 tbls) flour**
○ **30ml (2 tbls) parsley, coarsely**
  chopped
○ **40g (1¾ oz) butter**
○ **1 lemon**
○ **oil for frying**
○ **salt and pepper**

1. Rinse the fillets under running water, dry and lay in a dish; sprinkle with lemon juice and leave to marinate for 30 minutes.
2. Meanwhile, scald the tomatoes in boiling water for 10 seconds then drain, refresh in cold water and peel. Cut into halves, remove the seeds and crush to a pulp.
3. Melt the butter in a saucepan, sauté the onions until golden then add the tomatoes. Season with salt and pepper. Allow to cook gently for 15 minutes.
4. Lift out the fillets and roll them in flour. Heat the oil in a frying pan and sauté the fillets for 3 minutes on each side. Remove them, drain and put aside.
5. Add the wine and cream to the tomato sauce, mixing well. Allow to cook for 3 more minutes, then add the fillets to the sauce to simmer for 2 minutes. Arrange the fish on a serving dish, pour the sauce over, sprinkle with parsley and serve at once.

This fish is called by several different names in France: loup *in the Mediterranean,* louvine *or* loubine *on the Basque coast,* drenek *in Britanny. However, it is all the same fish, with delicate, succulent flesh which can be prepared in many ways. It is best grilled with its scales still on – no cleaning or washing – and served with melted butter or a sprinkling of olive oil. Cooked like that, its taste has no equal: protected by the scales, the flesh is cooked without being dried out and the only aroma it gives off is that of the sea . . .*

Anguilles au Vert à la Flamande

Eels with Spinach

Serves 4. Preparation: 25 min
Cooking: 15 min
★ ★

○ **1kg (2¼ lb) medium-sized eels**
○ **3 shallots**
○ **100g (4 oz) sorrel**
○ **100g (4 oz) spinach**
○ **10 sprigs parsley**
○ **6 sprigs chives**
○ **3 sprigs chervil**
○ **2 leaves sage**
○ **1 sprig tarragon**
○ **1 sprig thyme**
○ **2 mint leaves**
○ **1 bay leaf**
○ **100ml (½ cup) beer or white wine**
○ **100g (4 oz) cream**
○ **2 egg yolks**
○ **40g (1¾ oz) butter**
○ **salt and pepper**

1. Skin the eels, clean, wash and cut into 4cm (1½ inch) lengths. Dry the pieces on kitchen paper.
2. Remove the stalks from the various herbs. Wash the sorrel and spinach and shred finely. Wash the parsley, chervil, tarragon, sage, mint and chives and chop finely. Peel the shallots and chop finely.
3. Melt the butter in a frying pan, add the pieces of eel and shallots and sauté gently for 5 minutes, until golden brown. Remove the pan from the heat and pour away the butter; return to the heat and add the beer, bay leaf and thyme. Cover the pan and allow to cook slowly for 5 minutes.
4. Remove the bay leaf and thyme and add the remaining herbs. Season with salt and pepper. Cover the pan and simmer for a further 5 minutes. Meanwhile, beat together the cream and egg yolks with a fork in a bowl. Set aside.
5. When the eels are cooked, remove from the heat and quickly add the cream sauce, carefully turning the pieces of eel with a spatula to ensure they are evenly coated. Place eels and sauce in a serving dish and serve at once.

Serve this dish with lemon quarters. You can if you prefer omit the cream and eggs; it will be lighter but just as delicious. You can add other herbs besides the ones mentioned, such as watercress or white nettle – 100g (4 oz) of watercress and 50g (2 oz) of nettle.

Anguille en Cocotte

Eel Casserole

Serves 4. Preparation: 10 min Cooking: 30 min

★ ★

○ **1 large eel, weighing approximately 1kg (2¼ lb)**
○ **100g (4 oz) cream**
○ **250ml (9 fl oz) dry white wine**
○ **100ml (3½ fl oz) brandy**
○ **30g (1¼ oz) butter**
○ **30ml (2 tbls) oil**
○ **3 anchovy fillets**
○ **15ml (1 tbls) parsley**
○ **2 sprigs rosemary**
○ **1 sprig thyme**
○ **1 basil leaf**
○ **salt and pepper**

1. Skin the eel and cut off the head. Clean, wash and dry on kitchen paper. Cut into 5cm (2 inch) lengths.
2. Mash the anchovy fillets with a fork and tie the herbs together.
3. Heat the oil in a casserole, add the butter and anchovies. When the anchovies are softened, add the eel and sauté until golden brown, then add the bouquet garni. Season with salt and pepper. Sprinkle with brandy and set alight. Pour on the white wine, cover the pan and allow to simmer on a low heat for 15 minutes, checking occasionally.
4. After 15 minutes remove the bouquet garni and stir in the cream. Cook for 5 minutes over a high heat until the cream has reduced by a third, then turn off the heat.
5. Arrange the pieces of eel on a serving dish, pour over the sauce and serve at once.

Ideally, eel is best cooked and eaten immediately after being killed and skinned. If the fishmonger kills it for you, do not skin it until just before cooking.

Anguilles au Vert à la Flamande ▶

Baudroie à la Sétoise

Angler with Vegetables

Serves 4. Preparation and cooking: 40 min

★★

○ **4 slices of angler or lotte, approximately 250g (9 oz) each**
○ **10 celery leaves**
○ **2 leeks (white part only)**
○ **the green part of 2 beets**
○ **1 carrot**
○ **45ml (3 tbls) olive oil**
○ **salt and pepper**

For the aioli:
○ **1 clove garlic**
○ **1 egg yolk**
○ **2.5ml (½ tsp) mustard**
○ **150ml (6 fl oz) olive oil**
○ **salt**

1. Rinse the fish under cold water and dry on kitchen paper.
2. Wash and peel the carrots, leeks, beet and celery and chop finely.
3. Heat the oil in a saucepan and sauté the vegetables gently for 5 minutes without letting them brown. Season with salt and pepper. Add the slices of fish, cover and simmer over low heat for 20 minutes, turning them once.
4. Meanwhile, prepare the aioli: peel and crush the garlic in a mortar and add the mustard and egg yolk, mixing well. Beat the oil in gradually, little by little, and season with a little salt.
5. When the fish is cooked, remove 45ml (3 tbls) of the cooking juices – this fish gives out a lot of liquid – and stir it into the mortar. Arrange the fish and its cooking juices on a serving dish and spoon the sauce over it. Serve immediately.

Serve with small boiled potatoes and croûtons fried in oil or butter. If you can get the liver of the fish, add it to the saucepan for the last 10 minutes of cooking time. When the fish is cooked, lift out the liver, mash it with a fork and mix with the aioli.

Baudroie au Lait et à la Crème

Angler with Milk and Cream

Serves 4.
Preparation and cooking: 30 min approximately

★

○ **4 slices of angler or lotte, approximately 250g (9 oz) each**
○ **250ml (9 fl oz) milk**
○ **125g (4 oz) cream**
○ **1 bay leaf**
○ **45ml (3 tbls) parsley**
○ **5ml (1 tsp) thyme**
○ **1 clove**
○ **1 onion, finely chopped**
○ **50g (2 oz) butter**
○ **20g (¾ oz) flour**
○ **salt and pepper**
○ **nutmeg**

1. Wash the slices of angler under cold running water and dry on kitchen paper.
2. Pour the milk into a saucepan and add the bay leaf, parsley, thyme, onion and clove. Bring to the boil and simmer for 2 minutes. Remove from the heat and strain the milk through a sieve.
3. Melt the butter in another saucepan and stir in the flour with a wooden spoon. Pour in the flavoured milk and cream. Season with salt, pepper and nutmeg. Bring to the boil then add the slices of fish. Cover and simmer gently for 20 minutes over low heat. Arrange the fish on a serving dish and serve at once.

This dish can be served with thin slices of lemon and fresh spinach sautéed in butter.

Brill, which is often mistaken for turbot, is less delicate and not so highly prized, but nevertheless it is succulent, and can be prepared in the same way. It differs from turbot in that its shape is more oval and elongated; the skin is smooth. It can reach up to 80cm (3 ft) in length!

The angler can also be called diable de mer *(sea devil),* grenouille pêcheuse *(fishing frog),* crapaud de mer *(sea toad),* maranche *etc. It is almost always sold headless, and sometimes skinned, under the name of angler tail. It can be as long as 2m (6 ft) and with its round head, enormous for the size of its body, it resembles a huge toad, with numerous pointed teeth. Its flesh is boneless, white and succulent and tastes rather like lobster, but it reduces considerably when cooked. Allow 250 to 400g (9 to 14 oz) per person. The tail when it is whole looks like a leg of lamb, hence its other name: 'gigot de mer'.*

Brochet à la Crème et aux Noix

Pike with Cream and Walnuts

Serves 4. Preparation: 10 min
Cooking: 15 min
★

- ○ **4 fillets of pike, approximately 200g (7 oz) each**
- ○ **80g (3 oz) butter**
- ○ **100ml (3½ fl oz) white vermouth (Noilly, for example)**
- ○ **24 green walnuts**
- ○ **200g (7 oz) cream**
- ○ **salt and pepper**

1. Roughly chop the walnuts. Rinse the fillets under running cold water and dry them on kitchen paper.
2. Melt the butter in a frying pan and sauté the fillets for 1 minute on each side over a very low heat to prevent the butter burning. Season with salt and pepper and sprinkle with the vermouth. When the liquid has reduced, add the chopped walnuts and cream and cook very slowly over low heat for 10 minutes.
3. Arrange the fillets on a serving dish, pour over the walnut and cream sauce and serve at once.

Sauté de Brochet aux Champignons

Sauté of Pike with Mushrooms

Serves 4. Preparation: 15 min
Cooking: 15 min
★ ★

- ○ **1 pike, weighing approximately 1.2kg (2½ lb)**
- ○ **250g (9 oz) button mushrooms**
- ○ **100ml (3½ fl oz) brandy**
- ○ **2 egg yolks**
- ○ **30g (1 oz) butter**
- ○ **45ml (3 tbls) cream**
- ○ **15ml (1 tbls) flour**
- ○ **15ml (1 tbls) herbs, coarsely chopped**
- ○ **1 lemon**
- ○ **salt and pepper**
- ○ **nutmeg**

1. Clean and scale the pike and cut off the head. Cut into slices 4cm (1½ inches) thick. Rinse and dry on kitchen paper. Dust with flour and shake to remove excess. Cut off the mushroom stalks, rinse and chop into thin slices. Place them in a dish and sprinkle with lemon juice.
2. Melt the butter, sauté the slices of fish lightly for no more than 2 minutes, then add the brandy. When the liquid has reduced, add the mushrooms and season with salt, pepper and nutmeg. Cover and allow to simmer for 6 to 8 minutes, turning frequently, until the mushrooms have rendered all their liquid.
3. Meanwhile, beat the yolks and cream together with a fork.
4. When the fish and mushrooms are cooked, stir in the egg and cream mixture and cook for 2 to 3 minutes. The moment it begins to bubble, take it off the heat at once.
5. Arrange the fish with its sauce on a serving dish, sprinkle with herbs and serve immediately.

The flesh of the barbel is white and succulent, but beware of the bones! Barbel can be prepared in many ways, grilled, fried or cooked in wine. Its flesh, like many freshwater fish, is rather insipid, and it must be served with highly seasoned sauces.

The bonito, similar to a small tuna, can be found in almost all the oceans around the world. Its flesh is red, firm and tasty. It can be baked whole in the oven, with herbs and olive oil, or cooked in a court-bouillon (seasoned stock) and served cold in fillets moistened with olive oil and garnished with capers and gherkins. The boniton is smaller and even tastier than the bonito, but can be found only in the Mediterranean.

Bream has the same kind of flesh and number of bones as barbel. It is ideal for soups.

Pike is prepared mostly in dumplings (quenelles) or stuffed, but it is also delicious cooked in wine, au bleu (boiled in stock) or au vert (with spinach). Its white flesh is succulent, but make sure the fish is a young one; old pike are full of bones. The best pike is found in fast-flowing water; prepare it à la Nantaise, in stock with a little vinegar, and accompany it with beurre blanc – melted butter, beaten in reduced vinegar. See recipe for Sandre au Beurre Blanc, *pike-perch in melted butter, page 57.*

Filets de Dorade au Citron Vert

Serves 4. Preparation and cooking: 1 hr

Fillets of Dorado with Lime

★★★

○ **2 dorados, approximately 600g (1½ lb) each**
○ **15ml (1 tbls) coriander leaves, coarsely chopped**
○ **2 shallots**
○ **60g (2 oz) butter**
○ **1 lime**
○ **juice of one lime**

For the stock:
○ **150ml (5 fl oz) dry white wine**
○ **1 medium-sized onion**
○ **1 carrot**
○ **1 bouquet garni: bay leaf, thyme, celery stick**
○ **salt**
○ **6 peppercorns**

1. Scale and clean the fish and divide into fillets. Keep the heads and bones for stock.
2. Prepare the stock: peel the onion and carrot and slice finely. Tie the bouquet garni and place in a saucepan together with the heads and bones, the carrot, onion, pepper and wine. Cover with ½ litre (1 pint) of cold water and bring to the boil. Season with salt, cover and simmer for 20 minutes.
3. Meanwhile, peel the shallots and chop finely. Add the coriander and place the mixture in an ovenproof dish. Arrange the fillets on top. Set the oven to 220°C (425°F; gas mark 7).
4. When the stock is ready, strain over the fillets, cover with foil and bake for 15 minutes, basting the fillets occasionally.
5. When the fish is cooked, lift out and arrange on a serving dish; keep warm. Place the cooking dish on a high heat and boil down the cooking liquid to 200ml (7 fl oz) approximately. Remove from heat and add the lime juice and then the butter, cut into small knobs, beating until the sauce is smooth. Pour the sauce over the fillets, garnish with slices of lime and serve immediately.

If you cannot find fresh coriander, replace with parsley or tarragon.

Dorade aux Fines Herbes

Serves 4. Preparation: 10 min Cooking: 30 min

Dorado with Herbs

★

○ **1 dorado, 1.2kg (2½ lb)**
○ **1 sprig thyme**
○ **2 sprigs fennel**
○ **15ml (1 tbls) parsley, coarsely chopped**
○ **1 bay leaf**
○ **3 onions (pickling onions)**
○ **200ml (7 fl oz) dry white wine**
○ **45ml (3 tbls) oil**
○ **salt and pepper**

1. Scale, clean and rinse the fish under cold running water and dry on kitchen paper.
2. Set the oven to 220°C (425°F; gas mark 7). Chop the fennel and onions finely, and oil an ovenproof dish with 15ml (1 tbls) oil. Season the inside of the fish with salt and pepper and insert the bay leaf and thyme. Lay the fish in the oven dish and add a little salt, surround with the chopped onions, sprinkle with oil and bake for 10 minutes.
3. After 10 minutes pour the wine over and cook for another 15 minutes. Sprinkle with parsley and fennel, cook for 5 minutes and serve immediately.

The dorado is one of the best sea fish but much more difficult to find than one thinks, as many dorados sold on the market are not always the real ones!

The true dorado, with its dark blue back and silver sides, has a characteristic yellow spot on each side of its head and a crescent shaped mark on the forehead, between the two eyes – it looks like a crown and a pair of golden glasses. That is the royal dorado, or dorado with golden eyebrows! Its flesh is delicate and succulent, rare and very expensive. To appreciate it fully, prepare it simply: grilled with its scales, like the bass, en papillote *(in foil), or baked in salt.*

Cabillaud Grillé au Beurre d'Anchois

Serves 4. Preparation: 10 min
Cooking: 8 min
★

Grilled Cod with Anchovy Butter

○ **4 cod steaks, 200g (7 oz) each**
○ **100g (4 oz) butter**
○ **15ml (1 tbls) anchovy paste**
○ **15ml (1 tbls) capers**
○ **½ lemon**
○ **30ml (2 tbls) oil**
○ **salt and pepper**

1. Heat the grill. Wash the steaks under cold running water, dry, season with salt and sprinkle with oil. Finely chop the capers.
2. When the grill is hot, cook the fish for 3 to 4 minutes on both sides.
3. Meanwhile, melt the butter in a saucepan and add the anchovy paste, lemon juice and capers. Season with pepper, mix well and take off the heat.
4. Arrange the fish on a serving dish, pour over the sauce and serve at once.

Serve this dish with sautéed courgettes or aubergines.

Carpe à la Juive

Serves 4. Preparation: 15 min Cooking: 45 min

★ ★ ★

Carp Jewish-Style

○ **1 carp, weighing about 1.5kg (3¼ lb)**
○ **3 onions**
○ **2 shallots**
○ **2 cloves garlic**
○ **30ml (2 tbls) flour**
○ **200ml (7 fl oz) oil**
○ **1 litre (35 fl oz) white wine**
○ **1 bouquet garni: parsley, bay leaf, thyme**
○ **30ml (2 tbls) parsley, coarsely chopped**
○ **salt and pepper**

1. Clean and scale the fish and cut into thick slices. Peel the onions and shallots and chop finely. Tie up the bouquet garni and crush the garlic.
2. Heat half the oil in a large saucepan and cook the onions and shallots gently for 10 minutes. Add the fish and fry rapidly for 1 minute on both sides; dust with flour and cook gently for 2 minutes on each side, without browning. Add the garlic, bouquet garni and wine and cover with cold water. Season with salt and pepper. Bring to the boil, cover and allow to simmer for 25 minutes.
3. When cooked, drain the slices and transfer to an oval dish, carefully arranging them so as to reshape the fish.
4. Reduce the sauce to one-third by boiling over a high heat and remove the bouquet garni. Draw aside and stir in the rest of the oil, beating vigorously until the sauce is frothy. Adjust the seasoning if necessary and pour over the carp.
5. Allow to cool: the sauce will turn to a jelly. Sprinkle with chopped parsley before serving.

There are many ways of preparing this dish. Carp Jewish-style with parsley – add a large bunch of parsley while cooking; sweet and sour – add to the sauce 15ml (1 tbls) of sugar, 45ml (3 tbls) of alcohol vinegar, 100g (4 oz) of raisins or sultanas soaked in warm water; or oriental-style – add 60ml (4 tbls) of grated almonds and a pinch of saffron.

Suitable for pike or pike-perch.

Plaice belongs to the turbot and brill family. This succulent white fish is particularly recommended for invalids as it is fat-free and easy to digest. It is an attractive flat fish dotted with orange. Plaice can be prepared like turbot or brill: the smallest fried in butter à la meunière, *the biggest poached whole or in fillets.*

Lieu Grillé Sauce aux Câpres

Serves 4. Preparation: 5 min Cooking: 5 min

Grilled Saithe with Caper Sauce

★

○ **4 steaks of saithe, 200g (7 oz) each**
○ **80g (3 oz) butter**
○ **15ml (1 tbls) oil**
○ **5ml (1 tsp) vinegar**
○ **15ml (1 tbls) mustard**
○ **50g (2 oz) capers**
○ **salt and pepper**

1. Heat the grill. Rinse the fish, dry on kitchen paper, oil and season with salt. Grill for 2 minutes on each side.
2. Meanwhile, melt the butter in a saucepan, add the mustard and season with salt and pepper. Sprinkle with vinegar, add the capers, and mix well.
3. When the fish is cooked, arrange on a serving dish, pour over the sauce and serve at once.

Serve with boiled potatoes in their jackets and a green salad.

Limande aux Crevettes Grises

Serves 3-4. Preparation and cooking: 35 min

Dab with Prawns

★ ★

○ **2 dabs, approximately 500g (1¼ lb) each**
○ **250ml (9 fl oz) dry white wine**
○ **1 small chopped onion**
○ **1 clove**
○ **1 bay leaf**
○ **salt**

For the sauce:
○ **150g (6 oz) prawns, shelled**
○ **50g (2 oz) butter**
○ **20g (¾ oz) flour**
○ **1 egg yolk**
○ **100g (4 oz) cream**
○ **½ lemon**
○ **salt and white pepper**
○ **nutmeg**

1. Scale, clean and rinse the fish under running cold water. Remove heads and tails.
2. Place the wine and ½ litre (18 fl oz) of water in a saucepan large enough to contain the fish without overlapping. Add the onion, clove, bay leaf and the fish. Bring to the boil, season with salt and cover. Allow to simmer for 15 minutes.
3. When ready, lift out the dabs and keep warm on a serving dish. Strain the stock and boil down to a third.
4. Melt the butter in a saucepan, stir in the flour and cook very gently, until it is a pale yellow colour. Blend in the stock gradually, mixing continuously with a wooden spoon, and let it cook for 3 minutes. Remove from the heat.
5. Mix the cream and egg yolk together and add to the sauce. Sprinkle with lemon juice and season with salt, pepper and nutmeg. Add the prawns and stir gently. Pour the sauce over the fish and serve immediately.

You can tell if a fish sold in steaks is fresh – the white flesh should stick to the backbone and there should be no red halo around it.

There are several types of dab: the common or pale dab, the sole dab or limandelle *and the false dab. The colouring varies from light brown to grey, pale yellow or spotted brown. The best is undoubtedly the sole dab, which is similar to the sole in appearance and taste. It can be prepared like the sole or plaice and although its taste is not as delicate, you will appreciate it.*

Ling, also called long cod, is a long fish similar to the conger eel and can reach up to 1½ metres (5 ft). It is fished in the North Sea and sold mostly in fillets or salted. Its flesh is similar to that of the cod; it is rather insipid but very easy to digest. In northern countries, it is either smoked, salted or dried.

Merlu aux Poivrons

Hake with Peppers

Serves 4. Preparation and cooking: 55 min

★★

- ○ **4 hake steaks, about 200g (7 oz) each**
- ○ **3 red peppers**
- ○ **juice of 2 lemons**
- ○ **12 sage leaves**
- ○ **150ml (5 fl oz) oil**
- ○ **salt and pepper**

1. Light the grill. Wash and dry the peppers and place under the grill, turning frequently, until their skin turns black. Place the peppers in a saucepan, cover and leave on one side for 10 minutes.
2. Meanwhile, wash and dry the fish. Oil an ovenproof dish with 45ml (3 tbls) of oil and arrange the steaks in it. Sprinkle with lemon juice.
3. Set the oven to 200°C (400°F; gas mark 6). Peel the peppers, removing the black skin. Cut in halves and remove the seeds and centre. Cut into thin slices and place around the fish. Add the sage leaves and season with salt and pepper. Sprinkle over the rest of the oil and 15ml (1 tbls) of water.
4. Bake for 20 minutes and serve at once.

Suitable also for cod or tuna steaks.

Merlu à l'Orange

Hake with Orange

Serves 4. Preparation: 15 min Cooking: 20 min

★

- ○ **4 hake steaks, about 200g (7 oz) each**
- ○ **100ml (3½ fl oz) dry white wine**
- ○ **200g (7 oz) button mushrooms**
- ○ **3 oranges**
- ○ **45ml (3 tbls) breadcrumbs**
- ○ **50g (2 oz) butter**
- ○ **salt and pepper**

1. Wash the fish and dry on kitchen paper.
2. Remove the stalks of the mushrooms, wash and chop finely. Wash and slice the oranges without peeling.
3. Set the oven to 220°C (425°F; gas mark 7). Butter an ovenproof dish, lay in the fish steaks, sprinkle with white wine and place the mushrooms and oranges around. Sprinkle with breadcrumbs, dot with a few knobs of butter and season. Bake for 20 minutes and serve at once.

Morue au Lait et aux Pommes de Terre

Salt Cod with Milk and Potatoes

Serves 4. Preparation: 10 min
Cooking: 35 min

★

- ○ **600g (1½ lb) salt cod, soaked in water**
- ○ **500g (1 lb) potatoes**
- ○ **1 litre (2 pints) milk**
- ○ **100g (4 oz) cream**
- ○ **40g (1¾ oz) butter**
- ○ **30ml (2 tbls) parsley, coarsely chopped**
- ○ **salt and pepper**

1. Remove the skin and bones and cut the salt cod into small cubes. Peel and slice the potatoes.
2. Butter a saucepan; put in the fish and potatoes. Cover with the milk and cream, season with pepper and a little salt. Bring to the boil, reduce the heat and allow to cook for 30 minutes without the lid.
3. When ready, place on a serving dish, sprinkle with parsley and serve immediately.

The merou *is the common name for a lovely fish, found in the Mediterranean and South Atlantic coastal waters, which can only be fished with a harpoon. Its delicate white flesh is like shellfish. Delicious in* bouillabaisse, *it has no equal when served cold.*

Merlans aux Épinards

Serves 4. Preparation and cooking: 35 min

Whiting with Spinach

★★

- ○ **4 whiting, about 300g (11 oz) each**
- ○ **100ml (3½ fl oz) water**
- ○ **100ml (3½ fl oz) dry white wine**
- ○ **2 cloves**
- ○ **4 mint leaves**
- ○ **250g (9 oz) spinach**
- ○ **salt and peppercorns**
- ○ **15ml (1 tbls) coarse salt**
- ○ **1 lemon**

For the sauce:
- ○ **40g (2 oz) butter**
- ○ **15ml (1 tbls) flour**
- ○ **200g (7 oz) cream**
- ○ **salt**
- ○ **nutmeg**

1. Scale, clean and rinse the fish under cold water. Dry on kitchen paper.
2. Place the fish in a saucepan, together with the cloves, mint and 6 peppercorns. Add the wine and water, bring to the boil and season with salt; cover and allow to simmer on low heat for 15 minutes.
3. Meanwhile, wash the spinach thoroughly, place in a saucepan without draining and season with salt. Cover tightly and place on a high heat for 4 minutes. Drain well and pass through the fine sieve of a moulinette (or vegetable mill). Reserve.
4. Lift out the fish and arrange in a deep serving dish.
5. Prepare the sauce: melt the butter, stir in the flour with a wooden spoon and add the cream. Season with salt and nutmeg. Let this sauce cook gently for 6 minutes, stirring continuously. Remove from the heat and add the spinach to the sauce, stirring well, then pour over the whiting.
6. Serve hot or cold with lemon quarters.

Merlans Farcis aux Champignons

Serves 4.
Preparation and cooking: 1 hr

Stuffed Whiting with Mushrooms

★★★

- ○ **4 whiting, about 250g (9 oz) each**
- ○ **250g (9 oz) button mushrooms**
- ○ **70g (3 oz) white bread, crusts removed**
- ○ **200ml (7 fl oz) dry white wine**
- ○ **2 anchovy fillets in oil**
- ○ **2 onions**
- ○ **15ml (1 tbls) parsley, coarsely chopped**
- ○ **15ml (1 tbls) basil, coarsely chopped**
- ○ **1 clove garlic**
- ○ **1 egg**
- ○ **80g (3½ oz) butter**
- ○ **salt and pepper**

1. Scale the whiting, slit along the front and clean through the opening; remove the backbone without separating the fillets. Rinse under cold water and dry. Remove stalks from the mushrooms, wash and chop finely.
2. Melt 20g (1 oz) of the butter in a frying pan and sauté the mushrooms over a high heat for 15 minutes, stirring frequently.
3. Meanwhile, prepare the stuffing: mix 45ml (3 tbls) of wine with the bread and mash with a fork; peel the onion and garlic, chop finely and add to the mixture; chop the anchovy fillets finely and add. Stir everything well together and add the basil, parsley, and egg. Season with salt and pepper.
4. When the mushrooms are cooked, mix into the stuffing and blend all well together.
5. Set the oven to 200°C (400°F; gas mark 6). Stuff the fish, reshape and stitch with white thread to prevent the stuffing from coming out during the cooking.
6. Butter an ovenproof dish and lay the fish in, sprinkle over the rest of the wine, dot with the remaining butter and bake for 25 minutes, basting frequently with the cooking liquid. Serve hot.

A purée of artichokes, celery or spinach goes very well with this dish.

To prepare raw fish the Japanese way: clean, cut into fillets and then in fine strips; served with soya sauce, grated black radish, thin slices of ginger, and green mustard with horseradish, it becomes the wonderful Japanese Sashimi, *which will convince anybody who tries it that raw fish is a feast.*

Mulet Rôti aux Aromates

Serves 4. Preparation: 15 min Cooking: 30 min

Roast Grey Mullet with Herbs

★

○ **1.2kg (2½ lb) grey mullet**
○ **1 small pimento**
○ **2 cloves garlic**
○ **5ml (1 tsp) rosemary**
○ **2.5ml (½ tsp) thyme**
○ **2.5ml (½ tsp) fennel seeds**
○ **30ml (2 tbls) breadcrumbs**
○ **100ml (3½ fl oz) olive oil**
○ **juice of 1 lemon**
○ **salt and pepper**

1. Scale, clean and wash the mullet and dry on kitchen paper. Season with salt and pepper inside and out. Oil an ovenproof dish with 15ml (1 tbls) of oil, lay in the fish and sprinkle with lemon juice.
2. Set the oven to 200°C (400°F; gas mark 6). Prepare the seasoned oil: peel and crush the garlic in a mortar with 2.5ml (½ tsp) salt, the pimento, rosemary, fennel and thyme; mix well with the remaining oil.
3. Coat the fish with this oil, dust with breadcrumbs and bake for 30 minutes, basting from time to time with the cooking juices. Serve very hot.

Muge en Raïto

Serves 3-4. Preparation and cooking: 50 min

Grey Mullet Provençal-Style

★★

○ **1.2kg (2½ lb) grey mullet**
○ **30ml (2 tbls) flour**
○ **100ml (3½ fl oz) peanut oil**

For the sauce:
○ **3 ripe tomatoes or 15ml (1 tbls)**
   tomato purée
○ **2 onions**
○ **2 cloves garlic**
○ **1 bouquet garni: bay leaf,**
   5 sprigs parsley
○ **200ml (7 fl oz) red wine**
○ **100ml (3½ fl oz) boiling water**
○ **30ml (2 tbls) capers**
○ **24 black olives**
○ **45ml (3 tbls) olive oil**
○ **salt and pepper**

1. Scale and clean the mullet and cut into 5cm (2 inch) thick slices. Dip the fish in flour and shake to remove excess. Reserve.
2. Prepare the sauce: scald the tomatoes for 10 seconds in boiling water, drain and refresh in cold water. Peel, cut in halves and remove the seeds. Crush to a pulp. Peel the onions and garlic and chop finely.
3. Heat the olive oil in a saucepan, sauté the onions for 5 minutes on a low heat, then add the wine, turn up the heat and reduce for 5 minutes. Add the boiling water, crushed tomatoes, chopped garlic and bouquet garni and season with salt and pepper. Reduce the heat and leave to cook gently for 10 minutes, stirring from time to time with a wooden spoon.
4. Meanwhile, heat the peanut oil in a frying pan and fry the slices of fish for 2 minutes on each side until golden, then lift out and drain on kitchen paper.
5. When the sauce has cooked for 10 minutes, add the fish, capers and olives and allow to simmer for a further 10 minutes. Remove the bouquet garni.
6. Place the slices of mullet on a serving dish, coat with the sauce and serve at once.

Croûtons fried in oil or butter can accompany this recipe.

Mullet Provencal-style is the main course of the traditional meal served in the region of Arles on Christmas Eve, before the midnight mass. Other firm-fleshed fish can be prepared in the same way: bass, brill, salt cod or cod. It can be either fried, baked or boiled in stock, but is invariably left to simmer for 10 minutes in the sauce before serving.

Rougets en Sauce Tomate

Serves 4. Preparation: 15 min Cooking: 35 min

Red Mullet with Tomato Sauce

★★

○ **8 medium-sized red mullet**
○ **30ml (2 tbls) flour**
○ **oil for frying**

For the sauce:
○ **500g (1 lb) ripe tomatoes**
○ **45ml (3 tbls) oil**
○ **1 clove garlic**
○ **1 onion**
○ **1 bouquet garni: thyme, basil, bay leaf**
○ **15ml (1 tbls) parsley, coarsely chopped**
○ **100ml (3½ fl oz) dry white wine**
○ **salt**

1. Scale, clean and wash the mullet under cold running water and dry. Dip in flour.
2. Peel the garlic and onion and chop finely. Tie up the bouquet garni. Scald the tomatoes for 10 seconds in boiling water, drain and refresh in cold water; peel, cut into halves and press to remove seeds. Crush to a pulp with a fork and reserve.
3. Fry the red mullet in oil for 2 minutes on each side then lift out and drain on kitchen paper. Pour away the frying oil and wipe the frying pan clean.
4. Heat the 45ml (3 tbls) of oil in the frying pan and gently sauté the garlic and onion for about 5 minutes. Add the tomatoes, bouquet garni, white wine and chopped parsley. Season with salt and bring to the boil. Allow to simmer for 20 minutes, stirring from time to time with a wooden spoon.
5. After 20 minutes add the red mullet to the sauce and leave to cook for a further 2 minutes on each side. Serve hot or cold.

Rougets à l'Orientale

Serves 4. Preparation: 15 min Cooking: 10 min, 12 hr in advance

Red Mullet Oriental-Style

★

○ **8 small mullet**
○ **300ml (10 fl oz) dry white wine**
○ **4 sprigs parsley**
○ **1 fennel stem**
○ **1 sprig thyme**
○ **1 bay leaf**
○ **12 coriander seeds**
○ **6 peppercorns**
○ **2 cloves**
○ **2 pinches of saffron**
○ **15ml (1 tbls) oil**
○ **1 lemon**
○ **salt**

1. Scale and wash the red mullet but do not gut them. Dry on kitchen paper and season with salt.
2. Oil a big flameproof dish and lay the fish in side by side.
3. Pour the white wine over the fish and add water to cover if necessary. Add the parsley, fennel, thyme, bay leaf, coriander, saffron, cloves and peppercorns. Season with a little salt.
4. Place the dish over a low heat. The minute it begins to boil lower the heat and allow to simmer for 5 minutes. Remove from the heat.
5. Cut the lemon in thin slices and garnish the dish. Allow to cool for at least 12 hours before serving.

This can be kept in the fridge without ruining its flavour, and it makes a delicious first course. In winter, add thin slices of oranges with the lemon; in summer, add roughly chopped tomatoes to the red mullet before pouring over the wine.

There are two types of red mullet: rougets-barbets *and* surmulets. *Both are small, no more than 30cm (12 inches) in length, with two long barbels on the lower jaw; the brown-green back and silvery flanks become red when taken out of the water. The* surmulets *are rock mullets whereas the others inhabit the muddy bottom of the sea. They are best fried without being cleaned or scaled and try the liver: it is delicious.*

Filets de Perche à la Sauge

Serves 4. Preparation: 5 min Cooking: 15 min

Perch Fillets with Sage

★

○ **8 perch fillets**
○ **250g (9 oz) cream**
○ **10 sage leaves (fresh)**
○ **40g (1¼ oz) butter**
○ **salt and white pepper**

1. Wash and dry the fillets.
2. Set the oven to 220°C (425°F; gas mark 7). Pour the cream into a saucepan and bring to the boil.
3. Butter an ovenproof dish with 20g (¾ oz) of butter, cover the base with sage leaves, place the fillets on top and season with salt and pepper. Pour over the cream, dot with butter and bake for 15 minutes.
4. When the fillets are ready, serve at once.

Braised celery hearts or steamed potatoes are suitable with this dish.

Perches à la Crème et aux Champignons

Serves 4.
Preparation and cooking: 50 min

Perch with Cream and Mushrooms

★★

○ **1.2kg (2½ lb) perch**
○ **300g (10 oz) button mushrooms**
○ **30g (1¼ oz) butter**
○ **30ml (2 tbls) oil**
○ **250ml (9 fl oz) dry white wine**
○ **200g (7 oz) cream**
○ **2 shallots**
○ **15ml (1 tbls) parsley, coarsely chopped**
○ **salt and pepper**

1. Scale, clean and wash the fish under cold running water and dry.
2. Remove the stalks of the mushrooms, wash and chop finely. Peel the shallots and chop finely.
3. Heat the oil in a frying pan, and add the butter and mushrooms. Dust with half of the parsley and cook for 10 minutes on a high heat, stirring with a wooden spoon.
4. Set the oven to 220°C (425°F; gas mark 7). Lay the shallots at the bottom of an ovenproof dish, add the mushrooms, the remaining parsley and the fish, sprinkle with wine and season with salt and pepper.
5. Bake for 20 minutes, basting frequently with the cooking juices. When cooked, pour the cream over the fish and allow to cook for a further 5 minutes.
6. Serve immediately.

Perch can be found in small or large rivers. Small ones can be deep fried whereas the large ones are cut into fillets or served in batter. If not scaled immediately, perch must be skinned like an eel.

The brown hog-fish, called small because it is not longer than 30cm (12 inches), is exquisite in fish soup and indispensable in bouillabaise. It can be found among seaweed-covered rocks in the Mediterranean and Gulf of Gascony regions – its colours of brown, pink and grey often cause it to be mistaken for weed. Its cousin the red hog-fish is larger and less appreciated.

There is a third type, called the dorado hog-fish, which can be found in the rocky depths of the North Atlantic and can weigh up to 2kg (4½ lb). It is served in fillets which are fried or poached because its flesh is very oily.

Saint-Pierre aux Poireaux

Serves 4. Preparation: 15 min Cooking: 30 min

John Dory with Leeks

★★

○ **2 John Dorys, about 800g (2 lb) each**
○ **8 leeks**
○ **200g (7 oz) cream**
○ **50g (2 oz) butter**
○ **100ml (3½ fl oz) white vermouth**
○ **salt and pepper**

1. Clean and skin the fish and separate into fillets. Wash under cold running water and dry on kitchen paper.
2. Discard the green parts of the leeks. Wash and slice into thin rounds.
3. Melt the butter in a saucepan and gently sauté the leeks for 10 minutes. Season with salt and pepper, sprinkle with the vermouth and let it evaporate.
4. Pour on the cream and when it starts to bubble, add the fillets. Leave to cook gently for 10 minutes, turning them halfway through.
5. Lift out the fillets and arrange on a serving dish. Keep warm.
6. Reduce the sauce for 2 minutes over a high heat and pour over the fish. Serve at once.

Fillets of sole, turbot or brill can be prepared in the same way.

Sandre au Beurre Blanc

Serves 4. Preparation and cooking: 30 min

Pike-Perch with Butter Sauce

★★★

○ **1 pike-perch, about 1.5kg (3¼ lb)**
○ **250g (9 oz) slightly salted butter**
○ **4 shallots**
○ **100ml (3½ fl oz) white wine vinegar**
○ **150ml (5 fl oz) white wine**
○ **white pepper**

1. Ask your fishmonger to clean the fish through the gills. Do not scale. Light the grill.
2. When the grill is hot enough, grill the fish for 5 minutes on each side. Set the oven at 200°C (400°F; gas mark 6) and bake the pike-perch for 15 minutes.
3. Meanwhile, prepare the butter sauce: peel and finely chop the shallots. Put them in a heavy-based saucepan and add the vinegar and white wine.
4. Place the saucepan on a medium heat and allow to reduce until there is 15ml (1 tbls) of liquid left and the sauce has become syrupy. Remove from the heat. Cut the butter into cubes.
5. Away from the heat, add a nut of butter, whisking vigorously, and then beat in the rest of the butter, one nut after the other, keeping the saucepan just on a low heat. It is easier if you stand the saucepan on an asbestos sheet over a low heat: your sauce will be smooth, warm and velvety.
6. When the sauce is ready, add the freshly ground white pepper and pour into a sauce boat.
7. Arrange the pike-perch on a serving dish and serve the sauce separately.

Fish cooked in this way will keep its flavour. The skin comes off easily and the flesh is soft, succulent and delicious. Salmon or bass can be prepared in the same way.

Filets de Sole aux Nouilles Fraîches

Serves 4. Preparation and cooking: 30 min

Sole Fillets with Fresh Tagliatelle

★ ★

○ **8 fillets of sole**
○ **8 scallops**
○ **250g (8 oz) cream**
○ **30ml (2 tbls) white vermouth**
○ **5ml (1 tsp) tomato purée**
○ **250g (8 oz) tagliatelle**
○ **30g (1 oz) butter**
○ **nutmeg**
○ **salt and pepper**

1. Ask your fishmonger to prepare the scallops. Wash the fillets under running water and dry on kitchen paper. Season with salt, pepper and nutmeg. Place a fillet around each scallop, shiny side inside and secure with a toothpick or cocktail stick.
2. Put the cream and vermouth into a saucepan large enough to contain the fish, lay in the fillets, season with salt and pepper, bring to the boil and cook gently for 5 minutes. Remove the fillets, drain and keep warm.
3. Return the saucepan to a low heat and add the tomato purée. Boil down to half the liquid for about 10 minutes.
4. Meanwhile, boil some water in a large saucepan, add salt and plunge in the tagliatelle. Cook for 5 to 6 minutes, until it is *al dente*. Drain, stir in the butter and arrange on a serving dish. Place the fillets on top, coat with the sauce and serve immediately.

Serve with freshly ground pepper. Fresh tagliatelle can sometimes be bought in delicatessen shops.

Sole au Muscadet

Serves 2. Preparation and cooking: 35 min

Sole with Muscadet

★ ★

○ **1 large sole, about 600g (1½ lb)**
○ **250ml (9 fl oz) Muscadet**
○ **60g (2 oz) butter**
○ **2 shallots**
○ **30ml (2 tbls) cream**
○ **salt and pepper**

1. Skin, clean and dry the sole. Peel and finely chop the shallots. Set the oven to 200°C (400°F; gas mark 6).
2. Butter an ovenproof dish large enough to contain the fish. Sprinkle with the chopped shallots, then place the fish in and season with salt and pepper. Pour over the white wine, add a few knobs of butter, cover with aluminium foil and bake for 15 minutes.
3. When the fish is cooked, arrange on a serving dish, cover with aluminium foil and keep warm in the oven, with the heat turned off and the door ajar.
4. Place the cooking dish over a high heat and reduce the liquid until you have 60ml (4 tbls) left. Whisk in the cream and leave to cook gently for 2 minutes. Remove from the heat and stir in the remaining butter, beating constantly.
5. Strain this sauce over the sole and serve at once.

When in season sprinkle with fresh chopped tarragon or chives.

You can add wine, champagne, vermouth or cream to the stock which can be used to cook whole fish or fillets (baked or stewed). Once cooked, reduce the liquid, add the butter, egg yolks or cream to thicken it and season with chives or herbs of your choice.

Bouillabaisse

Bouillabaisse

Serves 6 to 8. Preparation: 25 min Cooking: 30 min

★★

- ○ **2.5kg (5½ lb) fresh fish: scorpion-fish, John Dory, weever, gurnard, conger eel, angler, sea-bass etc**
- ○ **12 small shellfish: crabs, prawns**
- ○ **1 chopped onion**
- ○ **1 leek, white part, chopped**
- ○ **4 cloves garlic, peeled**
- ○ **3 tomatoes**
- ○ **1 sprig fennel**
- ○ **1 sprig thyme**
- ○ **1 bay leaf**
- ○ **1 piece dried orange peel**
- ○ **200ml (7 fl oz) olive oil**
- ○ **4 pinches saffron**
- ○ **2.5 litres (4 pints) boiling water**
- ○ **salt and pepper**

To garnish
- ○ **24 slices of toast**

1. Scale and clean the fish. Rinse under running water and chop the large ones into pieces. Peel the tomatoes, remove the seeds, and crush with a fork.
2. Heat the oil in a large saucepan and put in the onion, leek, tomatoes, crushed garlic, fennel, thyme, bay leaf and orange peel. Gently sauté for 8 minutes, mixing well, and add the crabs and prawns. Pour on the boiling water, season and boil for 5 minutes: this is to allow the oil and water to form an emulsion, giving a smooth sauce.
3. After 5 minutes, add the scorpion-fish, conger eel and angler. Allow to boil for 5 minutes then add the soft-fleshed fish: John Dory, weever, gurnard, sea-bass. Continue to boil for 10 minutes and taste for seasoning. Add the saffron and remove from the heat.
4. Serve the fish and soup in the same dish.

Bouillabaisse can be served with a sauce prepared as follows: crush together 2 small pimentos, 2 garlic cloves, salt, pepper, saffron and 50g (2 oz) white bread soaked in milk – or even better – soaked in the bouillabaisse stock. Blend finely then beat in 250ml (9 fl oz) olive oil, as for mayonnaise.

Waterzoï

Flemish Fish-Pot

Serves 6. Preparation and cooking: 1 hr

★★★

- ○ **2kg (4½ lb) white fish: whiting, conger, dorado, gurnard, angler, John Dory, brill**
- ○ **1 celery stick**
- ○ **3 carrots**
- ○ **3 leeks**
- ○ **2 onions chopped into 4**
- ○ **juice of ½ lemon**
- ○ **250ml (9 fl oz) dry white wine**
- ○ **1 sprig thyme**
- ○ **1 bay leaf**
- ○ **6 sprigs parsley**
- ○ **2 egg yolks**
- ○ **125g (4 oz) cream**
- ○ **30ml (2 tbls) chopped chives**
- ○ **salt and pepper**

1. Skin or scale the fish, clean and rinse under running water. Cut into thin slices. Put the heads and bones in a large saucepan and cover with 1 litre (2 pints) of water and the white wine. Add the thyme, bay leaf, parsley and onions, and season. Bring to the boil, then simmer for 20 minutes.
2. Meanwhile, boil 1 litre (2 pints) of water. Peel the carrots, leeks, and celery. Rinse quickly, shred the carrot, quarter the celery heart and roughly chop the leeks. When the water is boiling, add salt and the vegetables. Cook over a high heat with the lid on for 15 minutes.
3. When the fish stock is ready, strain and add to the vegetables. Bring back to the boil and add the fish. Leave to cook gently for 5 minutes, remove from the heat, lift out the fish and vegetables and arrange on a serving dish or in a soup-tureen.
4. Whisk together the cream, lemon juice and egg yolks, add to the stock, sprinkle with chives and pour over the fish and vegetables. Serve immediately.

Slices of toasted bread go very well with this Flemish dish. Suitable for river fish: eel, perch, pike etc.

Soupe de Poissons à la Tomate

Fish Soup with Tomatoes

Serves 4. Preparation: 25 min Cooking: 30 min

★★

○ **1.5kg (3¼ lb) fish: scorpion-fish, John Dory, weever, gurnard, conger, angler, whiting**
○ **20 mussels**
○ **4 Dublin Bay prawns**
○ **1 very small octopus**
○ **500g (1 lb) ripe tomatoes**
○ **1 onion**
○ **1 white of leek**
○ **1 clove garlic**
○ **1 small fresh red pimento**
○ **150ml (5 fl oz) olive oil**
○ **200ml (7 fl oz) dry white wine**
○ **salt and pepper**

1. Scale the fish, clean, and cut the large ones into chunks of equal size. Rinse under running water and dry on kitchen paper. Scrub and rinse the mussels. Split the Dublin Bay prawns lengthwise. Clean the octopus, removing ink sac, rinse and chop into small pieces.
2. Wash the leek, peel and finely chop the leek, onion and garlic. Wash the tomatoes and crush to a pulp.
3. Heat the oil in a pan and gently sauté the garlic, onion, leek and small pimento. Add the octopus, mussels, Dublin Bay prawns and the fish with firm flesh, fry for another 5 minutes, then add the rest of the fish and cook for a further 5 minutes. Season with a little salt and pepper. Pour on the crushed tomatoes and white wine and cover with water. Leave to cook for 15 minutes over a high heat. Serve the soup in a bowl.

Serve this soup hot with toasted bread rubbed with garlic and, if you wish, an *aïoli* sauce or *rouille* sauce.

Bourride Provençale

Provençal Fish-Pot

Serves 6. Preparation and cooking: 1 hr 10 min

★★★

○ **2kg (3½ lb) white fish: whiting, bass, brill, turbot, conger, John Dory etc**
○ **2 chopped onions**
○ **2 leeks, white part only**
○ **1 carrot**
○ **1 celery stick**
○ **1 sprig fennel**
○ **2 cloves garlic**
○ **1 bay leaf**
○ **6 coriander seeds**
○ **1 small piece of dried orange peel**
○ **30ml (2 tbls) olive oil**
○ **salt**

For the aïoli
○ **6 egg yolks**
○ **400ml (14 fl oz) olive oil**
○ **6 cloves garlic**
○ **salt**

To garnish
○ **6 slices of bread toasted in the oven**

1. Clean and scale the fish. Rinse under running water and cut into 4cm (2 inch) slices. Reserve the heads. Wash the leeks and carrot and chop finely together with the celery.
2. Place 30ml (2 tbls) of olive oil in a large saucepan, add the vegetables and fish heads and sauté gently for 5 minutes without browning. Add 2 litres (4 pints) of water and the whole garlic cloves, bay leaf, coriander seeds, fennel and orange peel. Season with salt, bring to the boil and allow to simmer for 20 minutes.
3. Meanwhile, prepare the *aïoli*: peel and crush the garlic with 4 pinches of salt, add the 2 egg yolks and the oil a drop at a time and beat the sauce like a mayonnaise. When the sauce is ready, take half of it and add the 4 remaining egg yolks, beating vigorously.
4. When the stock has cooked for 20 minutes, strain and return to the large saucepan, bring to the boil and add the fish in the following order: brill, turbot, conger, whiting, bass, John Dory. Allow to boil for 10 minutes.
5. Arrange the fish on a serving dish. Strain the stock and put the saucepan on a low heat. Add a ladle of stock to the *aïoli* sauce which has the 4 egg yolks, mix well and beat this mixture into the stock to obtain a smooth sauce; do not allow to boil. Pour into a soup-tureen and serve. Each guest will moisten his toasted bread with this stock and help himself to the fish with the *aïoli*.

The water can be replaced with the same quantity of dry white wine.

Filet à la Robespierre
Fillet Grilled with Rosemary

Serves 4. Preparation and cooking: 10 min

★

- ○ **2 slices of fillet, 180g (6 oz) each**
- ○ **olive oil**
- ○ **salt and freshly ground pepper**
- ○ **rosemary**

1. Sprinkle the meat generously with oil and pepper. Cook on a heated grill for 2-3 minutes each side, turning once, and adding the salt at the end of cooking.
2. Arrange sprigs of fresh rosemary on a warmed serving dish and sprinkle with oil. When the meat is cooked, place on the dish and turn 2 or 3 times in the rosemary so that the herb flavours the meat.
3. Finally, cut the meat into thin slices, having removed the rosemary. Pour over the cooking juices and serve immediately.

Rosbif aux Fruits
Roast Beef with Fruit

Serves 4. Preparation and cooking: 50 min

★ ★

- ○ **1 piece of sirloin, 800g (1¾ lb)**
- ○ **15ml (1 tbls) oil**
- ○ **salt and pepper**
- ○ **juice of 1 lemon**
- ○ **2 apples**
- ○ **2 bananas**
- ○ **3 oranges**
- ○ **50g (2 oz) butter**

1. Bind the meat with kitchen thread so it will keep its shape during cooking. Place in a dish, baste with oil, add salt and pepper and put aside. Preheat the oven to 230°C (450°F; gas mark 8).
2. Prepare the fruit. Pour the lemon juice into a bowl. Slice and core the apples and place in the lemon juice to prevent discolouring. Peel the bananas, cut into rounds and add to the apples. Peel the oranges, divide into segments, remove the pith and put aside.
3. Butter an ovenproof dish large enough to hold all the fruit in one layer 1cm (½ inch) thick. Remove the fruit from the lemon juice and mix with the orange segments. Melt the remaining butter and pour evenly over the fruit. Spread the fruit over the base of the ovenproof dish. Arrange the meat on top of the fruit and place the dish in the oven for 35 minutes. Remove the meat from the oven, allow to rest for 5 minutes, then slice and arrange on a serving dish. Surround the meat with the fruit.

Pièce de Boeuf à l'Oignon
Pot Roast with Onions

Serves 4. Preparation: 30 min Cooking: 2 hr 30 min

★

- ○ **800g (1¾ lb) rolled brisket or silverside**
- ○ **1kg (2¼ lb) red onions**
- ○ **200g (7 oz) butter**
- ○ **1 beef stock cube**
- ○ **salt and pepper**

1. Place the meat in a large saucepan, with the butter which has been cut into small pieces. Chop the onion finely, and cover the meat with them. Place over a low heat and turn the meat frequently.
2. Dissolve the stock cube in hot water. When the butter and the juice from the onions has nearly evaporated, add a little of the stock, and season. Leave to cook for about 2 hours 30 minutes. Remove the meat and pass the onions through a sieve or blender.
3. Slice the meat. Arrange on a serving dish and pour the hot purée over. Serve at once.

Châteaubriands Béarnaise

Serves 4. Preparation and cooking: 40 min

Porterhouse Steaks with Béarnaise Sauce

★★★

- ○ **4 porterhouse steaks, 200g (7 oz) each**
- ○ **200g (7 oz) butter**
- ○ **3 egg yolks**
- ○ **100ml (3½ fl oz) white wine**
- ○ **100ml (3½ fl oz) tarragon vinegar**
- ○ **15ml (1 tbls) shallots, chopped very fine**
- ○ **5ml (1 tsp) freshly ground pepper**
- ○ **1 sprig tarragon**
- ○ **salt**

1. Cut the butter into small cubes and place it in a small saucepan. Wash and chop the tarragon. Put aside.
2. Place the shallots, vinegar, wine and pepper into another saucepan and place over a low heat. Allow this mixture to boil slowly until 15ml (1 tbls) liquid remains (this takes about 10 minutes), then remove from the heat and allow to cool for 2 minutes.
3. While this mixture is cooling, place the saucepan containing the butter on the heat until it is completely melted.
4. Heat the grill. Place the egg yolks into the saucepan containing the shallot mixture. Place on an asbestos mat on a very low heat and beat continuously with a whisk for 5-6 minutes, until the mixture is creamy. If the heat is too high in spite of the asbestos mat, remove the saucepan from the heat at intervals. It is essential that the heat is very gentle for this sauce.
5. When the mixture is creamy, add salt to taste, then the butter in small pieces, beating constantly. When the butter has been absorbed, the sauce is ready. Pass the sauce through a sieve into a sauceboat, pressing with the back of a spoon to extract all the shallot juices. Add the tarragon.
6. Grill the steaks for 4 minutes (rare) to 7 minutes (well done). Arrange them on a serving dish and serve immediately. Serve the sauce separately.

Faux-Filet à l'Infusion d'Herbes

Serves 2. Preparation: 10 min
Cooking: 4-6 min Marinade: 20 min

Sirloin Steak with Herbs

★

- ○ **2 slices sirloin steak, 200g (7 oz) each**
- ○ **10ml (2 tsp) thyme**
- ○ **10ml (2 tsp) rosemary**
- ○ **2 bay leaves, crumbled**
- ○ **2 cloves**
- ○ **2 chili peppers, crumbled**
- ○ **1 star anise, sliced**
- ○ **8ml (1 heaped tsp) salt**
- ○ **5ml (1 tsp) freshly ground pepper**

1. Place thyme, rosemary, bay leaves, cloves, star anise, chili peppers, salt and pepper in a small saucepan. Add 150ml (5 fl oz) water and place the saucepan over a medium heat. Boil for 1 minute, remove from the heat and allow to cool.
2. When the mixture is cold, strain through a fine strainer into a bowl and place the steaks on top. Allow them to marinate for 20 minutes, turning once. Meanwhile, heat the grill to a high temperature.
3. When the grill is very hot, drain the steaks without wiping them dry, and seal them for 1 minute each side, then cook for a further 3 minutes (rare) to 5 minutes (well done).
4. When the steaks are cooked, arrange them on individual plates and serve immediately.

Serve with a selection of vegetables in season: buttered green beans, sautéed courgettes, baked tomatoes, grilled mushrooms.

Entrecôte à l'Échalote

Serves 2. Preparation: 10 min Cooking: 10 min

Rib Steak with Shallots

★ ★

○ **1 rib steak, 500g (18 oz)**
○ **8 shallots**
○ **100ml (3½ fl oz) wine vinegar**
○ **5ml (1 tsp) freshly ground pepper**
○ **5ml (1 tsp) French mustard**
○ **5ml (1 tsp) chopped tarragon**
○ **80g (3¼ oz) butter**
○ **salt**

1. Peel and finely chop the shallots. Place them in a small saucepan with the pepper, 2.5ml (½ tsp) salt, tarragon and vinegar.
2. Heat the grill. When it is very hot, place the steak on it and grill for 5 minutes (rare) to 8 minutes (well done).
3. Meanwhile, place the saucepan over a high flame and reduce the vinegar mixture for 3 minutes until only 7-8ml (½ tbls) remains. Remove from the heat and add the mustard and the butter cut into small pieces, beating constantly with a fork. The mixture should be creamy.
4. When the steak is cooked, place it on a board and cut it crosswise into 8 thin slices. Arrange on a serving dish. Coat the meat with the shallot butter and serve immediately.

Côte de Boeuf au Beurre Bercy

Serves 4-5. Preparation: 15 min
Cooking: 20-25 min

Rib of Beef with Bercy Butter

★ ★

○ **1 rib of beef, about 1.2kg (2½ lb)**
○ **200g (7 oz) beef marrow**
○ **150ml (5 fl oz) dry white wine**
○ **4 grey shallots**
○ **120g (4½ oz) soft butter**
○ **15ml (1 tbls) chopped parsley**
○ **15ml (1 tbls) lemon juice**
○ **salt and pepper**

1. Ask the butcher for one of the first cuts off the side, so that you get a piece that is very wide and not too thick in relation to its weight. Trim the fat off but leave the knuckle bone attached.
2. Heat the grill or prepare a barbecue. Peel the shallots and chop as finely as possible. Cut the beef marrow into small cubes, 1cm (½ inch) square.
3. When the grill is hot, seal the beef for 2 minutes on each side, then, according to the thickness of the meat, cook for 15 to 20 minutes. Once sealed, either place the meat further away from the heat or lower the heat to avoid burning. When it is cooked, the meat is puffed up but firm to the touch.
4. While the meat is cooking, prepare the Bercy butter. Heat some salted water in a saucepan. When it starts to bubble, poach the marrow for 5 minutes. Do not let it boil. Remove from the heat with a skimmer and drain in a strainer. Place the shallots in a saucepan with the wine and reduce to half their quantity over a low heat, allow to cool to lukewarm, then add the butter while beating with a fork. Add the parsley, salt, pepper and lemon juice. Mix well and add the marrow. Mix again and pour the sauce into a sauceboat.
5. When the meat is cooked, serve in one piece or cut the meat in thin slices crosswise first but re-form as one whole piece on the dish. Serve the sauce separately.

To make a *marchand de vin* sauce, substitute a full-bodied red wine for the white, and increase the quantity of butter by 100g (4 oz). Omit the marrow.

Filet aux Trois Légumes Glacés

Serves 6. Preparation: 20 min Cooking: 40 min

Fillet with Three Glazed Vegetables

★★

- ○ **1kg (2¼ lb) fillet steak, barded and bound**
- ○ **24 small new onions**
- ○ **24 small new carrots**
- ○ **24 small new turnips**
- ○ **1 large onion**
- ○ **1 large carrot**
- ○ **15ml (1 tbls) granulated sugar**
- ○ **15ml (1 tbls) oil**
- ○ **150g (5 oz) butter**
- ○ **100ml (3½ fl oz) Madeira**
- ○ **salt and pepper**

1. Peel the large carrot and cut into thin rounds. Oil an ovenproof dish and cover it with the carrot rounds. Peel the large onion, mince it very finely and add to the dish. Place the roast on top.
2. Preheat the oven to 230°C (450°F; gas mark 8). Peel the new vegetables and cut them into rounds or ovals of the same size, to ensure that they cook evenly.
3. Place the roast in the oven. Take 3 saucepans, just large enough to hold each sort of new vegetable in one layer. Place each vegetable with 40g (1¾ oz) butter in a separate pan and sauté over a medium heat until the vegetables are golden brown, about 5 minutes, turning with a spatula.
4. When the vegetables are golden, sprinkle each with 5ml (1 tsp) sugar and 2.5ml (½ tsp) salt and cover with water. Allow to cook for 20-25 minutes, according to their size, until there is no water left in the pan and the vegetables are tender and glazed. Keep them hot until the meat is done.
5. After 30 minutes of cooking the roast is rare. After 35 minutes it is medium. When it is cooked as desired, turn the oven off and leave the roast to rest in the closed oven for at least 10 minutes.
6. Arrange the roast on a serving dish, untie the string and surround the meat with the glazed vegetables. Keep warm in the oven while you prepare the gravy: add 100ml (3½ fl oz) water and the Madeira to the ovenproof dish and place the dish over a high heat, scraping the bottom to make a gravy. Turn off the heat and add the remaining 30g (1¼ oz) butter. Mix, add salt and pepper to taste, and pour into a sauceboat through a fine strainer. Serve at once.

Filet en Croûte

Serves 4. Preparation and cooking: 1 hr 40 min

Fillet Steak in Puff Pastry

★★

- ○ **400g (14 oz) puff pastry, frozen or home-made**
- ○ **50g (2 oz) dried mushrooms**
- ○ **120g (4½ oz) butter**
- ○ **salt and pepper**
- ○ **300ml (10 fl oz) beef stock**
- ○ **700g (1½ lb) fillet in 1 piece**
- ○ **brandy**
- ○ **French mustard**
- ○ **100g (4 oz) raw ham**
- ○ **1 egg yolk**

1. Thaw the pastry, if frozen. Meanwhile, soak the dried mushrooms in tepid water for 30 minutes. Wash thoroughly, drain and sauté in 40g (1¾ oz) melted butter. When lightly browned, add salt and pepper and pour in a ladleful of hot beef stock. Cook for 20 minutes, adding more stock if necessary. Then remove from the heat. Pour into a liquidizer and blend to a purée.
2. Preheat the oven to 200°C (400°F; gas mark 6). Melt the remaining butter in a sauté pan. When almost black, add the fillet and brown lightly on all sides, trying not to pierce the meat. Sprinkle brandy over the meat, allow to evaporate, then add salt and pepper to taste. Remove from the heat and put aside. Roll out the pastry in one piece, not too thin but large enough to cover the fillet.
3. Remove the meat from the pan and place on a dish. Spread completely with a thin layer of mustard, then wrap in slices of raw ham. Spread some of the mushroom purée on the pastry, place the meat on top and cover with the remaining mushroom purée. Fold the pastry over the meat to form a roll and flatten slightly. Decorate this with shapes made from any remaining pastry. Glaze with beaten egg yolk. Lift the roll carefully and place on a moistened baking sheet.
4. Place in the oven and cook for 40 minutes. When cooked, remove from the oven, place on a hot serving dish and serve immediately. Carve in front of your guests.

Filet en Croute ▶

Rosbif au Yorkshire Pudding

Serves 6. Preparation and cooking: 2 hr

Roast Beef with Yorkshire Pudding

★★

○ **1 side of beef, 2kg (4½ lb), bound**
○ **220g (8 oz) flour**
○ **400ml (14 fl oz) milk**
○ **3 eggs**
○ **5ml (1 tsp) salt**

1. Preheat the oven to 280°C (525°F; gas mark 11). Prepare the Yorkshire pudding: place the flour in a bowl and break the eggs into the centre. Add salt and milk, whisking with a spatula. Leave to stand until ready to cook.
2. When the oven is hot, place the meat, fat side up, on a rack placed over a roasting pan. Allow to cook for 15 minutes at 280°C, then lower the heat to 200°C (400°F; gas mark 6) and allow another 40 minutes to 1 hour for cooking, according to whether the meat is preferred rare or well done.
3. When the meat is cooked, turn off the oven and leave the meat to rest inside for 5 minutes, then take it out, wrap it in several layers of aluminium foil and leave it in the drawer at the bottom of the oven or in some other warm place.
4. Relight the oven to 230°C (450°F; gas mark 8). Take 45ml (3 tbls) dripping and pour into a gratin dish large enough to contain the batter. Spread the fat evenly over the base and round the edges of the dish. Pour the batter in and place the dish in the oven for 15 minutes, then lower the heat to 220°C (400°F; gas mark 6) and continue cooking for another 15 minutes.
5. When the pudding is golden and well risen, place the meat on a board, cut the string, slice thickly and serve with the pudding.

This typically English roast can be served with a horseradish sauce prepared with 150g (5 fl oz) double cream, whipped and mixed with salt, pepper, a pinch of sugar, 5ml (1 tsp) mustard and 45ml (3 tbls) grated horseradish, fresh or dried.

Rôti en Cocotte

Serves 4. Preparation: 15 min Cooking: 45 min

Casseroled Roast Beef

★

○ **1 piece of rump for roasting, 2kg (4½ lb), bound**
○ **3 medium-sized carrots**
○ **2 medium-sized onions**
○ **1 celery heart**
○ **1 sprig thyme**
○ **1 bay leaf**
○ **30ml (2 tbls) oil**
○ **50g (2 oz) butter**
○ **salt and pepper**

1. Preheat the oven to 250°C (475°F; gas mark 9). Peel the carrots and slice them so thinly that they are transparent, or grate them. Peel the onions and mince them as finely as possible. Wash the celery heart and, without pulling off the outside stalks, cut into very thin slices. Mix all the vegetables together.
2. Heat the oil in an oval pot just large enough to hold the roast. Quickly brown the meat all over on a high heat for 5 minutes, taking care not to pierce the meat while it is being turned.
3. When the meat is lightly browned, remove it from the pot and place on a plate. Season the meat. Discard the oil in which it was cooked and replace this with the butter. Add the vegetables to the pot. Cook over a high flame for 2 minutes, add salt, pepper, the thyme and the bay leaf. Place the meat over the bed of vegetables. Cover the pot and place in the oven. Allow to cook for 25 minutes (rare) to 35 minutes (well done).
4. When the roast is cooked, cut the string, arrange the meat on a serving dish and surround it with the still slightly crisp vegetables.

Tournedos Farcis
Stuffed Tournedos

- ○ **4 tournedos, 150g (5 oz) each, not barded**
- ○ **2 slices raw ham**
- ○ **150g (5 oz) Gruyère cheese**
- ○ **12 pitted green olives**
- ○ **12 medium-sized mushrooms**
- ○ **juice of ½ lemon**
- ○ **100ml (3½ fl oz) Pineau des Charentes (an aperitif)**
- ○ **45ml (3 tbls) double cream**
- ○ **30g (1¼ oz) butter**
- ○ **15ml (1 tbls) oil**
- ○ **salt and pepper**

1. Make a horizontal slit in the middle of each tournedos, without cutting right through the meat. Cut the cheese into 4 slices, slightly smaller than the tournedos. Cut 4 pieces of ham the same size as the tournedos. Slip both ham and cheese into the steaks. Chop the remainder of the ham, with its fat, finely.
2. Cut the olives into small rounds. Trim off the earthy base of the mushrooms, wash and drain them and cut them into very fine slivers. Sprinkle with lemon juice to prevent them changing colour.
3. Tie the steaks up crosswise like a parcel, salt them and pepper them lightly. Heat the oil in a frying pan, add the butter; as soon as it melts, sauté the steaks over a very low heat, to allow the cheese to melt, 2 or 3 minutes each side, depending on their thickness.
4. When the steaks are cooked, remove them from the pan, cover and keep warm.
5. Add the chopped ham to the pan, brown lightly for 1 minute, then add the drained mushrooms and increase the heat. After about 3 minutes, when the mushrooms no longer give out water, add the olives, the Pineau des Charentes and the cream. Add salt and pepper and leave to reduce for 1 minute. Return the steaks and their juices to the pan, reheat them for 30 seconds, turning once, then arrange them on a hot serving dish, coat with their sauce and serve.

Paupiettes de Boeuf
Beef Olives with Anchovies

- ○ **8 slices chuck steak**
- ○ **3 hard-boiled eggs**
- ○ **3 red, ripe tomatoes**
- ○ **200g (7 oz) minced beef**
- ○ **50g (2 oz) breadcrumbs**
- ○ **6 anchovy fillets**
- ○ **salt and pepper**
- ○ **50g (2 oz) butter**
- ○ **150ml (5 fl oz) white wine**
- ○ **150ml (5 fl oz) beef stock**
- ○ **150ml (5 fl oz) single cream**

1. Pound the meat slices to flatten them as much as possible. Immerse the tomatoes into boiling water for 10 seconds, drain, peel, remove the seeds and chop roughly.
2. Place the mince, finely chopped hard-boiled eggs, tomatoes, breadcrumbs, finely chopped anchovy fillets, and a pinch each of salt and pepper into a bowl. Mix carefully until well blended, then divide into 8 equal parts and arrange in the middle of each slice of meat. Roll the slices up, having folded the side edges inwards to prevent the mixture escaping during cooking. Bind the rolls with white thread.
3. Melt the butter in a frying pan, add the beef olives and brown on all sides. Sprinkle with white wine and, when this has evaporated, add the hot stock and salt and pepper to taste. Allow to cook for about 25 to 30 minutes, turning often.
4. When cooked, place the beef olives on a serving dish. Add the cream to the contents remaining in the pan, bring to the boil and let thicken. Pour this over the beef olives and serve immediately.

Entrecôte au Beurre Rouge
Rib Steak with Red Butter

Serves 4. Preparation and cooking: 30 min

★

- ○ **1 rib steak, 900g-1kg (2-2¼ lb)**
- ○ **4 shallots**
- ○ **15ml (1 tbls) wine vinegar**
- ○ **240ml (9 fl oz) red wine: Beaujolais, Cahors, Gigondas, etc**
- ○ **15ml (1 tbls) oil**
- ○ **100g (4 oz) butter**
- ○ **salt and pepper**

1. Preheat the oven to 200°C (400°F; gas mark 6). Heat the oil in a sauté pan, add 20g (¾ oz) butter and brown the steak for 5 minutes on each side, over a low heat, to avoid burning the butter.
2. When the steak is browned, add salt, place the meat on a rack above a roasting pan and allow to cook for 15 to 20 minutes, according to its thickness and to taste. When the steak is cooked, leave it in the turned-off oven for 10 minutes.
3. 10 minutes before serving the meat, prepare the red butter in the sauté pan. Discard the fat from the roasting pan. Peel the shallots, chop them very finely and add them to the pan with the caramelized juices from the meat. Add the vinegar and place the pan over a medium heat. Allow the vinegar to boil until it evaporates, then add the wine and boil over a high heat until only 100ml (3½ fl oz) remains. Add salt and pepper. Take the pan off the heat and allow to cool for 1 minute before adding the butter, cut into small pieces, stirring with a spatula until the mixture is creamy. If the pan is too hot the butter will melt and prevent the mixture becoming creamy.
4. Remove the steak from the oven, cut it into thin slices crosswise, arrange in its original shape on a serving dish and coat with the red butter which has been passed through a strainer.

Aloyau Jardinière
Sirloin with Tomatoes and Olives

Serves 4. Preparation and cooking: 20 min

★★

- ○ **4 red, ripe tomatoes**
- ○ **60ml (4 tbls) oil**
- ○ **2 cloves garlic, sliced**
- ○ **4 slices sirloin, 150g (7 oz) each**
- ○ **salt and pepper**
- ○ **70g (3 oz) black olives**
- ○ **2 peppers in oil, sliced**
- ○ **1 stick celery, sliced**
- ○ **small handful oregano**
- ○ **30ml (2 tbls) vinegar**

1. Immerse the tomatoes in boiling water for 10 seconds. Peel them, halve them, remove the seeds and cut into slices. Pour the oil into a large frying pan and lightly brown the sliced garlic. Add meat slices and brown on both sides over a low heat. Season.
2. Add the pitted olives, sliced peppers, celery and tomatoes, and cook over a high heat, turning the meat a few times.
3. Sprinkle with oregano, baste with vinegar and leave to cook. When ready, place the meat and the vegetables on a hot serving dish and serve at once.

A delicious roast for 12 to 15 people can be made with a rib steak weighing 2.5kg (5½ lb). This cut is marbled and soft so it is not necessary to oil it or bard it before putting it in the oven, just tie it round and place the meat in a very hot oven, gradually lowering the heat to obtain perfect results. The meat can be punctured, like a leg of lamb, and garlic slivers with salt and pepper, sprigs of thyme and rosemary inserted. If there are 24 or more guests and if you have a very large oven, make a sumptuous roast with several ribs of beef on the bone prepared as above.

Boeuf aux Poivrons à la Chinoise

Beef with Peppers, Chinese Style

Serves 4. Preparation: 15 min
Cooking: 10 min
★★

○ **500g (18 oz) sirloin or rump steak**
○ **2 green peppers**
○ **1 medium-sized onion**
○ **1 piece ginger root, 3cm (1¼ inch) long**
○ **15ml (1 tbls) rice wine or sherry**
○ **45ml (3 tbls) soya sauce**
○ **2.5ml (½ tsp) sugar**
○ **5ml (1 tsp) cornflour**
○ **45ml (3 tbls) oil**

1. Ask the butcher for 1 or 2 slices of meat 4cm (1½ inches) thick. Cut each slice into rectangles 2cm (1 inch) by 4cm (1½ inches) and 3cm (1¼ inches) thick. Mix the cornflour, wine, soya sauce and sugar in a bowl. Add the slivers of beef and turn to ensure they are well covered by the mixture.
2. Wash the peppers, cut them into 4 lengthwise, remove the seeds and white filaments, and cut each quarter into fine slivers 3mm (⅛ inch) wide. Peel the onion and mince as finely as possible. Peel and grate the ginger.
3. Heat 30ml (2 tbls) oil in a wok (a Chinese pan with rounded bottom) or a deep-sided sauté pan and cook the onions for 2 minutes, until they become transparent. Add the peppers and sauté for 3 minutes, stirring often with a spatula, till they are tender but not golden. Remove the vegetables with a skimmer and put aside.
4. Add the rest of the oil to the pan and heat. Add the ginger. Stir for 3 seconds and add the meat, and sauté over a high heat for 3 minutes, until no liquid is left in the pan. Put the vegetables back, stir for 10 seconds and remove from the heat. Serve very hot.

You may add to this recipe 100g (4 oz) Chinese vermicelli cut in pieces 10cm (4 inches) long and fried briskly for several seconds, until they are lightly browned.

Faux-Filet au Beurre d'Anchois

Serves 2. Preparation: 5 min Cooking: 5-6 min

Sirloin Steaks with Anchovy Butter

★

○ **2 sirloin steaks, 200g (7 oz) each**
○ **4 anchovies in salt**
○ **15ml (1 tbls) wine vinegar**
○ **15ml (1 tbls) oil**
○ **50g (2 oz) butter**
○ **pepper**

1. Wash the anchovies in running water to remove all the grains of salt. Separate into fillets, remove the bones and cut into small cubes. Put aside on a plate.
2. Heat the oil in a frying pan. Add 20g (¾ oz) butter and cook the steaks in this over a medium heat for 1-2 minutes on each side, according to their thickness and to taste.
3. Arrange the steaks on individual plates and discard all the cooking fat from the pan. Lower the heat and add the vinegar and then the anchovies. Scrape the bottom of the pan with a spatula to detach the crusty bits from the meat, and after 30 seconds, when the anchovies have been reduced to a purée, remove the pan from the heat.
4. Away from the heat, add the rest of the butter to the pan in small pieces, turning with the spatula until the mixture becomes creamy. Pepper generously, coat the steaks with the sauce and serve immediately.

Serve with *tomates à la provencale* (tomatoes stuffed with garlic, herbs and breadcrumbs), sautéed aubergine, sautéed or battered and deep-fried onion rings.

Tournedos Rossini

Tournedos in Madeira Sauce

Serves 4. Preparation and cooking: 30 min

★★★

○ **4 tournedos, 150g (5 oz) each**
○ **4 slices bread (from a cottage loaf)**
○ **200g (7 oz) butter**
○ **salt and pepper**
○ **150ml (5 fl oz) Madeira**
○ **15ml (1 tbls) flour**
○ **150ml (5 fl oz) beef stock**
○ **4 round slices of goose liver pâté**
○ **4 slices black truffle**

1. Bind the tournedos to preserve their shape during cooking.
2. Cut the slices of bread to fit the tournedos, brown in 50g (2 oz) butter and keep warm.
3. Heat 100g (4 oz) butter in a large frying pan, add the tournedos and cook on both sides over a high heat for about 3 minutes. Then season, remove from the pan and keep warm on a serving dish.
4. Add the Madeira to the remaining cooking juices and bring to a boil. Mix the remaining butter with the flour and stir into the sauce, which will thicken. Dilute with the boiling Madeira mixture and allow to cook until a thick sauce is formed (about 5 minutes).
5. At this point, top each piece of bread with a tournedos, then a slice of pâté, then a slice of truffle. Pour over the Madeira sauce and serve immediately.

Tournedos à l'Anglaise

Tournedos English Style

Serves 4. Preparation and cooking: 40 min

★★

○ **300g (10 oz) cèpes (boletus mushrooms)**
○ **100g (4 oz) butter**
○ **1 clove garlic, sliced**
○ **100g (4 oz) cooked ham**
○ **salt and pepper**
○ **2.5ml (½ tsp) meat extract**
○ **4 tournedos weighing 150g (5 oz) each**

1. Scrape the cèpes with a sharp knife to remove all traces of earth, clean with a damp cloth, dry carefully and cut into thin slices.
2. Melt 50g (2 oz) butter. Add the sliced garlic and allow to colour, then add the ham, which has been roughly chopped, and allow to brown over a low heat. Then add the mushrooms, season with salt and pepper, and stir. Cook for several minutes over a high flame to evaporate any liquid. Add 75ml (2½ fl oz) lukewarm water in which the meat extract has been dissolved and allow to cook for 15-20 minutes over a low heat.
3. Shortly before the end of this time, melt the remaining butter in a pan and cook the tournedos on both sides over a high flame for 3-4 minutes. Season. Place the tournedos on a serving dish, cover with the cèpes and their sauce and serve.

Hamburgers à l'Oignon

Hamburgers with Onions

Serves 4. Preparation: 20 min Cooking: 10 min

★

○ **400g (14 oz) minced beef**
○ **1 large onion**
○ **2 eggs**
○ **salt and pepper**
○ **pinch nutmeg**
○ **15ml (1 tbls) oil**

1. Cut the onion in half. Chop one half very finely and slice the other into rings. Put the meat in a bowl and add the chopped onion, the eggs, and a pinch of salt, pepper and nutmeg.
2. Mix the ingredients together very carefully and divide the mixture into four. If you have a 'hamburger press', use it to shape the burgers, otherwise use your hands.
3. Brush both sides of the hamburgers generously with oil and cook under a very hot grill for about 10 minutes. Arrange on a heated serving dish and garnish with onion rings.

Boeuf Bourguignon

Serves 8. Preparation: 45 min Cooking: 4 hr

Beef Burgundy Style

★ ★

○ **1.8kg (4 lb) beef: ⅓ rump, ⅓ silverside, ⅓ chuck**
○ **1 litre (1¾ pints) red Burgundy wine**
○ **250g (9 oz) bacon**
○ **36 small onions**
○ **36 small button mushrooms**
○ **30ml (2 tbls) marc or cognac**
○ **10ml (2 tsp) cornflour or arrowroot**
○ **50g (2 oz) butter**
○ **15ml (1 tbls) oil**
○ **juice of ½ lemon**
○ **salt and pepper**

1. Peel the onions. Cut the bacon into sticks 1cm (½ inch) across. Cut the meat into cubes 4cm (1½ inches) square, and season.
2. Bring to the boil 2 litres (3½ pints) water in a saucepan, immerse the bacon sticks and blanch for 5 minutes, drain.
3. Heat the oil in a large stewpan and lightly brown the bacon sticks over a low heat for about 8 minutes, till the bacon fat is transparent. Remove with a skimmer and put aside in a bowl.
4. Add 20g (¾ oz) butter to the pan and add the onions. Lightly brown over a low heat for about 15 minutes. Remove with a skimmer and add to the bacon.
5. Add several of the cubes of beef to the pan and brown lightly (about 5 minutes), then remove and put aside. Repeat until all the meat is browned. Then discard the fat from cooking and pour the wine into the pan while scraping up the crusty bits with a spatula. Bring the wine to the boil, set alight, and when the flame is extinguished, return the beef to the pan. Bring back to the boil, cover and simmer over a very low heat, without boiling, for about 4 hours.
6. After 3 hours, add the bacon sticks and onions. Trim the earthy base off the mushrooms, wash, wipe and place in a sauté pan with the lemon juice and the remainder of the butter. Brown over a high heat until they give out no more liquid and are lightly browned, then add the mushrooms and their juices to the stew.
7. After about 4 hours, when the meat is almost tender, pour the contents of the stewpan into a saucepan through a strainer. Return the contents of the strainer to the stewpan and cover. Allow the sauce to stand for 5 minutes, then skim off the fat with a spoon.
8. Dilute the cornflour or arrowroot with 30ml (2 tbls) cold water and pour the mixture into the saucepan, stirring with a wooden spoon. Bring the sauce to the boil, then heat the marc or cognac in a small saucepan, set alight and add to the sauce. Boil over a high heat until the sauce thickens enough to coat the spoon and reduce until just enough is left to cover the pieces of meat (5 to 10 minutes). Add salt and pepper to taste, pour into the stewpan and simmer for 10 minutes, then serve immediately.

Boeuf Bourguignon should be served very hot on hot plates, accompanied by steamed or gratinéed potatoes. This dish is best when prepared with a large quantity of meat and better still when reheated: so prepare two meals at once, one to serve tonight and one to refrigerate.

In former times, a whole side of beef rump steak was prepared à la bourguignonne. *Try making it with a piece of rump steak weighing 1.6kg (3½ lb), larded and bound by the butcher. After the wine has been added to the stewpan, cover and cook in a preheated oven for 4 hours at 140°C (275°F; gas mark 1).*

Tournedos à l'Anglaise (p69) ▶

Daube aux Oeufs

Serves 4. Preparation and cooking: 3 hr

Beef with Golden Eggs

○ **250g (9 oz) onions**
○ **2 cloves garlic**
○ **bunch of mint**
○ **bunch of parsley**
○ **60ml (4 tbls) oil**
○ **salt**
○ **2.5ml (½ tsp) saffron**
○ **10ml (2 tsp) powdered ginger**
○ **800g (1¾ lb) neck of beef**
○ **4 eggs**

1. Peel and finely chop the onion. Peel and crush the garlic. Cut the meat into large chunks.
2. Tie the mint and parsley together.
3. Put the oil into a stewpan, add the garlic, salt, half the saffron, the ginger and 150ml (5 fl oz) water. Beat together with a fork until it becomes creamy. Add the meat and stir, then add the onion and mix all together.
4. Baste with 300ml (10 fl oz) water. Add the bunch of herbs and cover. Place the dish over a high flame until it boils, then lower the heat as much as possible and cook for two hours. The meat will be extremely tender. Remove the meat and the bunch of herbs from the dish. Put the meat in a warm place; discard the herbs.
5. Reduce the remaining juices to a syrupy sauce. This will take about 10 minutes. Meanwhile hard boil the eggs, then remove them from the water and shell them. In another saucepan, boil 480ml (18 fl oz) water with the remaining saffron. Plunge the eggs into this for 2 minutes: they will become yellow. Drain them and cut in half.
6. Now place the meat on a heated serving dish, cover with its sauce and garnish with the eggs. Serve immediately.

Boeuf à la Milanaise

Serves 4. Preparation and cooking: 4 hr 30 min

Beef Milan Style

★★

○ **1kg (2¼ lb) chuck**
○ **50g (2 oz) ham**
○ **100g (4 oz) butter**
○ **300ml (10 fl oz) full-bodied red wine**
○ **1 pinch of mixed spice**
○ **2 cloves**
○ **2 mushroom broth cubes**
○ **nutmeg**
○ **salt and pepper**
○ **1 onion**
○ **1 carrot**
○ **1 stick celery**
○ **1 leek**
○ **2 cloves garlic**
○ **bunch of aromatic herbs: marjoram, sage, rosemary and basil**
○ **4 ripe tomatoes**

1. Chop finely together the vegetables, garlic and herbs. Lard the meat with the ham which has been cut into small strips, then brown in melted butter in a stewpan.
2. When it is well coloured, sprinkle with the wine and cover with the chopped vegetables. Add the mixed spice and the cloves and, gradually, the mushroom broth cubes dissolved in 480ml (18 fl oz) water. Flavour with a little grated nutmeg, salt and pepper. Cook, covered, over a low heat.
3. After 4 hours (or 1½ hours in a pressure cooker), the dish is ready. There should be sufficient gravy – add a little water during cooking if necessary.

This stew is even better reheated.

Goulache
Goulash

Serves 4. Preparation: 30 min Cooking: 2 hr

★★

- ○ **300g (10 oz) onions**
- ○ **50g (2 oz) lard**
- ○ **15ml (1 tbls) vinegar**
- ○ **10ml (2 tsp) paprika**
- ○ **800g (1¾ lb) neck of beef**
- ○ **300g (10 oz) tomatoes**
- ○ **1 clove garlic**
- ○ **marjoram**
- ○ **1 bay leaf**
- ○ **cumin**
- ○ **salt and pepper**

1. Chop the onions and brown in the lard in a stewpan. Baste them with the vinegar and sprinkle with paprika.
2. Add the meat, cut into large chunks the size of walnuts, stir and continue cooking.
3. Chop the tomatoes and add, together with the garlic, bay leaf and marjoram and cumin to taste. After about 30 minutes, season with salt and pepper. Continue cooking over a low heat until the meat is well cooked (about 1½ hours). The sauce should be thick but plentiful: if necessary add a little hot water while cooking.

Serve with boiled potatoes.

Daube aux Noix
Beef Stew with Walnuts

Serves 4. Preparation and cooking: 3 hr 30 min
Marinade: 12 hr

★★

- ○ **800g (1¾ lb) neck of beef**
- ○ **200g (7 oz) onions**
- ○ **1 clove garlic**
- ○ **15ml (1 tbls) chopped parsley**
- ○ **1 bay leaf**
- ○ **2 cloves**
- ○ **salt and pepper**
- ○ **75ml (2½ fl oz) oil**
- ○ **75ml (2½ fl oz) vinegar**
- ○ **2.5ml (½ tsp) sugar**
- ○ **1 strip orange peel**
- ○ **12-16 walnut halves**

1. Cut the meat into large chunks, and place in an enamel or earthenware stewpan, together with the parsley, bay leaf, cloves, salt and pepper. Finely chop the garlic and onions and add to the meat.
2. Mix together the oil and vinegar and pour over the meat. Stir well, then cover and leave to marinate for 12 hours.
3. Preheat the oven to 160°C (300°F; gas mark 2). Add the sugar, orange peel and walnuts to the meat and its marinade, and stir well. Seal the pan with luting paste. Place in the preheated oven and cook for 1 hour at 160°C, then lower the heat to 120°C (250°F; gas mark ½) and cook 2 hours longer. When the meat is tender, remove the pan from the oven and, with a spoon, skim off any fat which has risen to the surface. Serve immediately from the cooking pot.

To skim off fat from a bouillon, let it stand for 15 minutes or more after removing from the heat. Then skim the top with a spoon. To degrease completely, pour the bouillon through a sieve lined with fine dampened white muslin which will hold all the fat. If you have the time, place the bouillon in the refrigerator. The fat will solidify on the surface and can easily be lifted off.

Bouilli à la Bretonne

Serves 8. Preparation: 30 min Cooking: 4 hr 30 min

Boiled Beef Breton Style

★ ★ ★

- ○ **1.5kg (3¼ lb) chuck**
- ○ **3 carrots**
- ○ **3 turnips**
- ○ **1 stick celery**
- ○ **1 onion**
- ○ **2 cloves**
- ○ **thyme**
- ○ **1 bay leaf**
- ○ **10 coriander seeds**
- ○ **5ml (1 tsp) peppercorns**
- ○ **5ml (1 tsp) coarse salt**
- ○ **250g (9 oz) buckwheat flour**
- ○ **100g (4 oz) butter**
- ○ **75ml (2½ fl oz) milk**
- ○ **1 egg**
- ○ **120ml (4 fl oz) cream**
- ○ **15ml (1 tbls) sugar**
- ○ **100g (4 oz) raisins**
- ○ **1 small savoy cabage**
- ○ **salt and pepper**

1. Bring to the boil 3 litres (5¼ pints) water in a large saucepan. Add the meat and return to the boil. Then lower the heat and cook for 30 minutes, skimming often. In a small bowl, soak the raisins in hot water to cover.
2. Meanwhile, clean the carrots, turnips and celery. At the end of 30 minutes, add them to the beef, along with the onion spiked with cloves, thyme, bay leaf, coriander, peppercorns and coarse salt. Put the flour into a bowl. Take 1 ladleful of the broth and mix it with 60g (2¼ oz) butter. Add this mixture to the flour. Mix well and add milk, cream, egg and sugar, stirring continuously. Add the drained raisins and mix again.
3. Enclose this mixture in a white cloth, forming a roll. Make a knot at each end. Cook the meat for a further 2½ hours, then plunge the roll into the soup and cook for 1½ hours.
4. Meanwhile, prepare the cabbage. Cut into 4 and boil for 5 minutes in salted water, then drain.
5. Melt the remaining butter in a pot, add the cabbage and salt and pepper to taste and cook, covered, over a low heat (adding a little soup if necessary) until it is tender. At this time the mixture in the cloth roll should be cooked, so remove it from the soup.
6. Remove the meat from the soup and slice. Arrange the meat on a warmed serving dish. Unroll the cloth and crumble its contents around the meat. Complete the dish with the well-drained vegetables from the soup and the cabbage. Pour the soup into a tureen and serve separately; it will provide a sauce.

It is always best to prepare a stew with the same wine you intend to serve with the meal.

Daubes *are very delicious, and very popular in France. This method of cooking meat is very ancient and still deserves to be appreciated today. It involves cooking in a covered pot, as slowly and for as long as possible, meat which may or may not have been marinated. The marinade would usually consist of red or white wine, sometimes seasoned with vinegar, with a bouquet garni, spices and chopped or sliced vegetables. Sometimes the meat is sealed in hot oil before it is placed in its marinade. All* daubes *are better when reheated and all can be eaten cold with salads and garlic* croûtons. *If you prefer a jellied* daube, *add 1 or 2 calf's feet (preferably blanched) when you cook it.*

Boeuf à la Milanaise (p72) ▶

Langue de Boeuf Gros Sel

Serves 4-6. Preparation and cooking: 2 hr 30 min

Boiled Tongue with Vegetables

★★

- ○ **1 trimmed beef tongue**
- ○ **6 carrots**
- ○ **6 turnips**
- ○ **6 leeks**
- ○ **6 potatoes**
- ○ **1 onion spiked with 1 clove**
- ○ **3 sprigs parsley**
- ○ **1 small stick celery**
- ○ **1 small sprig thyme**
- ○ **½ bay leaf**
- ○ **coarse salt**
- ○ **table salt**

1. Wash the tongue very carefully, then place in a pan, cover generously with cold water and bring to the boil over a medium heat. Then lower the heat and allow to simmer gently, skimming the froth as it appears, for 30 minutes.
2. At the end of this time, remove the tongue from the pan and drain well. Allow the meat to cool a little, then peel and return to the washed pan, cover with 2½ litres (4½ pints) cold water and bring to the boil. Tie together the parsley, celery, thyme and bay leaf and add this bouquet garni to the pan, along with the spiked onion. Add 10ml (2 tsp) coarse salt and allow to boil gently for 2 hours, partially covered.
3. At the end of 1 hour, peel the carrots, leeks and turnips and add them to the pan. Peel the potatoes and place in a small saucepan. Cover with cold water, add salt and cook on a low heat. When the potatoes are tender turn off the heat and cover to keep warm
4. After the vegetables have cooked for 45 minutes, they and the tongue should be tender. Remove the tongue from the pan, cut into slices ½cm (¼ inch) thick and arrange on a hot serving dish. Surround the meat with the vegetables and the drained potatoes. Baste everything with a little bouillon. Serve the bouillon separately as soup, accompanied by coarse sea salt, gherkins, various kinds of mustards and small pickled onions.

You can serve the soup with croûtons (slices of bread cut into triangles or other shapes and sautéed in butter) and grated cheese, and the tongue with a tomato or spicy onion sauce.

Flanchet Farci au Vert

Serves 6. Preparation: 30 min Cooking: 3 hr 30 min

Stuffed Beef Flank

★★★

- ○ **1.5kg (3¼ lb) flank**
- ○ **250g (9 oz) minced silverside**
- ○ **150g (5 oz) chard leaves**
- ○ **150g (5 oz) spinach**
- ○ **15ml (1 tbls) chopped parsley**
- ○ **100g (4 oz) grated Gruyère cheese**
- ○ **1 egg**
- ○ **50g (2 oz) white bread, crusts removed**
- ○ **100ml (3½ fl oz) milk**
- ○ **6 carrots**
- ○ **3 turnips**
- ○ **6 small leeks**
- ○ **1 head celery**
- ○ **1 onion spiked with 3 cloves**
- ○ **1 sprig thyme**
- ○ **1 bay leaf**
- ○ **4 sprigs parsley**
- ○ **nutmeg**
- ○ **salt and pepper**

1. Ask your butcher to make a slit in the meat, forming a pocket. Wash the spinach and remove the stalks. Wash the chard. (If chard is not available, use double the amount of spinach.) Place the spinach and the chard, with the water still clinging to their leaves, in a large saucepan. Salt lightly, cover and cook over a high flame for 4 minutes. Then drain thoroughly, pressing to extract all the water, and chop finely. Place in a bowl with the minced silverside, chopped parsley, grated cheese, egg and salt, pepper and nutmeg to taste.
2. Heat the milk in a small saucepan, add the bread which you have broken up, boil for 1 minute and add to the salad bowl. Mix well.
3. Stuff the meat with this mixture and sew up the opening with coarse white thread. Cut off the celery leaves and tie them together with the thyme, bay leaf and parsley to form a bouquet garni.
4. In a large pan, place the meat, spiked onion and bouquet garni. Cover generously with cold water and place over a medium heat. When it boils, skim, add salt, lower the heat and allow to simmer gently for 3½ hours.
5. 1 hour before the end of cooking, add the peeled vegetables.
6. When meat and vegetables are tender, remove from the pan and arrange on a hot serving dish. Slice the meat and keep warm. Remove and discard the onion and bouquet garni, pass the stock through a fine strainer, pour into a soup bowl and serve very hot.

Marmite Milanaise en Sauce Verte

Milanese Stew with Green Sauce

Serves 12.
Preparation and cooking: 4 hr 30 min
★ ★

○ **1kg (2¼ lb) rump, larded and bound by the butcher**
○ **1kg (2¼ lb) rib of beef, bound**
○ **1 ox tongue, trimmed**
○ **800g (1¾ lb) shin of veal, boned and bound**
○ **1 small chicken**
○ **500g (18 oz) Italian spiced sausage (cotechino) or Lyons sausage**
○ **salt**

For the green sauce:
○ **2 small onions**
○ **1 clove garlic**
○ **6 anchovies in salt**
○ **45ml (3 tbls) capers**
○ **60ml (4 tbls) chopped parsley**
○ **30ml (2 tbls) lemon juice**
○ **30ml (2 tbls) vinegar**
○ **150ml (5 fl oz) olive oil**
○ **pepper**

1. Place the rib in a large saucepan, cover generously with cold water and bring to the boil over a low heat, skimming as necessary. When boiling point is reached, add salt and the bound piece of rump. Leave to cook for 1½ hours before adding the chicken.
2. Meanwhile, blanch the tongue in boiling water for 10 minutes.
3. 30 minutes after the chicken is added, add the veal and tongue. To recap: 4½ hours for the rib, 4 hours for the rump, 2½ hours for the chicken and 2 hours for the tongue and the veal. Skim every time meat is added to the pot. If necessary, add more boiling water, but only in small quantities, because the bouillon must be very reduced and only barely cover the meat. Traditionally, not even aromatic herbs are added to the bouillon – this is an all-meat stew. You might add 1 carrot, 1 onion, 1 stick celery and a tiny bouquet garni, but nothing else.
4. 1 hour before the end of cooking, pierce the sausage with a fork and place in a saucepan of cold water. Boil gently for 1 hour. When cooked, add the sausage to the other meats, which will also be cooked by then.
5. Meanwhile, prepare the green sauce: peel the onions and cloves of garlic and chop finely. Wash the anchovies, separate into fillets and chop into small pieces, likewise the capers. Put these ingredients into a bowl with the parsley, add vinegar, lemon juice and pepper and incorporate the oil very slowly by beating with a fork, as if making a mayonnaise. Refrigerate until you are ready to serve it.
6. When everything is ready, peel the tongue and slice thinly. Cut up the chicken. Arrange all the different types of meat on a hot serving dish, baste with bouillon and serve. Serve the green sauce separately, and some of the bouillon in a soup bowl.

This dish may be served with spinach or mashed potatoes, as they do in the Piedmont region of northern Italy, where they also serve fruits pickled in vinegar, known as *mostarda*.

Don't cook cabbage with boiled beef without having blanched it first, as its flavour will dominate everything. In addition, a stock in which cabbage was boiled will not last as long as one cooked without it. For best results, cook the cabbage separately in some of the stock with, perhaps, a piece of bacon.

Boiled beef should cook uncovered: its delicious smell will spread through the whole house, creating a warm, cosy atmosphere. If you want to have good soup, put the meat into cold water; if you want the meat to be especially savoury, then put it into boiling water. Meat plunged into cold water gives all its juices and flavour to the soup; in boiling water it is immediately sealed. If you want both good stock and savoury meat, plunge the first type of meat (for instance the ribs) into cold water, then when the water boils add the rest of the meat. Save the former for the next day to mince or to make a salad with; the second lot of meat is best served very hot with the vegetables it was cooked with.

Steak Tartare

Steak Tartare

Serves 4. Preparation: 20 min

★ ★

- ○ **500g (18 oz) fillet**
- ○ **salt and pepper**
- ○ **mustard**
- ○ **75ml (2½ fl oz) oil**
- ○ **juice of 1 lemon**
- ○ **few drops Tabasco sauce**
- ○ **2 dashes Worcestershire sauce**
- ○ **4 eggs**
- ○ **2 onions**
- ○ **few sprigs parsley**
- ○ **large handful capers**
- ○ **12 pickled gherkins**

1. Mince the fillet in a mincer (or better still, use a large knife). Place in a bowl and season with salt and pepper.
2. In another bowl, mix the mustard with the oil, then add lemon juice, Tabasco and Worcestershire sauce. Add to the minced meat, season well and divide the meat into 4 equal portions. Form into round patties and place on 4 plates.
3. Make a hollow in the centre of each patty and stand half an eggshell in it with 1 egg yolk in each. Finely chop the onions; chop the parsley. Leave the capers whole; slice the gherkins.
4. Surround each patty with small heaps of onion, parsley and capers, alternating with gherkins. Serve cool but not very cold. To eat, each person mixes the egg yolk into the meat, discarding the shell, and adds the other ingredients to taste.

Bifteck Haché à la Russe

Russian Hamburgers

Serves 4. Preparation and cooking: 20 min

★ ★

- ○ **400g (14 oz) minced flank**
- ○ **100g (4 oz) butter**
- ○ **salt and pepper**
- ○ **nutmeg**
- ○ **oil**
- ○ **75ml (2½ fl oz) yogurt**

1. Place the minced meat in a bowl and add 70g (3 oz) soft butter, cut into small pieces, and a pinch each of salt, pepper and grated nutmeg. Mix the ingredients carefully so that the butter mixes properly with the meat.
2. Make hamburgers with this mixture, coat them with oil and arrange under a very hot grill. Cook on both sides for 10 minutes then place on a hot serving dish.
3. Just before they are cooked, melt the remaining butter, mix with the yogurt and stir for a few seconds. Pour this sauce over the hamburgers and serve immediately.

Galettes aux Beurre

Beef Pancakes with Butter

Serves 4-5. Preparation: 15 min Cooking: 10 min

★

- ○ **600g (1 lb 5 oz) minced steak**
- ○ **200g (8 oz) soft butter**
- ○ **30ml (2 tbls) Madeira**
- ○ **1 egg**
- ○ **15ml (1 tbls) flour**
- ○ **30ml (2 tbls) white breadcrumbs**
- ○ **150g (6 oz) fresh cream**
- ○ **7.5ml (1½ tsp) oil**
- ○ **pinch nutmeg**
- ○ **salt and pepper**

1. Put the meat in a dish, moisten with 15ml (1 tbls) of Madeira, and season. Add a pinch of nutmeg, 150g (6 oz) of soft butter and blend all together well with a wooden spoon, two forks or – better still – your hands, until perfectly smooth.
2. Beat the egg well in a bowl with a little salt and pepper. Put the flour on one flat plate and the breadcrumbs on another.
3. Divide the mixture into 8 equal parts, roll them into balls between your hands, then flatten into thin cakes 1.5cm (½ inch) thick. Dip them in the flour, then the beaten egg, then the breadcrumbs, and leave on a board.
4. Heat the oil in a frying pan, add to it the remaining 50g (2 oz) of butter and fry the cakes over a low heat until they are golden brown, about 2 minutes each side. Remove with a spatula and arrange around a serving dish kept hot over a pan of boiling water.
5. Pour away the cooking fat, glaze the frying pan with the other 15ml (1 tbls) of Madeira. When it has evaporated add the fresh cream. Boil for 30 seconds and pour into the centre of the cakes in the dish, and serve.

Palets du Poitou à la Moelle

Serves 6. Preparation: 20 min Cooking: 15 min

Beef Marrow Rissoles

★

- ○ **600g (21 oz) minced steak**
- ○ **300g (10 oz) beef marrow**
- ○ **100g (4 oz) white bread, crusts removed**
- ○ **150ml (5 fl oz) milk**
- ○ **2 eggs**
- ○ **2 medium-sized onions, finely chopped**
- ○ **45ml (3 tbls) oil**
- ○ **50g (2 oz) butter**
- ○ **30ml (2 tbls) white wine**
- ○ **juice of 1 lemon**
- ○ **15ml (1 tbls) chopped parsley**
- ○ **nutmeg**
- ○ **salt and pepper**

1. Heat the milk in a saucepan, add the crumbled bread, stirring with a spatula until a smooth and sticky paste is obtained, then remove from the heat and allow to cool.
2. Place onions in a pan with 25g (1 oz) butter over a low heat. Cook, stirring occasionally, until slightly browned, then remove from the heat.
3. Mash the marrow in a bowl with a fork, add the mince, mix and add the bread and browned onions. Break in the eggs, add salt, pepper and nutmeg to taste and work the mixture with one hand until well blended.
4. Divide the mixture into 8 equal parts, roll into balls, then flatten into rissoles 1.5cm (slightly more than ½ inch) thick. Moisten your hands with water to prevent the mixture from sticking to your fingers.
5. Heat the oil in a frying pan, add the remaining butter and, when melted, brown the rissoles for 15 minutes over a low heat, turning once. When cooked, place on a serving dish and keep warm (they must be eaten very hot) in a low oven.
6. Discard the cooking fat, deglaze the pan with the white wine, scraping up the crusty bits on the bottom, allow the wine to evaporate then add the lemon juice and parsley. Pour over the rissoles and serve immediately.

Croquettes aux Champignons

Serves 4. Preparation: 30 min Cooking: 20 min

Meatballs with Dried Mushrooms

★★

- ○ **40g (1¾ oz) dried mushrooms**
- ○ **400g (14 oz) minced flank**
- ○ **100g (4 oz) mortadella sausage**
- ○ **100g (4 oz) Emmenthal cheese, grated**
- ○ **small bunch basil**
- ○ **2 eggs**
- ○ **salt and pepper**
- ○ **1 pinch grated nutmeg**
- ○ **flour**
- ○ **½ onion**
- ○ **40g (1¾ oz) butter**
- ○ **45ml (3 tbls) oil**
- ○ **30ml (2 tbls) tomato purée**

1. Soak the dried mushrooms in tepid water for ½ hour. Then wash them thoroughly and chop very finely.
2. Meanwhile, place the meat in a bowl and add the mortadella (put twice through a mincer), mushrooms, grated cheese, chopped basil, eggs, a pinch each of salt, pepper and grated nutmeg. Mix with a wooden spoon until well blended, then divide into balls the size of an apricot. Coat these in flour.
3. Brown the chopped onion in the butter and hot oil in a large pan. Add the meatballs, brown them on all sides, then add 150ml (5 fl oz) water mixed with the tomato purée. Add salt and pepper and cook for about 20 minutes over a low heat, turning often. Then turn into a hot serving dish and serve immediately.

Terrine aux Poireaux et à la Menthe

Minced Beef with Leeks and Mint

Serves 5-6. Preparation: 25 min
Cooking: 2 hr Refrigeration: 8 hr
★★

○ **500g (18 oz) minced chuck or silverside**
○ **1kg (2¼ lb) leeks**
○ **50g (2 oz) bread, crusts removed**
○ **100ml (3½ fl oz) double cream**
○ **1 egg**
○ **15ml (1 tbls) chopped mint**
○ **100g (4 oz) shelled peas (petits pois if available)**
○ **nutmeg**
○ **15ml (1 tbls) oil**
○ **salt and pepper**

1. Peel the leeks, cut part of the green away, weigh and keep 500g (18 oz). Cut into rounds 3mm (⅛ inch) long. Bring some water to the boil in a large pan, add salt and blanch the leeks for 3 minutes, then drain in a sieve, pressing to extract all the water.
2. Heat the cream in a small saucepan, crumble in the bread and mix to obtain a sticky paste, then remove from the heat.
3. Place the meat in a bowl, sprinkle generously with nutmeg, salt and pepper, add the bread paste and knead with your hands until well blended. Add the leeks, mix again, then the egg and mint, and work until you have a compact mixture.
4. Preheat the oven to 140°C (275°F; gas mark 1). Lightly oil an ovenproof dish. Place in it a layer of one-third of the beef mixture, press down well, scatter peas here and there, then put in another third of the mixture, then the rest of the peas and finish with a layer of meat. Press down well and brush the top with oil. Cover and bake for 2 hours.
5. At the end of this time, remove from the oven and allow to cool at least 8 hours before serving.

Accompany with a sweet-and-sour tomato sauce.

Rillettes de Queue de Boeuf

Potted Oxtail

Serves 6. Preparation: 20 min Cooking:4-5 hr
Refrigeration: 8 hr
★★

○ **1.5kg (3¼ lb) oxtail (the fleshy part)**
○ **750ml (1 bottle) red wine: Beaujolais or Côtes du Rhône**
○ **2 large ripe tomatoes**
○ **200g (7 oz) carrots**
○ **250g (9 oz) onions**
○ **6 shallots**
○ **2 cloves garlic**
○ **100g (4 oz) button mushrooms**
○ **juice of ½ lemon**
○ **3 cloves**
○ **6 sprigs parsley**
○ **1 stick celery**
○ **1 bay leaf**
○ **1 sprig thyme**
○ **1 slice orange peel, 2cm (¾ inch) by 3cm (1¼ inches)**
○ **15ml (1 tbls) chopped fines herbes: a mixture of parsley, chives, tarragon, chervil**
○ **45ml (3 tbls) oil**
○ **salt and pepper**

1. Cut the oxtail into pieces 4cm (1½ inches) long. Cut the tomatoes in half, press to remove the seeds and crush. Peel the carrots and cut into rounds. Leave 1 onion whole and spike it with cloves. Peel and roughly chop the shallots and the remainder of the onions. Trim the earthy base off the mushrooms. Wash, wipe dry, cut into quarters and sprinkle with lemon juice. Wrap the orange peel, thyme and bay leaf in the celery and parsley and bind with thread to form a bouquet garni.
2. Heat the oil in a pan and lightly brown the pieces of oxtail, removing them when they are done, and put aside. Add to the pan the carrot rounds, shallots and chopped onions and allow to brown lightly, then add the oxtail, bouquet garni, peeled garlic, tomatoes, mushrooms and their juice, and barely cover with wine. Add salt. Bring to the boil, cover the pan and allow to simmer for 4-5 hours, until the flesh is tender and comes away from the bone easily.
3. Remove the pieces of oxtail, sieve the juice, put the vegetables aside and reduce the juice until only about 240ml (9 fl oz) remains. Remove from the heat.
4. Remove the meat from the bones and shred with a fork. Put the vegetables – except the onion spiked with cloves and the bouquet garni – through a vegetable mill. Skim the fat from the gravy, add vegetable purée, meat and *fines herbes*. Add pepper to taste, mix and place in an earthenware dish. Leave to cool for 8 hours before serving.

Accompany with a green or mixed salad, gherkins, small pickled onions and toast.

Daube de Joue en Gelée

Jellied Beef Cheek

Serves 6. Preparation: 20 min Cooking: 2½-3 hr
Refrigeration: 8 hr
★★

○ **1kg (2¼ lb) cheek of beef**
○ **2 calf's feet**
○ **24 small onions**
○ **3 carrots**
○ **1 clove garlic**
○ **1 sprig thyme**
○ **1 bay leaf**
○ **6 sprigs parsley**
○ **1 piece orange peel, 2cm**
   (¾ inch) by 3cm (1¼ inches)
○ **15ml (1 tbls) cognac**
○ **½ litre (18 fl oz) white wine**
○ **5ml (1 tsp) peppercorns**
○ **salt**

1. Halve the calf's feet and blanch in boiling water for 10 minutes. Peel the carrots and cut into cubes 1cm (½ inch) square. Peel the onions. Peel and crush the garlic and wrap in the parsley sprigs, together with the orange peel, thyme and bay leaf. Tie together with white thread to make a bouquet garni.
2. In a stewpan, place the calf's feet, pieces of cheek, carrots, onions, bouquet garni, salt, pepper and cognac, and moisten with white wine, which should just cover the stew. If it does not, add water. Cover and bring to the boil. Simmer for 2½ to 3 hours, until the meat is very tender.
3. Remove the calf's feet from the pan, take out the bones, cut the flesh into small cubes and return to the pan. Discard the bouquet garni. Leave to cool, then pour everything into a terrine, mixing so that the contents are distributed equally. Put in a cold place for at least 8 hours. Dip the dish in hot water for 3 minutes then turn out.

Serve with a salad and garlic bread.

Terrine de Foie

Calf's Liver Terrine

Serves 6. Preparation: 30 min Cooking: 1 hr 30 min
Refrigeration: 12 hr
★★

○ **500g (18 oz) calf's liver**
○ **200g (7 oz) mild-cure bacon**
○ **200g (7 oz) sausagemeat**
○ **250g (9 oz) sliced bacon**
○ **50ml (1¾ fl oz) cognac**
○ **50ml (1¾ fl oz) Madeira**
○ **2 pinches mixed spice**
○ **1 clove garlic**
○ **3 sprigs thyme**
○ **3 bay leaves**
○ **2.5ml (½ tsp) thyme leaves**
○ **30ml (2 tbls) chopped parsley**
○ **salt and pepper**

1. Cut the liver into cubes 1cm (½ inch) square. Place in a bowl, add salt and pepper, mixed spice and thyme leaves and mix.
2. Chop the mild-cure bacon into small pieces. Peel the garlic and put through a garlic press into the bowl.
3. Add the sausagemeat and chopped bacon to the bowl. Mix well, then moisten with cognac and Madeira and mix again.
4. Cover the bottom and sides of a terrine just big enough to contain the mixture with slices of bacon. Preheat the oven to 230°C (450°F; gas mark 8).
5. Pour the contents of the bowl into the terrine. Thinly slice the rest of the bacon and criss-cross the slices over the meat mixture. Decorate with thyme sprigs and bay leaves. Cover. Place the terrine in a larger pan containing hot water and cook for ½ hour at 230°C, then lower the heat to 200°C (400°F; gas mark 6) and cook for 1 hour.
6. When the terrine is cooked, remove from the oven, leave to cool completely, then refrigerate for 12 hours before serving.

Serve with pickled gherkins and small pickled onions.

Pâtés always shrink a little during cooking. It is very useful to have in your kitchen the same type of dish in several sizes so a pâté cooked in one dish can be served in another, slightly smaller one.

Croquettes aux Champignons (p80) ▶

Poulet Rôti Farci

Serves 6. Preparation: 30 min Cooking: 1 hr 30 min

Roast Chicken with Basic Stuffing

★★★

○ **1 chicken, about 1.8kg (4 lb)**
○ **15ml (1 tbls) oil**
○ **4 slices white bread**
○ **100ml (3½ fl oz) boiling milk**
○ **3 finely chopped shallots**
○ **100g (4 oz) pork sausagemeat**
○ **100g (4 oz) minced, cooked ham**
○ **the chicken liver**
○ **200g (7 oz) frozen spinach, cooked and drained**
○ **30ml (2 tbls) finely chopped herbs or parsley**
○ **1 egg**
○ **salt, pepper and nutmeg**
○ *quatre épices* **or mixed spice**
○ **20g (¾ oz) butter**

1. Cut the crusts off the bread, dip in the boiling milk, then place in a bowl and mash with a fork.
2. Put the butter in a small frying pan, add the shallots and sauté over a low heat. Then add the sausagemeat and fry gently, mashing it up with a fork. Pour the sausage and onion into a bowl and add the minced ham.
3. Chop the spinach and add to the ingredients in the bowl together with the herbs. Season to taste with salt, pepper and grated nutmeg. Sprinkle with a pinch of *quatre épices* and mix well.
4. Dice the liver and add to the stuffing. Add the egg and mix it in well with a fork.
5. Fill the chicken with the stuffing and sew up the vent with a trussing needle and a strong piece of string.
6. Preheat the oven to 220°C (425°F; gas mark 7). Brush the chicken with oil and place in a roasting tin. Place in the centre of the oven, reduce the oven to 200°C (400°F; gas mark 6) and roast for 30 minutes. Then reduce to 190°C (375°F; gas mark 5) and cook for a further 30 minutes. Reduce the oven once more to 180°C (350°F; gas mark 4) and cook for 30 minutes more. Add a little water from time to time if it looks as if the chicken is drying out. After 1 hour 30 minutes check if the chicken is done by pricking the leg with a fork: the juices should run clear yellow.
7. Place the chicken on a serving dish. Carve, and cut the stuffing into slices. Serve the cooking liquid separately in a sauceboat.

A few suggestions for vegetables to serve with roast chicken: puréed vegetables either individually or mixed, such as carrots, celery, turnip, cauliflower, courgettes or green peas, depending on the time of year.

Fricassée de Poulet au Citron

Serves 6. Preparation: 15 min Cooking: 1 hr

Chicken Fricassée with Lemon

★

○ **1 1.6kg (3½ lb) chicken, cut into 12 pieces**
○ **1 large onion**
○ **80g (3 oz) butter**
○ **15ml (1 tbls) flour**
○ **1 chicken stock cube**
○ **½ litre (18 fl oz) hot water**
○ **250g (9 oz) cream**
○ **2 egg yolks**
○ **2 lemons**
○ **salt and pepper**

1. Peel the onion and cut into thin slices.
2. Melt the butter in a flameproof casserole over a low heat. Gently sauté the onion and chicken joints, sprinkle in the flour and blend well in.
3. Dissolve the stock cube in hot water and pour over the chicken pieces. Cover and simmer for 45 minutes, turning the meat occasionally.
4. Squeeze the juice from the lemons and add it to the cream and egg yolks, beating with a fork. Pour into the casserole and stir rapidly for 30 seconds. Check the seasoning, add some freshly ground pepper and serve at once.

Serve with boiled rice, dried in the oven.

Before you cook most kinds of meat cut off the fat first.

To make canapés, and for certain recipes which require bread, cut the crusts off the bread first.

Jambonneaux de Poulet aux Cèpes

Stuffed Chicken Legs with Mushrooms

- ○ **4 large chicken legs**
- ○ **1 chicken breast**
- ○ **100g (4 oz) pork sausagemeat**
- ○ **100g (4 oz) Gruyère cheese**
- ○ **10 sprigs parsley**
- ○ **1 egg**
- ○ **salt and pepper**
- ○ **pinch nutmeg**
- ○ **50g (2 oz) unsmoked bacon**
- ○ **1 medium-sized onion**
- ○ **400g (14 oz) mushrooms**
- ○ **50g (2 oz) butter**
- ○ **30ml (2 tbls) groundnut oil**
- ○ **100ml (3½ fl oz) dry white wine**
- ○ **5 sprigs parsley**
- ○ **5 sprigs chervil**
- ○ **1 sprig tarragon**
- ○ **10 chives**

1. Bone the chicken legs, using a sharp knife and keeping the skin intact. Cut the chicken breast into thin strips, then dice. Grate the cheese and chop the parsley.
2. Place the diced chicken breast, sausagemeat, cheese and parsley in a bowl. Break in an egg. Season with salt, pepper and grated nutmeg. Mix all the ingredients together well, using a fork.
3. Divide into 4 and fill each leg with the stuffing, pushing it in. Sew up the skin with a needle and thread. They should look like knuckle joints of ham.
4. Cut the bacon into strips approximately 0.5cm (¼ inch). Peel and chop the onion finely. Take off the mushroom stalks; wash and slice.
5. Pour the oil and butter into a frying pan. Gently fry the chicken legs for 10 minutes, turning occasionally. Remove from heat. Then brown the onion and bacon lightly in the pan. Add the mushrooms and gently fry for 5 minutes more or until their juices have begun to run. Put the chicken legs back into the pan.
6. Preheat the oven to 200°C (400°F; gas mark 6). Pour the contents of the pan into an ovenproof dish. Pour in the wine and cook in the oven for 30 minutes; turn the chicken legs once and baste twice with the cooking juices.
7. Meanwhile, prepare the herbs: wash, wipe dry and strip off the stalks. Finely chop the leaves. When the meat is cooked remove the dish from the oven and sprinkle with the chopped herbs.

Serve at once with sautéed potatoes or polenta.

Poule au Pot

Chicken in the Pot

- ○ **1 2½kg (4½-5 lb) boiling fowl**
- ○ **6 carrots**
- ○ **3 turnips**
- ○ **3 leeks**
- ○ **1 celery heart**
- ○ **1 medium-sized onion**
- ○ **3 cloves**
- ○ **salt**

Bouquet garni:
- ○ **1 sprig thyme**
- ○ **1 bay leaf**
- ○ **4 sprigs parsley**

1. Peel and wash the vegetables.
2. Spike the onion with the cloves. Tie the leeks in a bunch. Tie the herbs together to make the bouquet garni.
3. Place the chicken in a large saucepan. Cover with cold water. Bring to the boil over a medium heat. Skim when necessary.
4. Season with salt. Add the vegetables and bouquet garni.
5. Boil slowly for 2 hours. Then remove the chicken and carve. Serve surrounded by the vegetables.

The gravy should be served separately. Accompany with coarse sea salt and small gherkins.

Polenta, either yellow or white, makes a delicious accompaniment to any roast or meat dish with a sauce. Corn meal made from dried, ground maize, polenta is easy to cook: just boil it in milk or stock and serve at once. Or leave it to cool and then cut into shapes (squares, rectangles, triangles etc) and cook au gratin, *ie in the oven with butter and cheese. These small dumplings are known as* gnocchi.

Poulet au Genièvre

Chicken with Juniper Berries

Serves 4. Preparation: 5 min Cooking: 1 hr

★★

- ○ 1 1.2kg (2½ lb) chicken, cut into 8 pieces
- ○ 10 finely chopped shallots
- ○ 60g (2½ oz) butter
- ○ 200ml (7 fl oz) dry white wine
- ○ 20 juniper berries
- ○ 5ml (1 tsp) cornflour
- ○ 30ml (2 tbls) cold water
- ○ 200g (7 oz) cream
- ○ salt and pepper

1. Melt the butter in a frying pan and sauté the chicken pieces, turning them with a spatula. Add the shallots and cook until it is all golden brown. This must be done over a low heat to prevent the shallots burning.
2. Add the wine and juniper berries. Season. Cover the pan and simmer for 35 minutes.
3. Remove the chicken pieces and keep warm on a serving dish.
4. Reduce the cooking juices to 30ml (2 tbls) over a high heat.
5. Mix the cornflour with the cold water and add to the cream. Pour into the frying pan and boil for 2 minutes, then pour over the chicken pieces and serve at once.

Serve with sauté potatoes.

Curry de Poulet

Curried Chicken

Serves 6. Preparation: 10 min Cooking: 1 hr 10 min

★★★

- ○ 1 1.6kg (3½ lb) chicken, cut into 12 pieces
- ○ 300g (11 oz) onions
- ○ 60ml (4 tbls) oil
- ○ 1 cooking apple
- ○ 1 unripe banana
- ○ 60ml (4 tbls) curry powder
- ○ 15ml (1 tbls) flour
- ○ 100g (4 oz) cream or natural yoghurt
- ○ ½ lemon
- ○ salt
- ○ ¼ litre (9 fl oz) milk
- ○ 70g (3 oz) grated coconut

1. Bring the milk to the boil in a saucepan and sprinkle in the grated coconut. Turn the heat off and cover the saucepan. Leave to soak. Peel the onions and cut into thin slices.
2. Heat the oil in a flameproof casserole, brown the chicken pieces on both sides and reserve. Put the onions in the casserole and gently sauté until they become transparent.
3. Peel the apple and banana and grate them. Add to the casserole, and once they have taken on a golden brown colour sprinkle in the flour and the curry powder. Then add the coconut and milk mixture, passing it through a sieve; squeeze well to extract all the milk. You can substitute an equal amount of water for this if you wish.
4. Put the chicken pieces back into the casserole. Season and cover with a lid. Simmer for 45 minutes, turning the meat occasionally. Check to make sure the sauce does not burn.
5. 5 minutes before the end of the cooking time add the cream or yoghurt. Then remove the chicken pieces and place on a serving dish. Keep warm.
6. Add the juice of ½ a lemon to the sauce and liquidize it (or pass it through a fine meshed sieve) to obtain a creamy sauce. Pour over the chicken pieces.

Curried chicken may be served with boiled rice (dried slightly in a warm oven), slices of banana with lemon juice, fresh pineapple cut into cubes, diced fresh mangoes, and slices of cucumber mixed with natural yoghurt that has been salted and flavoured with chopped mint.

To bard a chicken is to cover the breast with thin sheets of pork fat (the best type is back fat) or with rashers of streaky bacon. This is necessary to prevent the meat becoming too dry when roasting.

Poularde à la Farce Blanche

Braised Chicken with White Stuffing

Serves 6. Preparation: 20-40 min
Cooking: 1 hr 45 min
★ ★ ★

○ **1 large 1.5kg (3¼ lb) pullet**
○ **2 chicken breasts**
○ **1 veal sweetbread**
○ **80g (3 oz) double cream**
○ **1 egg white**
○ **salt and white pepper**
○ **200g (7 oz) barding fat (thin slices of pork fat)**
○ **50g (2 oz) butter**
○ **100g (4 oz) raw ham**
○ **24 small onions (or pickling onions)**
○ **30ml (2 tbls) cognac**
○ **30ml (2 tbls) Liqueur de Vervaine**

1. Have the chicken boned by your butcher, if possible. If you want to bone it yourself, make a cut down the centre of the back, using a sharp knife. Then cut the flesh away from the bones. You can remove the lower part of the wings, the feet and lower leg, or leave them attached, as you wish.
2. Poach the sweetbread in simmering water with vinegar added for 5 minutes. Drain and dice. Chop the raw chicken breasts with a sharp knife. Dice the ham and peel the onions.
3. Mix the ingredients for the stuffing in a bowl: chicken breasts, sweetbread, cream, egg white, salt and white pepper. Stuff the chicken and truss it. Bard it by covering with slices of the pork fat and securing with string.
4. Melt the butter in a large flameproof casserole and brown the chicken on all sides. Add the diced ham. Season with pepper and a little salt. Add 2 tablespoons of water. Cover the casserole and simmer over a low heat for 30 minutes; turn the chicken frequently, and add a little water when necessary.
5. After 30 minutes, add the onions to the casserole and continue cooking for a further 30 minutes. Then remove the chicken from the casserole. Discard the string and barding fat and put the chicken back into the casserole. Continue to cook over a low heat for another 30 minutes, turning frequently so that it browns on all sides.
6. When cooked pour the cognac and Liqueur de Vervaine into the casserole. Simmer for 2 minutes, turning the chicken all the time in the sauce. Add a little water to deglaze the sauce, scraping up the cooking juices from the bottom of the pan.
7. Place the chicken on a serving dish and surround with the onions. Pour the sauce over the chicken and serve at once.

The Liqueur de Vervaine may be omitted if it is not available.

Blancs de Poulet à la Cannelle

Fried Chicken Breasts with Cinnamon

Serves 4. Preparation: 5 min Cooking: 25 min
★

○ **4 chicken breasts**
○ **30ml (2 tbls) flour**
○ **50g (2 oz) butter**
○ **1 medium-sized onion**
○ **salt and pepper**
○ **2ml (½ tsp) cinnamon**
○ **2 cloves**
○ **100ml (3½ fl oz) white wine vinegar**
○ **60ml (4 tbls) double cream**

1. Peel and finely chop the onion.
2. Cut each chicken breast into two. Flatten them with the blade of a knife.
3. Sprinkle a little flour onto each slice.
4. Melt the butter in a frying pan. Add the onion and chicken and brown lightly over a medium heat.
5. Then add the vinegar, cloves, cinnamon, salt and pepper. When the vinegar has completely evaporated pour in the cream. Cover the frying pan.
6. Simmer over a low heat for 15 minutes turning from time to time with a spatula.

Serve with sautéed vegetables: carrots, turnips, celery hearts.

A pullet is a young bird (5½ to 9 months old) which has not laid eggs. Its flesh is slightly fattier than that of a chicken and is therefore suitable for poaching; but you may stuff and roast it in the oven, or cook it in a casserole.

Poulet aux Écrevisses

Serves 6. Preparation and cooking: 1 hr 15 min

Chicken with Crayfish

★★★

○ 1 1.6kg (3½ lb) chicken, jointed in 8 pieces
○ 30g (1¼ oz) butter
○ 1 unpeeled garlic clove crushed
○ 100g (4 oz) fresh tomato pulp
○ 30ml (2 tbls) cognac
○ 100ml (3½ fl oz) dry white wine
○ 125g (5 oz) cream
○ salt and pepper
○ 15ml (1 tbls) chopped parsley and tarragon

For the crayfish:
○ 24 crayfish, washed and gutted
○ 1 finely chopped onion
○ 2 finely chopped shallots
○ 1 sliced carrot
○ 40g (1¼ oz) butter
○ 1 pinch thyme
○ ½ bay leaf
○ 30ml (2 tbls) cognac
○ 250ml (9 fl oz) dry white wine
○ salt and pepper

1. Melt the butter in a flameproof casserole and gently fry the chicken joints over a very low heat until lightly browned. Season, pour in the cognac, wine, garlic and tomato pulp. Cover with a lid and simmer for 40 minutes, over a low heat.
2. Meanwhile, prepare the crayfish in the 'Bordeaux' manner: melt the butter in a pan and sauté the onion, carrot and shallots until lightly browned. Then add the crayfish, salt, pepper, thyme and bay leaf. Sauté the crayfish over a high heat until they turn red. Then pour in the cognac and wine. Cover the pan and cook for 10 minutes.
3. At the end of that time, shell 18 crayfish. Put the remaining 6 aside for garnishing. Reserve the cooking juices.
4. When the chicken is cooked, put on one side with the crayfish. Add the cooking juices from the crayfish to the stock in the casserole. Reduce uncovered over a high heat until 200ml (7 fl oz) of liquid remains. Stir in the cream and put the chicken joints and crayfish back into the casserole. Simmer for 5 minutes. Check the seasoning.
5. Place the chicken joints and crayfish on a serving dish. Garnish with the 6 remaining crayfish. Pour over the sauce, passing it through a sieve. Sprinkle with herbs and serve at once.

Chicken with crayfish is one of the great classic dishes of French cuisine. Before cooking the crayfish you must be sure to clean them thoroughly. To do this, tug very strongly on the central ribs of the tail, and the guts will come out cleanly.

Petit Sauté de Poulet aux Girolles

Serves 4. Preparation: 15 min
Cooking: 30 min

Sautéed Chicken Breasts with Mushrooms

★

○ 4 chicken breasts
○ 50g (2 oz) butter
○ juice of ½ lemon
○ 500g (1 lb 2 oz) chanterelle mushrooms
○ 200g (7 oz) cream
○ 15ml (1 tbls) chopped herbs: parsley, chervil, tarragon, chives
○ salt and pepper

1. Clean the mushrooms.
2. Cook the mushrooms in a frying pan over a medium heat, stirring from time to time so that the juices run.
3. When all the juices have run add a knob of butter to the mushrooms and simmer for 15 minutes.
4. Meanwhile, prepare the chicken breasts. Slice them in two and flatten each side with the blade of a knife.
5. Melt the rest of the butter in a heavy pan over a low heat and brown the chicken breasts on both sides. Add the lemon juice and season to taste. Cover and simmer for 10 minutes.
6. Then add the mushrooms to the chicken in the pan. Pour in the cream, stir well and simmer, uncovered, for 5 minutes. The cream should turn a slightly golden colour.
7. Serve very hot sprinkled with herbs.

You can replace the chanterelles with other kinds of mushrooms for this recipe.

If you strip the stem from a sprig of garden thyme and roll the leaves and dried up flowers between your fingers, you will obtain a small quantity of what in France is known as fleurs de thym. *It has a stronger flavour than the dried thyme you can buy in most shops.*

Coquelets Farcis à la Broche

Serves 4. Preparation: 25 min Cooking: 40 min

Stuffed and Spit-Roasted Poussins

- ○ **2 poussins**
- ○ **300g (11 oz) lean minced pork**
- ○ **30ml (2 tbls) oil**
- ○ **1 large onion, finely chopped**
- ○ **1 egg**
- ○ **salt and pepper**
- ○ **pinch nutmeg**
- ○ **1 rasher 1.5cm (½ inch) thick smoked bacon**

1. Heat the oil in a frying pan. Gently fry the onion, then add the minced pork and brown over a low heat for 10 minutes. Transfer the contents of the frying pan to a bowl. Add the egg, season with salt, pepper and grated nutmeg. Mix well.
2. Divide the mixture into two and stuff each poussin. Sew the vent of each bird with a needle and thread.
3. Cut the bacon rasher into 6 pieces.
4. Thread onto a spit: two pieces of bacon, a poussin, two more pieces of bacon, the other poussin, and finish with the last two pieces of bacon.
5. Cook in the oven for 40 minutes, turning the spit from time to time.

Serve on a bed of buttered spinach.

Coq en Pâte

Serves 6. Preparation: 30 min Cooking: 1 hr 10 min

Cockerel Baked in Pastry

★★★

- ○ **1 1.5kg (3¼ lb) cockerel**
- ○ **4 shallots**
- ○ **4 sprigs parsley**
- ○ **the liver of the bird**
- ○ **100g (4 oz) chicken livers**
- ○ **30ml (2 tbls) brandy**
- ○ **2 eggs**
- ○ **80g (3 oz) butter**
- ○ **salt and pepper**
- ○ **500g (18 oz) frozen puff pastry**

1. Prepare the puff pastry, following the instructions on the packet.
2. Peel and finely chop the shallots. Wash the parsley, remove the stalks, and chop coarsely. Dice the livers. Beat one of the eggs well in a bowl.
3. In a frying pan melt 30g (1 oz) of butter. Gently fry the shallots and then brown the chopped livers. Pour in the beaten egg and brandy. Mix vigorously and remove from the heat. Add the chopped parsley and stuff the cockerel with this mixture.
4. Sew the vent of the bird with a needle and thread, and truss it, to secure the wings and legs.
5. Melt the remaining butter in a flameproof casserole. Brown the cockerel on all sides. Season. Remove from heat.
6. Preheat the oven to 220°C (425°F; gas mark 7). Grease a baking tray.
7. Divide the puff pastry into two pieces: one ⅓, the other ⅔. Roll out the smaller piece to a thickness of 0.5cm (¼ inch). Place on the greased baking tray and put the cockerel on top. Roll out the larger piece of puff pastry to the same thickness. Place over the cockerel and wet the edges. Seal the two pieces together using your fingertips.
8. Beat the other egg in a bowl and brush the pastry with it. Make a hole in the top and insert a rolled piece of greaseproof paper. This is to allow the steam to escape. Cook in the oven for 1 hour.
9. Serve at once. Carve at the table.

If you spit-roast a chicken, you should choose one with a good amount of fat. The fat will melt in the heat of cooking, and its flesh will be less dry. If you oven roast a chicken it is best to use one that is less fatty so that it does not swim in its own grease. But this does not necessarily mean one that is small.

Poulet Sauce Poulette

Serves 4. Preparation: 10 min Cooking: 1 hr 15 min

Chicken Sauce Poulette

★★

- ○ 1 1.2kg (2¾ lb) chicken, trussed
- ○ 2 medium-sized carrots
- ○ 1 celery stalk
- ○ 1 leek
- ○ 80g (3 oz) butter
- ○ 2 shallots, or pickling onions
- ○ 15ml (1 tbls) flour
- ○ 1 egg yolk
- ○ 30ml (2 tbls) cream
- ○ 15ml (1 tbls) chopped parsley
- ○ juice of 1 lemon

1. Prepare and wash the vegetables.
2. Place the chicken with the vegetables in a large saucepan. Cover with just enough cold water: you need about 2 litres (88 fl oz; 3½ pints). Cook over a medium heat.
3. When the water starts to boil, skim. Season with salt. Turn the heat down and simmer for about 1 hour.
4. 10 minutes before the end of the cooking time prepare the sauce. Peel and finely chop the onions. Melt the butter in a saucepan and gently sauté the onions, but do not let them brown. Remove from heat.
5. Remove the chicken from the stock. Place on a serving dish, carve, and keep warm.
6. Reserve ½ litre (18 fl oz; just under 1 pint) of the chicken stock. Put the rest back over a medium heat. Add the flour gradually and stir well; then slowly pour in the reserved stock, stirring continuously. Boil the sauce for 5 minutes, then remove from heat.
7. Beat the egg yolk and the cream together. Pour this mixture into the sauce, beating with a whisk for 1 minute. Add the juice of one lemon, together with the chopped parsley. Check the seasoning.
8. Pour some of the sauce over the chicken and serve the rest in a sauceboat.

Serve with boiled rice that has been allowed to dry slightly in the oven.

Blancs de Poulet Surprise

Serves 4. Preparation: 10 min Cooking: 20 min

Surprise Chicken Breasts

- ○ 4 chicken breasts
- ○ 4 thin slices ham
- ○ 8 thin slices Emmenthal or Gouda cheese
- ○ 8 fresh basil leaves
- ○ 80g (3 oz) butter
- ○ 100ml (3½ fl oz) port, dry marsala, or sherry
- ○ salt and pepper

1. Cut each chicken breast into two. Flatten each slice with the blade of a knife. Cut each slice of ham into two lengthways.
2. Place a slice of ham on each chicken breast then cover with a slice of cheese, and garnish with one basil leaf.
3. Fold each slice over, and secure the edge with 2 cocktail sticks.
4. Melt the butter in a heavy pan over a low heat. Gently fry the chicken pieces for 3 minutes on each side. Season, and moisten with wine. Cover the pan and simmer for 15 minutes over a very low heat. Turn the chicken pieces occasionally while cooking.
5. Place the chicken pieces on a serving dish. If necessary, deglaze the pan by adding 30ml (2 tbls) of water to the sauce. Pour the sauce over the chicken.

Serve with buttered peas or fresh spinach.

How to prepare fried chicken successfully. Cut into pieces of equal size. Dip them in batter or cover with breadcrumbs. To do this, coat each piece with flour. Then dip in beaten egg and roll in the breadcrumbs, pressing down well to ensure they adhere firmly to the meat.

Coquelets aux Herbes

Serves 6. Preparation: 5 min Cooking: 50 min

Poussins with Herbs

★

○ 3 poussins
○ 200g (7 oz) smoked streaky bacon
○ 30ml (2 tbls) oil
○ 50g (2 oz) butter
○ 2 bay leaves
○ 2 sprigs thyme
○ 10 sprigs parsley
○ 20 sprigs chervil
○ 2 sprigs tarragon
○ 1 small bunch chives
○ salt and pepper
○ 30ml (2 tbls) water

1. Rub the inside of the poussins with salt and pepper.
2. Cut the bacon into strips. Chop the herbs coarsely, having removed the stalks.
3. Heat the oil in a heavy pan and gently fry the bacon over a low heat for 10 minutes. Remove with a slotted spoon and put on one side.
4. Add half the butter to the fat in the pan. Brown the poussins on all sides over a low heat for about 15 minutes. Add the thyme and bay leaves. Season with salt and pepper. Cover with a lid and cook for another 15 minutes, stirring frequently.
5. When the poussins are cooked, put the bacon strips back into the pan. Add the chopped herbs, water and remaining butter. Continue cooking over a low heat for 5 minutes, turning the poussins in the sauce. Serve at once.

Serve with small sautéed potatoes.

Chapon à la Sauce aux Noix

Serves 8. Preparation and cooking: 2 hr 10 min

Roast Capon with Walnut Sauce

★ ★ ★

○ 1 2kg (4½ lb) capon
○ salt and pepper
○ 30ml (2 tbls) oil

For the sauce:
○ 4 finely chopped shallots
○ 50g (2 oz) butter
○ 15ml (1 tbls) flour
○ 1 chicken stock cube
○ 30ml (2 tbls) wine vinegar
○ 1 crushed clove
○ pinch cinnamon
○ pinch cayenne pepper
○ ½ bay leaf
○ 100g (4 oz) chopped walnuts
○ juice of ½ orange
○ pinch saffron
○ salt and pepper
○ 15ml (1 tbls) chopped parsley

For the garnish:
○ 16 green walnuts
○ ½ orange

1. Preheat the oven to 220°C (425°F; gas mark 7). Rub the inside of the capon with salt and pepper. Brush the outside with oil. Grease an ovenproof dish and place the capon in it.
2. Cook in the oven for 30 minutes, then turn the heat down to 200°C (400°F; gas mark 6) and cook for another 30 minutes, adding a little water to the dish whenever the cooking juices start to brown. Baste the capon with these juices frequently.
3. After 1 hour of cooking, reduce the heat further to 190°C (375°F; gas mark 5) and continue cooking for another hour, basting frequently.
4. 15 minutes before the end of the time, prepare the sauce. Dissolve the chicken stock cube in ½ litre (18 fl oz; just under 1 pint) of boiling water. Melt the butter in a saucepan and gently fry the shallots until lightly brown. Then sprinkle on the flour and pour in the hot stock, stirring all the time to prevent the sauce becoming lumpy. Add the vinegar, clove, cinnamon, cayenne pepper, bay leaf, parsley, and pinch of saffron for colouring. Season sparingly with salt (the stock will already have been salted) and add some pepper. Simmer for 10 minutes, stirring all the time; then add the juice from half an orange and the walnuts. Mix together well for another minute. Pour the sauce into a sauceboat.
5. Peel and slice the other half of the orange, then cut into small segments.
6. Arrange the capon on a serving dish, garnished with the green walnuts and orange segments.
7. Pour 100ml (3½ fl oz) of water into the dish the capon was cooked in. Deglaze the sauce and pour it into another sauceboat.
8. Serve the capon with the two sauces.

A few suggestions to accompany this dish: sautéed mushrooms, buttered green vegetables, braised chicory or celery hearts.

Dinde au Chocolat

Turkey with Chocolate Sauce

Serves 8-10. Preparation and cooking: 2 hr

★★★

- ○ 1 2.5kg (5½ lb) turkey, jointed (10 pieces)
- ○ 60ml (4 tbls) goose fat or dripping
- ○ salt

For the sauce:
- ○ ¾ litre (slightly over 1¼ pint) chicken stock, preferably home-made
- ○ 1 small chilli, flaked
- ○ 100g (4 oz) blanched almonds
- ○ 1 clove garlic, peeled
- ○ 1 medium-sized onion, finely chopped
- ○ 2ml (½ tsp) powdered cinnamon
- ○ 1 clove, crushed
- ○ 2ml (½ tsp) powdered coriander seeds
- ○ 30ml (2 tbls) sultanas
- ○ 2ml (½ tsp) aniseed
- ○ 15ml (1 tbls) sesame seeds
- ○ 60ml (4 tbls) unsweetened cocoa or 50g (2 oz) bitter chocolate
- ○ salt and pepper

1. Place the turkey pieces in a flameproof casserole, cover with cold water and bring to the boil. Season with salt and cook over a low heat for 1 hour 15 minutes.
2. Meanwhile, prepare the sauce. Put all the ingredients (except the chocolate or cocoa) in the bowl of an electric mixer and add half the stock. Blend at top speed until you obtain a purée.
3. Melt 15ml (1 tbls) of goose fat or dripping in a saucepan. Add the sauce, the remaining stock and the chocolate. Season with salt and pepper. Bring to the boil and simmer for 5 minutes, stirring all the time, then turn the heat off.
4. Remove the turkey pieces from the casserole, drain and wipe with kitchen paper.
5. Melt the remaining goose fat or dripping in the casserole and brown the turkey pieces on each side. Then simmer, uncovered, for 30 minutes, adding the sauce a little at a time, every 10 minutes.
6. When the turkey is cooked, place on a serving dish and cover with the sauce.

Serve this turkey the Mexican way: sprinkled with toasted sesame seeds and accompanied by _tortillas_. _Tortillas_ are pancakes made with a thick batter, rich in eggs. They are cooked in butter in a frying pan or a crêpe pan. As soon as you pour the batter into the frying pan, sprinkle with freshly cooked corn grains, then fold the pancake over. _Tortillas_ are served with fresh cream and sprinkled with chopped parsley.

Dinde Farcie aux Trois Fruits

Roast Turkey with Three Fruit Stuffing

Serves 8. Preparation: 20 min Cooking: 2 hr 15 min

★★

- ○ 1 young 2.5kg (5½ lb) turkey
- ○ 150g (5 oz) prunes
- ○ 12 chestnuts
- ○ 2 cooking apples
- ○ 200g (7 oz) pork sausagemeat
- ○ 200g (7 oz) ham
- ○ 30ml (2 tbls) Armagnac
- ○ the turkey liver
- ○ 1 egg
- ○ salt and pepper
- ○ nutmeg
- ○ 30ml (2 tbls) oil

1. Soak the prunes in lukewarm water for 1 hour, then stone them.
2. Chop the ham and dice the turkey liver. Flake the chestnuts. Peel and coarsely grate the apples.
3. Put all these ingredients into a bowl and add the sausagemeat and egg. Season with salt, pepper and grated nutmeg. Mix well, sprinkle over with Armagnac, and mix once more.
4. Preheat the oven to 200°C (400°F; gas mark 6). Rub the inside of the turkey with salt and pepper. Fill the turkey with the stuffing and sew the vent with a needle and thread. Brush with oil and place in an ovenproof dish.
5. Roast for 30 minutes at 200°C (400°F; gas mark 6), then for 1 hour at 190°C (375°F; gas mark 5), then reduce the heat to 180°C (350°F; gas mark 4) and cook for a further 45 minutes. Baste frequently with the cooking juices, adding a few tablespoons of water whenever the juices start to caramelize.
6. When the turkey is ready, place it on a serving dish. Deglaze the cooking juices with a little water and pour into a sauceboat. Serve at once.

Serve with corn salad (known also as lamb's lettuce) seasoned with olive oil and vinegar.

Coquelets aux Herbes (p93) ▶

Dindonneau Farci en Cocotte

Serves 8. Preparation: 15 min Cooking: 15 min

Braised Stuffed Turkey

★ ★ ★

○ **1 young 2.2kg (5 lb) turkey**
○ **200g (7 oz) cooked ham**
○ **200g (7 oz) pork sausagemeat**
○ **200g (7 oz) bread, crusts removed**
○ **200ml (7 fl oz) warm milk**
○ **2 small truffles or mushrooms**
○ **1 chicken stock cube**
○ **½ litre (1 pint) warm water**
○ **salt and pepper**
○ **nutmeg**
○ **100ml (3½ fl oz) groundnut oil**
○ **125g (4½ oz) butter**
○ **6 fresh sage leaves**
○ **1 small sprig rosemary**

1. Soak the bread in warm milk. Chop the ham.
2. Mash the bread in a bowl, using a fork. Add the sausagemeat and chopped ham. Mix all ingredients well. Cut one truffle into thin strips and add to the bowl. Season with salt, pepper and grated nutmeg and mix again.
3. Fill the turkey with the stuffing, and sew the vent with a needle and thread.
4. Dissolve the chicken stock in warm water.
5. Heat the oil in a large flameproof casserole. Add 50g (2 oz) of butter, the sage and rosemary. Brown the turkey on all sides over a medium heat, making sure the butter does not burn. Season with salt and pepper.
6. Pour half the stock into the casserole and cover tightly with a lid. Cook over a low heat for 2 hours, adding the remaining stock if necessary during the cooking. When the turkey is cooked, there should be hardly any cooking juices remaining – about 200ml (7 fl oz).
7. Remove the turkey from the casserole and place on a serving dish. Using a spoon, skim as much fat as possible from the cooking juices and reduce over a brisk heat if necessary, then turn the heat down.
8. Add the remaining butter to the casserole, beating it into the juices with a whisk. The sauce should be smooth and creamy. Cut the remaining truffle into thin strips, add to the sauce and pour over the turkey. Serve at once.

Serve with braised celery hearts, chicory or a smooth purée of celeriac.

Filets de Dinde au Marsala

Serves 4. Preparation: 5 min Cooking: 55 min

Turkey Breasts in Marsala

★ ★

○ **8 turkey breasts, about 100g (4 oz) each**
○ **80g (3 oz) butter**
○ **100ml (3½ fl oz) dry Marsala**
○ **100ml (3½ fl oz) milk**
○ **250g (9 oz) ripe tomatoes**
○ **30ml (2 tbls) cream**
○ **salt and pepper**
○ **nutmeg**

1. Wash the tomatoes and quarter them. Pass them through the fine mesh of a vegetable mill.
2. Melt the butter in a large frying pan and lightly brown the turkey breasts on both sides. Season with salt, pepper and grated nutmeg.
3. Add the Marsala, milk and tomato purée. Cover the frying pan loosely.
4. Simmer over a low heat for 35 minutes, turning the turkey in the sauce two or three times.
5. Remove the turkey breasts from the frying pan and place on a serving dish. Pour the cream into the pan, boil the sauce for 1 or 2 minutes until it thickens, then pour over the turkey. Serve at once.

Serve with french beans, sprinkled with parsley, or small sauté potatoes.

A sautéed fowl should always be cooked in a pan or casserole, uncovered; otherwise it is braised.

Estouffat de Dinde aux Oignons

Serves 4. Preparation and cooking: 1 hr 35 min

Casserole of Turkey with Onions

★

○ **900g (2 lb) legs and breasts of turkey**
○ **1kg (2¼ lb) onions**
○ **60g (2½ oz) butter**
○ **250ml (9 fl oz) beer**
○ **salt and pepper**

1. Peel and finely slice the onions. Put into a sauté pan (without any cooking fat), cover the pan and sauté for 20 minutes over a low heat, stirring from time to time.
2. Meanwhile, cut the turkey joints into square chunks, about 3 cm (1 inch) thick, and remove the bones.
3. Melt the butter in a frying pan and brown the turkey pieces on all sides. Season with salt and pepper.
4. When the onions have cooked for approximately 20 minutes, add the turkey pieces and mix well.
5. Pour over the beer, cover the sauté pan and cook for 1 hour over a low heat, until there is no liquid left in the pan.
6. Serve very hot.

Serve with *gnocchi au gratin* or polenta. *Gnocchi* are a kind of dumplings made of *pâté à choux* into which a purée is beaten. Polenta is corn meal, made from maize, which is dried and ground.

Saucisson de Dinde

Serves 6. Preparation: 25 min Cooking: 1 hr 15 min
To be served cold
★★★

Turkey Sausage

○ **1kg (2½ lb) turkey legs and breasts**
○ **200g (7 oz) ham**
○ **100g (4 oz) stale bread, without crusts**
○ **100ml (3½ fl oz) warm milk**
○ **100g (4 oz) grated Gruyère**
○ **2 eggs**
○ **salt and pepper**
○ **nutmeg**
○ **2 chicken stock cubes**
○ **1 onion**
○ **1 carrot**
○ **1 stalk celery**
○ **1 clove**

1. Remove the bones from the turkey legs, and discard the skin from the legs and breasts. Coarsely chop the meat. Finely chop the ham. Soak the bread in warm milk then mash it with a fork.
2. Put the turkey, ham, bread and Gruyère in a bowl. Season with salt, pepper and grated nutmeg. Add the eggs and mix all ingredients well, using a fork. Roll this mixture into a large sausage shape.
3. Wash and peel the vegetables. Spike the onion with the clove. Bring 2 litres (3½ pints) of water to the boil in a large saucepan. Add the vegetables and chicken stock cubes.
4. Lay the turkey sausage on a clean cloth and roll up tightly. Secure the ends with string. Plunge into the saucepan and cook for 1 hour 15 minutes over a low heat.
5. Remove the sausage from the saucepan and leave to cool, then remove string and cloth. Cut into thick slices.

Serve with mayonnaise: mayonnaise with lemon, or with herbs, and accompany with raw vegetables and salad.

A top quality fowl should have a smooth white skin, its flesh should be firm and its legs plump.

The flesh of a well cooked fowl should be neither bloody nor dry. To check whether the fowl is cooked or not, insert a needle into the flesh of the thigh – the juice which spurts out should be transparent. If it is slightly pink, continue cooking. If there is not much liquid left in the cooking dish, add a little water or white wine (this only applies to oven roast fowls). Mix the cooking juices into the liquid, boil for 1 minute, then add a knob of butter.

Pintade Farcie aux Olives Noires

Guinea Fowl with Black Olive Stuffing

Serves 4. Preparation: 30 min
Cooking: 1 hr 10 min
★ ★ ★

- ○ 1 1.2kg (2½ lb) guinea fowl
- ○ the guinea fowl liver
- ○ 250g (9 oz) button mushrooms
- ○ 150g (5 oz) black olives
- ○ 100g (4 oz) pork sausagemeat
- ○ 50g (2 oz) bread, without crusts
- ○ 100ml (3½ fl oz) warm milk
- ○ 1 egg
- ○ 1 chicken stock cube
- ○ ¼ litre (9 fl oz) boiling water
- ○ 60ml (4 tbls) oil
- ○ 80g (3 oz) butter
- ○ salt and pepper

1. Dissolve the chicken stock cube in the boiling water. Stone the olives and quarter them. Dice the guinea fowl liver; trim, wash and dry the mushrooms; cut them into thin strips.
2. Melt 20g (1 oz) of butter in a frying pan and sauté the mushrooms until golden; add the pork sausagemeat and mix it into the mushrooms with a fork. Add the liver, let it brown gently then remove the frying pan from the heat.
3. Soak the bread in warm milk. Put into a bowl and mash with a fork; then add the contents of the frying pan, together with the olives. Mix all ingredients well and season with a little salt and pepper. Add the egg and mix once more.
4. Stuff the guinea fowl and sew up the vent, using a needle and thread.
5. Heat the oil in a flameproof casserole. Add 20g (1 oz) of butter and brown the guinea fowl on both sides; then skim off three-quarters of the cooking fat and pour in half the stock. Cover and simmer over a low heat for 1 hour, turning the bird from time to time and basting it with the cooking juices.
6. When the guinea fowl is cooked, remove from the casserole and place on a serving dish.
7. Add the remaining butter to the casserole, beating it into the cooking juices with a whisk to obtain a smooth sauce. Pour the sauce over the guinea fowl and serve at once.

Serve with fresh spinach or any other green vegetables in season.

Pintade aux Pommes Vertes

Guinea Fowl with Apples

Serves 4. Preparation and cooking: 1 hr 15 min

★

- ○ 1 1.2kg (2½ lb) guinea fowl, cut into 8 pieces
- ○ 60g (2½ oz) butter
- ○ 4 medium-sized onions, thinly sliced
- ○ 4 green apples (cooking apples)
- ○ salt and pepper

1. Melt half the butter in a frying pan and sauté the guinea fowl pieces over a low heat, then remove from the pan and reserve.
2. Sauté the onions over a low heat until golden, stirring frequently.
3. Put the guinea fowl pieces back into the frying pan, season and pour over 100ml (3½ fl oz) water. Cover and simmer for 45 minutes, adding a little more water during the cooking, if necessary.
4. 15 minutes before the end of the cooking time, peel, core and halve the apples. Cut each half apple into 4.
5. Melt the remaining butter in a frying pan and gently sauté the apples until they start to turn brown. Then add to the guinea fowl and simmer for 10 minutes. Serve at once.

Dindonneau Farci en Cocotte (p96)

Pintade à la Brésilienne

Serves 4. Preparation and cooking: 1 hr 20 min

Guinea Fowl Brazilian-Style

★ ★ ★

○ 1 1.2kg (2½ lb) guinea fowl, cut into 4 pieces
○ 1 large onion
○ 45ml (3 tbls) groundnut oil
○ 1 chicken stock cube
○ ½ litre (1 pint) boiling water
○ 2 cooking apples (or green apples)
○ 30ml (2 tbls) curry powder
○ 60ml (4 tbls) concentrated milk, unsweetened
○ 10ml (2 tsp) cornflour
○ 15ml (1 tbls) honey
○ 100g (4 oz) cream
○ 30ml (2 tbls) sultanas
○ 30ml (2 tbls) almonds, flaked and grilled
○ 1 green banana
○ juice of ½ lemon
○ salt and pepper

1. Dissolve the chicken stock cube in the boiling water. Soak the sultanas in warm water. Peel and finely chop the onion.
2. Heat the oil in a flameproof casserole. Brown the guinea fowl on both sides over a high heat, then add the chopped onion and sauté until golden, stirring continuously.
3. When the onion has taken on a golden colour sprinkle in the curry powder, mix well and pour in the stock. Then peel the apples and cut into 4; remove the core and pips and dice; add to the ingredients in the casserole. Cover with a lid.
4. Simmer over a low heat for 40 minutes, turning the guinea fowl from time to time.
5. Remove the guinea fowl pieces from the casserole and reserve. Mix the cornflour with cold milk and add to the casserole. Season with a very little salt (the stock is already salted) and pepper. Add the honey and mix well. Simmer over a low heat for 10 minutes, uncovered, turning the meat from time to time.
6. Meanwhile, remove the bones from the guinea fowl and discard them. Put the meat back into the casserole and add the cream. Simmer for a further 5 minutes.
7. Peel and slice the banana and pour the lemon juice over it to prevent it from turning black. Drain the sultanas.
8. Place the guinea fowl and sauce on a serving dish and garnish with the sliced banana and sultanas. Sprinkle with almonds, and serve at once.

Serve with boiled rice.

Pintade aux Poireaux

Serves 4. Preparation: 10 min Cooking: 1 hr 20 min

Guinea Fowl with Leeks

★

○ 1 1.2kg (2½ lb) guinea fowl, cut into 8 pieces
○ 50g (2 oz) butter
○ 100g (4 oz) smoked streaky bacon
○ 8 large leeks
○ 5ml (1 tsp) curry powder
○ 1 bay leaf
○ salt

1. Cut the bacon into thin strips.
2. Wash the leeks and discard the green part. Cut the white of the leeks into thin slices and reserve.
3. Melt the butter in a flameproof casserole over a very low heat; add the bacon and guinea fowl pieces and brown gently, turning them all the time. Season with salt.
4. Add the leeks and bay leaf to the casserole, mix well for 5 minutes, then sprinkle in the curry powder. Mix once more.
5. Cover and simmer over a low heat for 1 hour, turning the guinea fowl and leeks from time to time. The liquid from the leeks should provide enough cooking juices, but if the ingredients start to dry up or stick to the casserole, add one or two tablespoons of water.
6. Serve very hot.

Canard à l'Orange

Serves 4. Preparation and cooking: 1 hr 20 min

Duck with Orange Sauce

★ ★ ★

- ○ 1 1.6kg (3½ lb) duck
- ○ 6 oranges
- ○ 2 lemons
- ○ 100g (4 oz) sugar
- ○ 60ml (2 fl oz) wine vinegar
- ○ 100ml (3½ fl oz) dry white wine
- ○ 5ml (1 tsp) cornflour
- ○ 60ml (4 tbls) curaçao
- ○ 30ml (2 tbls) kummel
- ○ 15ml (1 tbls) redcurrant jelly
- ○ salt and pepper
- ○ 15ml (1 tbls) oil

1. Preheat the oven to 220°C (425°F; gas mark 7).
2. Rub the inside of the duck with salt and pepper. Grease the outside with a little oil. Grease an ovenproof dish and place the duck in it. Cook in the oven for one hour. If the cooking juices start to brown during cooking, add some water to the dish.
3. Meanwhile, prepare the fruit. Peel 2 oranges and 1 lemon, cutting off the skin but leaving the white membrane. Cut the peel into thin strips. Bring some water to the boil and blanch the strips of peel for 3 minutes, drain and reserve. Squeeze the juice from the peeled oranges and lemon and mix together.
4. Peel the remaining 4 oranges and the lemon. Cut one orange into thin slices for garnish and the other 3 oranges and the lemon into segments.
5. Put the sugar and 30ml (2 tbls) of water into a saucepan. Cook over a medium heat until the sugar starts to caramelize, then add the vinegar and the orange and lemon juice. Boil for 1 minute, stirring with a spatula to dissolve the caramelized sugar, then turn the heat off.
6. When the duck is cooked pour the juice from the inside of the duck into the cooking juices. Place the duck on a serving dish and season with salt. Cover with a sheet of greaseproof paper or foil and keep warm.
7. Skim off the fat from the cooking dish, and place it over a medium heat. Pour in the white wine and scrape the coagulated cooking juices into it. Reduce the sauce by half.
8. Mix the cornflour with the curacao. Add this mixture to the cooking dish together with the kummel, the contents of the saucepan and the redcurrant jelly. Mix all ingredients well together. Boil this sauce for 1 minute until it thickens and the jelly melts. Then add the orange and lemon peel and the segments. Simmer for another minute and pour round the duck.
9. Garnish with the orange slices and serve immediately.

Canard au Poivre Vert

Serves 4. Preparation: 5 min Cooking: 1 hr

Duck with Green Pepper

★

- ○ 1 1.6kg (3½ lb) duck
- ○ ½ lemon
- ○ 15ml (1 tbls) green pepper
- ○ 1 sprig tarragon
- ○ salt and pepper

1. Rub the inside of the duck with salt and pepper. Place the green pepper and tarragon inside the bird and secure the vent with a skewer. Rub the skin of the duck with the half lemon and season with salt.
2. Spit roast the duck for approximately 1 hour, away from the flame. The duck should not be too well done and its flesh should be slightly pink.
3. When cooked, carve and place on a serving dish. Discard the tarragon but not the green pepper, which you eat with the duck.

Serve with a purée of turnips.

Canard Braisé aux Olives

Braised Duck with Olives

Serves 4. Preparation and cooking: 1 hr 20 min

★★

- ○ 1 1.6kg (3½ lb) duck
- ○ 1 medium-sized onion
- ○ 150g (5 oz) green olives, stoned
- ○ 150ml (5 fl oz) dry white wine
- ○ 20 sprigs parsley
- ○ 15ml (1 tbls) capers
- ○ the duck liver
- ○ 30ml (2 tbls) oil
- ○ 20g (¾ oz) butter
- ○ salt and pepper

1. Peel and finely chop the onion. Rub the inside of the duck with salt and pepper.
2. Heat the oil in a flameproof casserole, brown the duck on both sides and reserve.
3. Pour away the cooking fat and replace with the butter. When the butter has melted, put in the onion and gently sauté until slightly golden; pour in the wine and put the duck back into the casserole. Season with salt and pepper. Cover and cook over a low heat for 1 hour 10 minutes, turning the duck from time to time.
4. 15 minutes before the end of cooking time, coarsely chop the parsley; drain and chop the capers and chop the duck liver.
5. 10 minutes before the end of cooking time add the parsley, capers, duck liver and olives to the casserole. Simmer for 10 minutes.
6. When cooked place the duck on a serving dish, arrange the garnish around the duck and serve immediately.

Canard Farci aux Pignons

Duck with Pine Kernel Stuffing

Serves 4. Preparation: 20 min Cooking: 1 hr 20 min

★★★

- ○ 1 1.6kg (3½ lb) duck
- ○ 100g (4 oz) pine kernels
- ○ 150g (6 oz) *fromage blanc* (or very soft cream cheese)
- ○ 50g (2 oz) grated Gruyère
- ○ the duck liver
- ○ 100g (4 oz) chopped ham
- ○ 60ml (4 tbls) chopped chervil
- ○ 50g (2 oz) bread, without crusts
- ○ 30ml (2 tbls) Madeira
- ○ 1 egg
- ○ 100g (4 oz) larding fat (fresh fat back)
- ○ 15ml (1 tbls) oil
- ○ salt, pepper, nutmeg and *quatre épices* or mixed spice

1. Pour the Madeira into a bowl, add the bread and mash it with a fork. Add the *fromage blanc* and mix with the bread. Finely dice the duck liver and mix with the bread and cheese mixture, together with the ham, Gruyère and chervil. Season with salt, pepper and grated nutmeg. Add one pinch of *quatre épices* (or mixed spice) and the egg. Mix all the ingredients well, then add the pine kernels and mix once more.
2. Fill the duck with this stuffing and sew up the vent with a needle and thread.
3. Preheat the oven to 200°C (400°F; gas mark 6). Grease an ovenproof dish. Place the larding fat on the duck's breast and secure with string. Put the duck in the dish and cook in the oven for 40 minutes.
4. Remove the dish from the oven, discard the larding fat and pour away the cooking fat. Pour in 60ml (4 tbls) of water. Put the duck back into the dish, reduce the heat to 190°C (375°F; gas mark 5) and cook for 30 minutes more, basting the duck frequently with the cooking juices and adding a little water if the juices start to brown.
5. When the cooking is over, prick the duck with a fork; if the juice which spurts out is transparent, the duck is cooked, but if it is slightly pink continue cooking for a few more minutes.
6. When the duck is cooked, place on a board and carve, trying not to break the stuffing. Slice the stuffing and arrange round the duck on a serving dish. Deglaze the cooking juices with a little water and pour over the duck. Serve immediately.

To accompany this dish we suggest a green salad, such as corn salad or endive, or a fine vegetable purée.

Canard Braisé Sauce Bigarade

Serves 4. Preparation and cooking: 1 hr 30 min

Braised Duck with Bigarade Sauce

★ ★ ★

- ○ 1 1.5kg (3 lb) duck
- ○ 6 oranges
- ○ 1 carrot
- ○ 1 onion
- ○ 1 celery stalk
- ○ 1 bouquet garni: 1 sprig thyme, 1 bay leaf, 4 sprigs parsley
- ○ 150ml (¼ pint) dry white wine
- ○ 30ml (2 tbls) oil
- ○ 20g (¾ oz) butter
- ○ salt and pepper
- ○ 30ml (2 tbls) caramel
- ○ 15ml (1 tbls) vinegar
- ○ 5ml (1 tsp) cornflour
- ○ 15ml (1 tbls) curacao

1. Finely peel one orange, leaving the white membrane around the orange. Cut the peel into thin strips and reserve. Cut the peeled orange into 4 pieces and place inside the duck. Secure the vent with a skewer.
2. Wash the carrot, onion and celery, peel and cut into slices.
3. Heat the oil in a flameproof casserole, add the butter and brown the duck all over together with the vegetables, over a low heat. Pour on the white wine, add the bouquet garni and cover the casserole. Simmer over a low heat for 1 hour, turning the duck from time to time.
4. 15 minutes before the end of the cooking time, blanch the strips of peel in boiling water for 5 minutes. Drain and reserve. Squeeze the juice from 3 oranges and reserve. Peel the 2 remaining oranges and cut them into segments. Reserve.
5. Mix the caramel and vinegar in a saucepan; add the orange juice and stir in the cornflour.
6. When the duck is cooked, remove from the casserole and place on a serving dish. Remove the skewer and the orange pieces. Keep the duck warm.
7. Pour the contents of the saucepan into the cooking dish. Leave the sauce to thicken by boiling it for 2 minutes, then turn the heat off and add the curacao. Mix well, sieve and pour the sauce over the duck.
8. Garnish with orange segments and peel strips. Serve immediately.

Caneton à la Normande

Serves 4. Preparation and cooking: 1 hr 25 min

Duckling Normandy-Style

★

- ○ 1 1.5kg (3¼ lb) duckling
- ○ 150ml (¼ pint) Muscadet
- ○ 60ml (2 fl oz) calvados
- ○ 200g (7 oz) cream
- ○ 60g (2½ oz) butter
- ○ 30ml (2 tbls) oil
- ○ salt and pepper

1. Heat the oil in a flameproof casserole. Add 25g (1 oz) of butter and brown the duckling on both sides.
2. Pour out the cooking oil from the casserole and pour in the wine; season with salt and pepper and simmer over a low heat for 1 hour, turning the bird frequently.
3. When the duckling is cooked, place on a serving dish and keep warm. Reduce the cooking juice by more than half by boiling over a high heat; then add the calvados and cream. Stir well and boil until the sauce again reduces by half. Remove from the heat.
4. Away from the heat, add the remaining butter to the casserole and blend into the sauce, beating vigorously.
5. Carve the duckling and pour over the sauce. Serve at once.

Apples, sautéed in butter or caramelized, accompany this dish perfectly.

Before using green olives in a sauce or in a stuffing, blanch them for 5 minutes in boiling water. This removes their bitterness and enhances their delicate flavour.

104

Lapin Mariné

Marinated Rabbit

Serves 6. Preparation: 15 min Marinade: 3 hr Cooking: 1 hr 15 min

★ ★ ★

○ 1 1.5kg (3 lb) rabbit, cut into 9 pieces
○ 1 bottle dry white wine
○ 12 peppercorns
○ 3 cloves
○ 2 cloves garlic, unpeeled
○ 1 bouquet garni: 1 sprig thyme, 2 bay leaves, 6 parsley stalks, 1 sprig tarragon
○ salt
○ 15ml (1 tbls) flour
○ 45ml (3 tbls) oil
○ 70g (3 oz) butter

1. 3 hours before cooking the rabbit, prepare the marinade. Pour the wine into a saucepan and add the bouquet garni, cloves, garlic, peppercorns and 2ml (½ tsp) of salt. Bring to the boil and simmer over a low heat for 5 minutes, then remove from the heat and leave to cool.
2. Put the rabbit pieces into a dish and cover with the marinade. Leave to marinate for 3 hours.
3. Drain the rabbit pieces, wipe dry and rub lightly with flour. Strain the marinade through a fine sieve and reserve.
4. Heat the oil in a sauté pan. Add half the butter and brown the rabbit pieces all over.
5. When the rabbit is brown, pour over 100ml (3½ fl oz) of the marinade. When the liquid has evaporated, add the same again and so on until the end of the cooking time (about 1 hour). Turn the rabbit pieces constantly during the cooking.
6. When the rabbit is cooked, tender and golden, place on a serving dish. Put the remaining butter in the sauté pan and incorporate into the cooking juices, beating with a whisk. Pour this sauce (which should be thick) over the rabbit and serve at once.

Chips or sauté potatoes go very well with this dish.

Lapin au Petits Pois

Rabbit with Petits Pois

Serves 4. Preparation: 15 min Cooking: 1 hr 10 min

★

○ 1 1.2kg (2½ lb) rabbit, cut into 8 pieces
○ 150ml (¼ pint) dry white wine
○ 1kg (2½ lb) petits pois
○ 12 asparagus tips
○ 1 medium-sized onion
○ 250g (9 oz) cream
○ 30g (1 oz) butter
○ 200ml (7 fl oz) water
○ 1 sprig tarragon
○ salt, pepper and nutmeg

1. Shell the peas. Peel and finely slice the onion. Melt the butter in a flameproof casserole over a very low heat and brown the rabbit pieces. Season. Add the wine and turn the rabbit over a few times, so that the meat absorbs the flavour of the wine.
2. When the wine has completely evaporated, add the onion, asparagus tips, tarragon, peas and a little grated nutmeg. Stir in the cream and add the water. Cover and cook for 1 hour over a very low heat. If there is not enough liquid during the cooking, add a little more water.
3. When the rabbit is cooked, serve hot in the cooking dish.

Fresh herbs, such as parsley, chervil, chives, tarragon, basil and coriander, have such delicate flavours that when they are chopped too finely or in an electric mincer, they tend to loose some of their aromatic qualities. Try not to chop them too finely. When washed and dried on kitchen paper, put the leaves into a glass. Hold the glass in one hand and a pair of scissors in the other, then cut the herbs with the scissors, opening them as widely as the diameter of the glass allows, and turning the glass at the same time. Always chop fresh herbs at the last minute, to retain the maximum flavour.

Oie en Sauce Veloutée

Serves 6-8. Preparation and cooking: 3 hr

Goose in Cream Sauce

★★★

○ 1 2.5kg (5½ lb) goose, with giblets
○ 3 carrots
○ 2 leeks
○ 1 celery stalk
○ 1 onion
○ 3 cloves
○ 1 whole head of garlic, unpeeled
○ 1 bouquet garni: 1 sprig thyme, 1 bay leaf, 10 parsley stalks
○ 100g (4 oz) goose fat or dripping
○ salt

For the sauce:
○ ½ litre (1 pint) milk
○ ½ litre (1 pint) goose stock
○ 1 head of garlic
○ 100g (4 oz) bread, without crusts
○ 125g (5 oz) cream
○ 4 egg yolks
○ salt and pepper

1. Peel the onion and spike with 3 cloves. Peel and wash the carrots and turnips, clean and wash the leeks. Cut each vegetable into 4 pieces. Wash the celery and cut into 2.
2. Place the goose in a very large saucepan together with the giblets. Add the carrots, turnips, leeks, celery, onion and bouquet garni. Add also the head of garlic, unpeeled. Pour in enough cold water to barely cover the goose. Bring to the boil uncovered over a low heat. Skin off the froth which appears on top, season with salt and cook for 2 hours.
3. 30 minutes before the end of the cooking time, peel the second head of garlic and cook it in milk in a saucepan over a very low heat.
4. When the goose is cooked remove from the stock, place on a board and carve into 12 pieces.
5. Melt the goose fat in a sauté pan and brown the goose pieces over a high heat until they turn golden. Drain and keep warm.
6. Pour ½ litre (1 pint) of the goose stock into a saucepan and skim the fat off. Add to the garlic and milk in the other saucepan. Crumble the bread and sprinkle into the saucepan. Boil for 5 minutes then remove from the heat. Strain this sauce through a sieve (or fine mesh of a mill) or liquidize it. Add the egg yolks and mix well, then put back on the heat, beating all the time until the sauce starts to froth. Remove from the heat before it boils and stir in the cream. Check the seasoning.
7. Place the goose pieces on a serving dish and pour over some of the sauce. Serve the rest in a sauceboat.

Serve with salsify sautéed in butter or braised celery hearts.

Oie Rôtie Sauce Myrtilles

Serves 6. Preparation and cooking: 2 hr 40 min

Roast Goose with Bilberry Sauce

★

○ 1 2.5kg (5½ lb) goose
○ 250g (9 oz) bilberries, or a jar of puréed bilberries
○ 200ml (7 fl oz) red wine
○ 3 pinches cinnamon
○ the juice of ½ lemon
○ salt, pepper and nutmeg

1. Preheat the oven to 200°C (400°F; gas mark 6). Rub the inside of the goose with salt and pepper. Place in an ovenproof dish and roast for 1 hour, then reduce the heat to 180°C (375°F; gas mark 5) and cook for 1 hour 30 minutes.
2. When the goose is cooked, remove from the oven, place on a serving dish and keep warm.
3. Skim the fat from the cooking juices. Pour the wine into the cooking dish and bring to the boil, then add the puréed bilberries, cinnamon, salt, pepper and grated nutmeg. Mix well and boil until the sauce reduces by half, then turn the heat off and add the lemon juice.
4. Carve the goose. Sieve the sauce and pour it over the meat. Serve immediately.

A purée of celeriac, chestnuts sautéed in butter or sautéed sweet potatoes accompany this dish very well. The purée of bilberries may be replaced by redcurrant jelly.

Lapin Marinée (p105)

Pigeons Trois Étoiles

Serves 4. Preparation and cooking: 50 min

Pigeons with Truffle in Brandy and Foie Gras Sauce ★★★

○ **4 pigeons**
○ **60g (2½ oz) butter**
○ **100g (4 oz) foie gras**
○ **1 small truffle**
○ **60ml (2 fl oz) fine champagne or brandy**
○ **¼ litre (9 fl oz) chicken stock**
○ **salt and pepper**

For the croûtons:
○ **4 slices of white bread**
○ **80g (3 oz) butter**

1. Rub the inside of the pigeons with salt and pepper. Cut the truffle into very thin strips.
2. Melt the butter in a flameproof casserole and brown the pigeons over a very low heat. Season with salt and pepper and add 100ml (3½ fl oz) of chicken stock. Cover with a lid and simmer over a low heat for 30 minutes.
3. 10 minutes before the end of the cooking time, prepare the croûtons. Cut the crusts off the bread, melt the butter in a frying pan and gently fry the slices of bread on both sides. Keep warm in a serving dish.
4. When the pigeons are cooked, remove from the casserole and place each one on a slice of bread. Pour the brandy into the casserole together with the remaining chicken stock. Reduce to a third, by boiling the sauce over a brisk heat for 5 minutes.
5. Reduce the heat and stir in the foie gras, little by little, beating with a whisk to mix the ingredients well.
6. When the sauce is smooth, add the truffle strips and pour over the pigeons. Serve immediately.

Pigeons Suaves

Serves 4. Preparation: 10 min Cooking: 55 min

Pigeons in Creamy Sweet Sauce ★★

○ **4 pigeons**
○ **200g (7 oz) barding fat**
○ **30ml (2 tbls) oil**
○ **40g (1½ oz) butter**
○ **½ litre (1 pint) dry white wine**
○ **4 sage leaves**
○ **4 juniper berries**
○ **4 mint leaves**
○ **1 clove**
○ **2 pinches cinnamon**
○ **salt, pepper and nutmeg**
○ **250g (9 oz) cream**
○ **30ml (2 tbls) rum**

1. Rub the inside of the pigeons with salt and pepper. Place some barding fat on each pigeon breast, securing it with a piece of string.
2. Heat the oil in a flameproof casserole. Add the butter and brown the pigeons all over. Add the sage, mint, juniper berries, clove and cinnamon. Stir well and pour on the wine. Season with salt, pepper and grated nutmeg. Cover with a lid and cook over a medium heat for 30 minutes.
3. Remove the pigeons from the casserole. Discard the string and barding fat and put the pigeons back into the casserole. Cook uncovered until the wine evaporates and the pigeon breasts become brown, then pour on the cream and rum and boil for 5 minutes, until the cream takes on a golden colour.
4. When the pigeons are cooked, place on a serving dish and pour the sauce over.

Serve with rice, mixed with peas and lightly buttered.

A fowl which is spit-roasted should be basted with the cooking juices as often as possible. In the dripping pan underneath the fowl you can add salt, pepper, herbs and some white vermouth or port, but only during the last third of cooking time, when the skin of the fowl is crispy and golden. At the last minute, you can add a small glass of whisky, rum or cognac to the liquid and flame the fowl.

All recipes for chicken apply to pigeon, and vice versa; the same goes for guinea fowl and turkey, and also for goose and duck. Goose, turkey and duck have similar stuffings and similar garnishes.

Artichauts Farcis Gratinés

Gratin of Stuffed Artichokes

Serves 4. Preparation: 20 min Cooking: 40 min

★★

- ○ **8 young artichokes**
- ○ **50g (2 oz) smoked bacon**
- ○ **100g (4 oz) small sausages or sausagemeat**
- ○ **1 egg**
- ○ **1 peeled garlic clove**
- ○ **10 sprigs parsley**
- ○ **30ml (2 tbls) breadcrumbs**
- ○ **50g (2 oz) grated Parmesan or Gruyère cheese**
- ○ **juice of 1 lemon**
- ○ **60ml (4 tbls) oil**
- ○ **200ml (7 fl oz) water**
- ○ **salt and pepper**

1. Wash the artichokes and remove the toughest leaves. Slice off the remaining leaves halfway from the top. Spread the centre leaves and remove the choke to make room for the stuffing. Cut the stalk off near the base. Soak the artichokes in water containing lemon juice.
2. Prepare stuffing. Skin the sausages and mash them with a fork. Dice the bacon. Chop the garlic and parsley finely. Put all the ingredients in a bowl, add the egg and breadcrumbs, season with salt and pepper and mix well.
3. Set the oven at 200°C (385°F; gas mark 5½).
4. Pour the oil and water into a gratin dish, arrange the artichokes in it and place in oven for 40 minutes.
5. Serve very hot, or allow to cool.

If served cold, accompany with thin slices of red pepper and small spring onions.

Soufflé de Fonds d'Artichauts

Soufflé of Artichoke Hearts

Serves 4. Preparation and cooking: 1 hr 40 min

★★★

- ○ **6 artichokes 200g (7 oz) each**
- ○ **4 eggs (separated)**
- ○ **250ml (9 fl oz) milk**
- ○ **15ml (1 tbls) flour**
- ○ **30ml (2 tbls) grated Gruyère cheese**
- ○ **70g (3 oz) butter**
- ○ **juice of 1 lemon**
- ○ **salt**
- ○ **pinch nutmeg**

1. Wash and trim the artichokes. Bring some water with lemon juice added to the boil, add salt and cook the artichokes in it for 40 minutes, until they are very tender. Then put under cold running water and remove the leaves and choke.
2. Prepare béchamel sauce. Melt 50g (2 oz) butter in a saucepan; add flour, turning in with a wooden spoon, then add milk, stirring continuously. Add salt and nutmeg. Cook for 10 minutes stirring all the time. Remove from heat and allow to cool.
3. Meanwhile, put the artichoke hearts through a fine sieve or, better still, in the blender to get rid of all the fibres. Incorporate the purée with the béchamel sauce, mixing well. Add egg yolks and grated cheese.
4. Set the oven at 190°C (365°F; gas mark 4½).
5. Beat egg whites until stiff and fold in to the mixture gently.
6. Butter a soufflé dish of a capacity 1½ times the volume of the mixture. Pour in the mixture and put in oven for 35 minutes. Serve immediately.

Steaming vegetables – or cooking à l'anglaise *– is a very common practice in England. In France, only potatoes are normally cooked like this and are called* pommes de terre à l'anglaise. *This method is highly recommended, easy and quick, and requires no great skill. All you need is a special hermetically sealed pan to prevent any loss of heat. The water must boil continuously to ensure sufficient steam pressure. Steamed vegetables are delicious eaten hot with a knob of butter, or cold with a salad. This method of cooking is also best for soufflés, purées or gratins as the vegetables are not full of water.*

Artichauts Farcis au Riz
Artichokes Stuffed with Rice

Serves 4. Preparation: 35 min Cooking: 45 min

★★★

- ○ **8 artichokes**
- ○ **4 thin rashers of smoked bacon**
- ○ **60ml (4 tbls) cooked rice**
- ○ **100g (4 oz) raw ham**
- ○ **150g (6 oz) button mushrooms**
- ○ **100g (4 oz) sausagemeat**
- ○ **15ml (1 tbls) chopped parsley**
- ○ **4 ripe tomatoes**
- ○ **50g (2 oz) grated Gruyère cheese**
- ○ **1 small onion**
- ○ **50g (2 oz) butter**
- ○ **juice of 1 lemon**
- ○ **100ml (3½ fl oz) dry white wine**
- ○ **salt and pepper**

1. Wash artichokes and remove toughest leaves. Slice through the remaining leaves in one go, one-third from top. Spread the centre leaves to stuff, and remove choke. Cut off stalk near base. Bring water to boil in saucepan, add salt and lemon juice. Blanch artichokes for 5 minutes, then drain.
2. Peel onion and chop small. Chop ham. Trim the mushrooms and slice finely. Prepare the tomatoes by plunging in boiling water for 30 seconds, then hold under cold running water and peel. Cut in two, press to remove seeds, chop into large pieces, then mash roughly with a fork.
3. Melt 30g (1¼ oz) butter in a large frying pan. Lightly brown onion then add the ham, mushrooms and sausagemeat which has been mashed with a fork. Brown everything lightly. Add tomatoes to frying pan, then the salt and pepper. Cook over strong heat, turning often, until the liquid has completely evaporated. Remove from heat, add the rice, cheese and parsley, and mix well.
4. Set the oven at 205°C (400°F; gas mark 6). Stuff the artichokes. Cut each rasher of bacon in two to cover artichokes. Grease a gratin dish with remaining butter and arrange artichokes on it. Moisten with wine and cook in oven for 40 minutes, adding some spoonfuls of water to the dish if necessary. Remove from oven and serve.

Artichauts et Pommes de Terre en Cocotte
Artichoke and Potato Stew

Serves 4. Preparation: 20 min Cooking: 30 min approx

★★

- ○ **4 young artichokes**
- ○ **8 small potatoes**
- ○ **2 peeled garlic cloves**
- ○ **10 sprigs parsley**
- ○ **1 stock cube**
- ○ **½ litre (18 fl oz; 1 pint) hot water**
- ○ **juice of 1 lemon**
- ○ **60ml (4 tbls) oil**
- ○ **salt and pepper**

1. Wash the artichokes and remove toughest leaves. Slice through remaining leaves in one go, one-third from top. Cut into 8, remove choke, leave to soak in water with lemon juice added.
2. Peel and wash potatoes. Cut into 4 and soak in cold water.
3. Finely chop parsley and garlic. Dissolve stock cube in hot water. Drain artichokes and potatoes.
4. Place the oil in a heavy pan, add garlic and parsley mixture, potatoes and artichokes. Season with salt and pepper and cover with stock. Bring to the boil and cover.
5. Cook for 20 to 25 minutes until all the stock has disappeared and artichokes are tender. If any stock is left after cooking, reduce it over a high heat. Serve very hot.

Oie en Sauce Veloutée (p106) ▶

Aubergines à la Parmesane

Serves 4. Preparation and cooking: 1 hr 50 min

Aubergines with Parmesan Cheese

- ○ **1kg (2¼ lb) aubergines**
- ○ **1kg (2¼ lb) ripe tomatoes**
- ○ **300g (11 oz) Mozzarella cheese**
- ○ **100g (4 oz) grated Parmesan cheese**
- ○ **1 large onion**
- ○ **1 garlic clove**
- ○ **45ml (3 tbls) olive oil**
- ○ **groundnut oil for frying**
- ○ **salt and pepper**

1. Wash aubergines, but do not peel them. Cut them lengthways into slices 1cm (½ inch) thick. Put them in a sieve with salt on each layer. Leave to drain for 1 hour.
2. Meanwhile, plunge the tomatoes into boiling water for 30 seconds. Drain them, then hold under cold running water. Peel tomatoes, cut in half, squeezing to remove the seeds, and chop coarsely.
3. Peel the onion and garlic and chop finely. Heat some olive oil in a frying pan and lightly brown the garlic and onion. Add the tomato. Add salt and pepper. Cook the sauce for 30 minutes, turning often.
4. Wash the aubergines, drain and dry with a cloth. Heat 90ml (6 tbls) groundnut oil in a large frying pan and lightly brown the aubergine slices on both sides. Drain them on kitchen paper. Add oil as needed during cooking.
5. Set oven at 220°C (425°F; gas mark 7).
6. Slice the Mozzarella thinly. Pour a little tomato sauce into the bottom of a high-sided ovenproof dish, then add a layer of aubergines, more tomato sauce, grated Parmesan cheese and finally a layer of Mozzarella. Continue like this until all the ingredients have been used up, finishing with a layer of tomato sprinkled with Parmesan cheese.
7. Cover the dish with foil and place in the oven for 30 minutes. Then remove the foil and cook uncovered for a further 10 minutes. Serve hot in the dish.

Aubergines en Beignets

Serves 4. Preparation: 2 hr 20 min Cooking: 30 min approx

Aubergine Fritters

- ○ **6 small round aubergines**
- ○ **300g (11 oz) Gruyère or Gouda cheese**
- ○ **60g (2½ oz) anchovy fillets, canned**
- ○ **50g (2 oz) soft butter**
- ○ **10 sprigs parsley**
- ○ **6 leaves basil**
- ○ **50g (2 oz) flour**
- ○ **2 eggs**
- ○ **45ml (3 tbls) breadcrumbs**
- ○ **oil for frying**
- ○ **salt and pepper**

1. Wash but do not peel the aubergines. Cut them into slices widthways, 1cm (½ inch) thick. Arrange the slices in a sieve putting salt between each layer. Leave to drain for 2 hours.
2. At the end of this time, wash and wipe the aubergines. Slice the cheese thinly. Chop the herbs and mix with butter. Add salt and pepper.
3. On one slice of aubergine put a slice of cheese and an anchovy fillet. On another, spread some of the herb butter. Stick the two slices together, pressing firmly. Continue like this until all the ingredients are used up.
4. Beat the eggs well in a dish. Add the salt. Put the breadcrumbs and flour on two separate plates. Dip each aubergine 'sandwich', first in the flour, then in the egg and finally in the breadcrumbs.
5. Heat the oil in a frying pan and lightly brown the aubergine fritters over a medium heat for about 5 minutes on each side. Drain them on kitchen paper and keep them warm until all the fritters have been cooked. Serve hot.

Asperges Sauce Hollandaise

Serves 4. Preparation and cooking: 1 hr

Asparagus with Hollandaise Sauce

★ ★ ★

- ○ **1kg (2¼ lb) asparagus**
- ○ **100ml (3½ fl oz) wine vinegar**
- ○ **5ml (1 tsp) milled pepper**
- ○ **3 egg yolks**
- ○ **200g (7 oz) butter**
- ○ **juice of 1 lemon**
- ○ **200ml (7 fl oz) water**
- ○ **salt**
- ○ **15ml (1 tbls) coarse salt**

1. Place large saucepan three-quarters full of water on a high heat, and add coarse salt.
2. Scrape or peel and wash asparagus. Cut into equal lengths and tie in a bundle.
3. When water boils, place bundle upright in saucepan. The water should come to 1cm (½ inch) below the asparagus tips so that they are not spoiled during cooking. Simmer gently for about 20 minutes. Check cooking by pricking with a knife which should go in easily.
4. Meanwhile prepare Hollandaise sauce: put vinegar and pepper into a saucepan, bring to the boil and evaporate liquid until only 5ml (1 tsp) remains. Remove from heat and leave to cool. Away from heat add the egg yolks one by one, beating with a whisk, then add the water. Put saucepan back on a gentle heat and heat slowly, beating continuously. Remove again from heat, allowing the sauce formed to cool.
5. When asparagus is ready, remove from water, undo binding and drain on rack.
6. Prepare clarified butter: melt butter over low heat and skim. Use the transparent layer of butter and throw away the deposit which forms at the bottom. Allow to cool.
7. When the butter is at the same temperature as the sauce, blend together gently, beating lightly. Then pass the sauce through a very fine sieve, and add salt and lemon juice.
8. Arrange the asparagus on a suitable dish with a rack. Serve Hollandaise sauce separately – it should be lukewarm and of a firm consistency like mayonnaise.

Asperges Gratinées à la Hongroise

*Serves 4.
Preparation and cooking: 50 min*

Asparagus Gratin Hungarian-Style

★ ★

- ○ **1kg (2¼ lb) asparagus**
- ○ **2 egg yolks**
- ○ **15ml (1 tbls) sugar**
- ○ **30ml (2 tbls) flour**
- ○ **250g (9 oz) fresh cream**
- ○ **30ml (2 tbls) breadcrumbs**
- ○ **15ml (1 tbls) coarse salt**
- ○ **salt**

1. Place a large saucepan three-quarters full of water over a high heat, and add coarse salt.
2. Scrape or peel, wash and tie asparagus in a bundle.
3. When the water boils, place the bundle upright in saucepan. The water should come 1cm (½ inch) below the tips so that they are not spoilt during cooking. Simmer gently for 20 minutes. Check cooking by pricking with a knife which should go in easily.
4. Meanwhile, prepare sauce: in a bowl mix the egg yolks, salt, sugar and flour with whisk. Add fresh cream and beat further to mix well.
5. Set oven at 195°C (375°F; gas mark 5).
6. When the asparagus is cooked, remove from the water, tie and drain on rack.
7. Butter an ovenproof dish, arrange asparagus in it, and cover with sauce. Sprinkle with breadcrumbs and put on a few knobs of butter.
8. Heat for 15 minutes in the oven and serve immediately.

Asperges Gratinées au Jambon

Serves 6. Preparation and cooking: 50 min

Asparagus Gratin with Ham

★★

○ **1.5kg (3¼ lb) thin green asparagus**
○ **50g (2 oz) butter**
○ **30ml (2 tbls) flour**
○ **250ml (10 fl oz) milk**
○ **2 egg yolks**
○ **100g (4 oz) grated Gruyère cheese**
○ **100ml (3½ fl oz) dry white wine**
○ **6 slices cooked ham**
○ **15ml (1 tbls) coarse salt**
○ **salt and pepper**
○ **pinch nutmeg**

1. Place a large saucepan, three-quarters full of water, over a high heat, and add 15ml (1 tbls) coarse salt.
2. Scrape or peel, and wash asparagus. Cut into equal lengths and tie into 3 bundles.
3. When the water boils, place the bundles upright in the saucepan. The water should come to 1cm (½ inch) below asparagus tips to avoid spoiling them. Leave them in gently simmering water for about 20 minutes. They are cooked when the point of a knife pierces them easily.
4. Meanwhile, prepare the béchamel sauce. Melt the butter in a saucepan, gradually blend in the flour by mixing rapidly to avoid lumps. Pour in the milk all at once, stirring continuously. Bring to the boil and allow to cook for several minutes. Add salt, pepper, and nutmeg. Remove from heat, blend in the egg yolks, cheese and white wine. Leave to cool.
5. Set the oven at 230°C (450°F; gas mark 8).
6. When the asparagus is cooked, remove from water, untie, and drain on a rack. Divide into 6 small bundles and roll a slice of ham around each. Butter a gratin dish, arrange the parcels on it and sprinkle with béchamel sauce.
7. Put the dish in the oven for 10 minutes and serve very hot.

Asperges Sauce Gribiche

Serves 4. Preparation: 15 min Cooking: 20 min

Asparagus with Egg, Lemon and Herbs

★

○ **1kg (2¼ lb) asparagus**
○ **3 hard-boiled egg yolks**
○ **5ml (1 tsp) mustard**
○ **5ml (1 tsp) chopped capers**
○ **5ml (1 tsp) chopped herbs: parsley, chervil, tarragon**
○ **45ml (3 tbls) oil**
○ **juice of 1 lemon**
○ **15ml (1 tbls) coarse salt**
○ **salt and pepper**

1. Place a large saucepan, three-quarters full of water, on a high heat, and add coarse salt.
2. Scrape or peel, and wash asparagus. Cut the stalks to an equal length and tie up in a bundle.
3. When the water boils, place the bundle upright in the saucepan. The water should come 1cm (½ inch) below the tips so they do not get spoilt during cooking. Allow to simmer gently for about 20 minutes. They are cooked when the point of a knife pierces them easily.
4. Meanwhile, prepare the sauce. Place the egg yolks in a bowl and add the lemon juice, mustard and oil, mixing well, then add the capers, chopped herbs, salt and pepper.
5. When the asparagus is cooked, remove from water, untie and drain on a rack. Then arrange on a serving dish.
6. Serve the sauce in a sauceboat.

To clean asparagus stalks without causing any damage, place them flat on a table or a board and peel with a vegetable peeler from the tip towards the end. Always buy freshly picked stalks; their freshness is apparent on cutting. But on the other hand a fresh asparagus stalk breaks very easily and the juice will seep out.

Dôme de Courgettes

Serves 4. Preparation and cooking: 45 min approx

Courgettes with Veal

○ **600g (1 lb 5 oz) courgettes**
○ **400g (14 oz) thinly beaten veal escalopes**
○ **80g (3¼ oz) butter**
○ **100g (4 oz) grated Gruyère cheese**
○ **salt and pepper**

1. Cut off both ends of the courgettes. Wash and cut into circles 0.5cm (⅛ inch) thick.
2. Melt half the butter in a frying pan and lightly brown the courgettes, turning them often with a wooden spoon. Add salt and pepper. Drain them in a colander and keep warm.
3. In the same pan melt the rest of the butter and cook the escalopes for 3 minutes on each side. Add salt and pepper. Deglaze the juices with 30ml (2 tbls) hot water.
4. Set oven to 220°C (425°F; gas mark 7).
5. Pour the deglazed juices into a round ovenproof dish and arrange a layer of courgettes in it, topped by a layer of cheese and a layer of escalopes. Continue in this way, building a dome, until all the ingredients have been used up, finishing with a layer of courgettes. Put in the oven for 15 minutes and serve immediately.

Cardons au Gratin

Serves 4. Preparation and cooking: 1 hr 50 min

Gratin of Cardoons (type of Globe Artichoke)

★★

○ **1kg (2¼ lb) cardoons**
○ **100g (4 oz) butter**
○ **100g (4 oz) grated Gruyère cheese**
○ **juice of 1 lemon plus ½ lemon**
○ **15ml (1 tbls) flour**
○ **salt and pepper**

1. Take off tough outer stalks of the cardoons. Discard all other fibrous parts. Trim remaining stalks and cut into 8cm (3 inch) long segments. Rub with lemon juice and drop into cold water. Add lemon juice, 15ml (1 tbls) of flour and salt to a pan of water and bring to a boil. Cook the cardoons gently in this for 1 hour 30 minutes. Drain.
2. Melt 50g (2 oz) butter in a pan, add the cardoons and brown lightly. Add salt and pepper.
3. Set oven at 230°C (450°F; gas mark 8).
4. Butter a gratin dish and put in half the cardoons. Sprinkle with the grated Gruyère and dot with butter. Add the remaining cardoons and the rest of the Gruyère and butter.
5. Place in the oven for 5 minutes and serve hot.

The method of cooking au blanc is used for certain vegetables like cardoons, seakale or artichoke hearts which discolour rapidly when peeled. Once prepared, you should immediately rub them with half a lemon and plunge them into cold water with lemon juice added. Leave them until you need to use them. Place together in a pan 20g (¾ oz) flour, 10g (½ oz) salt, 1 litre (1¾ pints) of water and lemon juice. Bring to the boil, stirring well, then add the vegetables and cook for the length of time desired. If you are serving the vegetables cold, allow them to cool in the liquor. The lemon juice and the flour will prevent them from discolouring, the first because of its acidity and the second because it allows an inpenetrable skin to form. Such vegetables, which turn black on contact with the air, may also blacken your hands when preparing them. You will find you can remove the marks by rubbing with half a lemon.

Coeurs de Céleri Braisés aux Olives

Serves 4. Preparation and cooking: 50 min

Braised Celery Hearts with Olives

★★

- ○ **8 small heads of celery**
- ○ **100g (4 oz) pitted black olives**
- ○ **500g (1 lb 2 oz) ripe tomatoes**
- ○ **2 peeled garlic cloves**
- ○ **15ml (1 tbls) chopped parsley**
- ○ **30ml (2 tbls) oil**
- ○ **50g (2 oz) butter**
- ○ **salt and pepper**

1. Discard the tough, outer stalks of the celery, and trim the leaves of the heart. Cut the hearts into 4. String with a sharp knife. Blanch them for 15 minutes in salted boiling water.
2. Meanwhile wash the tomatoes, quarter them and put them through a sieve or blender. Chop the olives. Strain the celery.
3. Heat the oil in a heavy pan, add the butter and lightly brown the garlic, then add the tomato purée, olives and parsley. Cook this mixture for 5 minutes on a medium heat and add the celery hearts, turning them with a wooden spoon so that they absorb the sauce. Add salt and pepper. Cover, and leave to simmer for 20 minutes over a low heat.
4. At the end of this time the celery should be tender and the sauce have greatly reduced. If it has not, cook uncovered for a few more minutes over a higher heat.
5. Arrange the celery in a dish, and serve hot.

Purée de Céleri-Rave

Serves 4-6. Preparation and cooking: 50 min

Purée of Celeriac

★★

- ○ **2 large celeriac roots**
- ○ **300g (11 oz) potatoes**
- ○ **100g (4 oz) fresh cream**
- ○ **50g (2 oz) butter**
- ○ **juice of 1 lemon plus ½ lemon**
- ○ **15ml (1 tbls) flour**
- ○ **salt and pepper**
- ○ **pinch nutmeg**

1. Peel the celeriac roots, quarter and squeeze lemon juice over the pieces to prevent discoloration. Leave to soak in cold water.
2. Bring some water to boil in a large saucepan. Add the salt, flour and lemon juice and gently simmer for 35 minutes.
3. Wash, peel, and quarter the potatoes and put them in the pan with the celeriac. After 35 minutes, check by piercing with a fork to see if the celeriac and potatoes are ready.
4. When the vegetables are cooked, strain them and put through a sieve or blender. Put the purée into a saucepan, add the cream and mix with a whisk. Add salt, pepper and nutmeg. Add butter and serve immediately, or keep warm until later.

This delicious purée can accompany all roasts and is especially good with game. A handful of chopped sorrel lightly browned in butter may be added.

When braising vegetables such as cabbage, celery hearts, leeks, or chicory they should first be blanched. This aids the cooking and helps to remove bitterness. They can then be braised in a slow oven or over a low heat by the following method. Grease a thick-bottomed pan generously with butter and put in a layer of sliced carrot and onion if you like. Arrange the vegetable to be braised on top and cover a quarter of the way up with stock. Add salt and pepper. Put in a few knobs of butter and cover. When they are cooked, strain the vegetables and arrange on a serving dish. Quickly reduce the cooking liquid, pour the residue over the vegetables, and serve. You may stuff such vegetables first, and cover the base of the pan with squares of pork fat or slices of lean bacon.

Chou Farci

Stuffed Cabbage

Serves 6. Preparation: 30 min Cooking: 2 hr

★★★

- ○ **1 large green cabbage, about 1.5kg (3¼ lb)**
- ○ **100g (4 oz) sausagemeat**
- ○ **100g (4 oz) smoked bacon**
- ○ **300g (11 oz) pickled pork**
- ○ **50g (2 oz) grated Gruyère cheese**
- ○ **100g (4 oz) white breadcrumbs or**
- ○ **200g (8 oz) cooked rice**
- ○ **1 egg**
- ○ **1 stock cube**
- ○ **½ litre (18 fl oz) hot water**
- ○ **1 garlic clove**
- ○ **15ml (1 tbls) chopped parsley**
- ○ **salt and pepper**

1. Take off any damaged leaves and wash the cabbage. Bring to the boil some water in a saucepan big enough to hold the cabbage and add salt; blanch by simmering for 15 minutes. Strain, pressing down well in the colander to eliminate all the water.
2. Meanwhile, prepare the stuffing: peel and chop the garlic finely. Dice the pork and bacon as small as possible. Mash the sausagemeat with a fork. Mix everything together in a bowl and add the breadcrumbs, grated cheese and chopped parsley. Bind together with an egg. Season and mix again.
3. Gently open out the leaves of the cabbage from the heart outwards. Place a spoonful of stuffing in the centre and spread another spoonful between each layer of leaves. Use up all the stuffing. Tie the cabbage with string like a parcel, leaving the knot at the top so that you will be able to lift it from the pan.
4. Set the oven at 195°C (375°F; gas mark 5). Dissolve the stock cube in hot water.
5. Put the cabbage in a pan and cover with stock, adding more water if necessary. Bring to the boil over a high heat. Cover and place in the oven for 2 hours.
6. Remove the cabbage from the stock by the knot, then cut the thread. Place on a serving dish, pour the stock into a sauceboat, and serve.

Boiled or puréed potatoes make the perfect accompaniment to this dish.

Feuilles de Chou Farcies

Stuffed Cabbage Leaves

Serves 4. Preparation: 30 min Cooking: 50 min

★★★

- ○ **8 undamaged green cabbage leaves**
- ○ **100g (4 oz) sausagemeat**
- ○ **100g (4 oz) cooked ham**
- ○ **2 eggs**
- ○ **100g (4 oz) grated Gruyère cheese**
- ○ **100ml (3½ fl oz) milk**
- ○ **50g (2 oz) bread without crusts**
- ○ **60g (2½ oz) butter**
- ○ **salt and pepper**
- ○ **pinch nutmeg**
- ○ **1 tin (14 oz) peeled tomatoes (optional)**

1. Wash the cabbage leaves. Blanch in boiling, salted water for 3 minutes, cool under a running tap and drain. Place on a cloth.
2. Crumble the bread and soak it in milk.
3. Chop the ham as small as possible and mash the sausagemeat. Mix together in a bowl. Add the eggs and the Gruyère cheese and mix again.
4. Squeeze out the bread and mix with the stuffing. Add salt, pepper and nutmeg. Work well with a fork.
5. Put a little stuffing in each cabbage leaf. Fold the leaf in four and tie up with kitchen thread.
6. Purée the tinned tomatoes through a sieve or blender.
7. Melt the butter in a heavy pan. Add the cabbage parcels and lightly brown all over. Then add the tomato purée, salt, pepper and nutmeg. Cover the pan. Leave to cook for 45 minutes over a low heat turning the stuffed leaves once. Serve either hot or cold.

You may replace the tomato purée with 250ml (9 fl oz) beef or chicken stock.

Aubergines à la Parmesane (p113) ▶

Chou-Fleur au Gratin

Serves 4. Preparation and cooking: 35 min

Cauliflower Cheese ★★

○ **1 large cauliflower**
○ **50g (2 oz) flour**
○ **70g (3 oz) butter**
○ **½ litre (18 fl oz) milk**
○ **100g (4 oz) fresh cream**
○ **50g (2 oz) grated Gruyère
  cheese**
○ **salt and pepper**
○ **pinch nutmeg**

1. Wash the cauliflower and separate into small flowerets. Boil gently in salted water for 10 minutes.
2. Meanwhile, prepare the béchamel sauce. Melt 50g (2 oz) butter in a saucepan and blend in the flour gradually, stirring constantly to avoid any lumps. Pour in the milk slowly, stirring all the time. Bring to the boil and leave to cook for 5 minutes. Add salt, pepper and nutmeg. Remove from the heat and blend in the fresh cream.
3. Set oven at 230°C (450°F; gas mark 8).
4. Strain the cauliflower. Butter a gratin dish. Arrange the cauliflower on it and pour over the béchamel. Scatter with grated cheese and cook in the oven for 15 minutes before serving immediately.

Chou à l'Aigre-Doux

Serves 4. Preparation: 30 min Cooking: 1 hr approx

Sweet and Sour Cabbage ★★

○ **1 large white cabbage**
○ **1 large onion**
○ **50g (2 oz) smoked bacon**
○ **100ml (3½ fl oz) oil**
○ **50g (2 oz) butter**
○ **100ml (3½ fl oz) vinegar**
○ **1 stock cube**
○ **250ml (9 fl oz) hot water**
○ **5ml (1 tsp) sugar**
○ **salt and pepper**

1. Boil 2 litres (3½ pints) water.
2. Cut off the stalk and discard any damaged leaves. Quarter and slice the cabbage. Put in the boiling water and leave to get completely cool.
3. When cold, drain the cabbage carefully. Peel and chop the onion. Cut the bacon into sticks.
4. Put half the oil and half the butter into a heavy pan. Lightly brown the onion in it, together with the bacon. Add the cabbage, then the salt and pepper.
5. Dissolve the stock cube in hot water and pour into the pan. Cook over a low heat uncovered for about 20 minutes until no stock is left. Then add the rest of the oil and the butter, the vinegar and the sugar. Mix well. Cover and cook for a further 40 minutes over a low heat. If there is any liquor left, reduce for a few minutes over a high heat, stirring continuously.

This cabbage dish makes an excellent accompaniment for goose and roast sucking pig.

Chou-Fleur Sauté

Serves 4. Preparation and cooking: 30 min

Sautéed Cauliflower with Onions and Sausagemeat ★

○ **1 large cauliflower**
○ **40g (1¾ oz) butter**
○ **2 medium-sized onions**
○ **100g (4 oz) sausagemeat**
○ **salt and pepper**

1. Wash the cauliflower and separate it into small flowerets.
2. Boil some water in a large saucepan, add salt and cook the cauliflower by simmering gently for 15 minutes.
3. Meanwhile, peel the onions and chop into small pieces.
4. Melt the butter in a frying pan and brown the onions lightly. Add the sausagemeat and brown it lightly, using a fork to break it up.
5. When the cauliflower is cooked, strain and add to the frying pan, stirring all together well. Season with pepper and serve.

Endives Sautées à la Crème
Chicory Sautéed with Cream

Serves 4. Preparation and cooking: 50 min

★★

- ○ 1kg (2¼ lb) large heads chicory
- ○ 3 thin rashers smoked bacon
- ○ 30g (1⅛ oz) butter
- ○ 100ml (3½ fl oz) dry white wine
- ○ 100ml (3½ fl oz) water
- ○ 200g (7 oz) fresh cream
- ○ 15ml (1 tbls) chopped parsley
- ○ salt and pepper

1. Remove the outer leaves of the chicory, and wash carefully. Hollow out the bitter core with a small pointed knife. Blanch the heads for 10 minutes in salted boiling water.
2. Meanwhile, cut the bacon into sticks 1cm (½ inch) wide. Melt the butter in a heavy pan, add the bacon and lightly brown over a low heat to prevent the butter burning.
3. When the chicory is blanched, strain, and add to the pan. Lightly brown them on all sides by turning continuously. Add the water and the wine. Add salt, pepper and cook uncovered for 20 minutes over a low heat; turn the chicory two or three times during the cooking.
4. At the end of this time, add the fresh cream and reduce it for 5 minutes over a high heat. Sprinkle with chopped parsley and serve hot.

Endives au Lait
Chicory with Milk

Serves 4. Preparation and cooking: 35 min

★★

- ○ 4 good heads chicory
- ○ 1 large chopped onion
- ○ 250ml (9 fl oz) milk
- ○ 50g (2 oz) grated Parmesan or Gruyère cheese
- ○ 30ml (2 tbls) oil
- ○ salt and pepper
- ○ pinch nutmeg

1. Remove the outer leaves of the chicory, and wash carefully. Hollow out the bitter core with a small pointed knife. Blanch the heads for 5 minutes in salted boiling water.
2. Pour the oil into a heavy pan, and add the well-chopped onion. Brown lightly over a low heat.
3. Carefully strain the chicory and add to the pan on top of the layer of onion. Add salt, pour in the milk and cook uncovered for 20 minutes over a low heat.
4. Mix the grated cheese with the pepper and nutmeg and sprinkle over the chicory. Allow the cheese to melt and serve immediately.

Salade d'Endives aux Noix
Chicory and Walnut Salad

Serves 4. Preparation: 15 min

★

- ○ 4 medium-sized heads chicory
- ○ 50g (2 oz) shelled walnuts
- ○ 45ml (3 tbls) oil
- ○ 30ml (2 tbls) vinegar
- ○ 2.5ml (½ tsp) sugar
- ○ salt and pepper

1. Roughly chop the walnuts. Remove the outer leaves of chicory. Hollow out the bitter core with a small pointed knife. Wash the heads quickly with cold water, dry them in a cloth and cut them into rounds 1cm (½ inch) thick.
2. Prepare the dressing. In a bowl mix the vinegar, sugar, salt and pepper with a fork. Add the oil, mixing all the time.
3. Put the chicory into a salad bowl, add the walnuts and pour over the dressing. Mix everything very well and serve immediately.

In Italy they do not blanch spinach by boiling in an uncovered saucepan, in a large quantity of salted water. Instead, having washed the spinach, they put it into a large saucepan without draining it. Salt is added, and the pan is covered and placed over a high heat. After 5 minutes, the spinach is fané *(limp) and ready to be used as you want.*

Choux de Bruxelles au Jambon
Brussels Sprouts with Ham

*Serves 4. Preparation: 15 min
Cooking: 30 min approx*
★

- ○ **500g (1 lb 2 oz) Brussels sprouts**
- ○ **100g (4 oz) thin rashers smoked bacon**
- ○ **100g (4 oz) cooked ham**
- ○ **50g (2 oz) butter**
- ○ **1 stock cube**
- ○ **½ litre (18 fl oz) hot water**
- ○ **salt and pepper**
- ○ **pinch nutmeg**

1. Pull off the outer leaves, then wash the sprouts in lots of water and drain. Slice the ham finely. Butter an ovenproof dish, and line it, first with the bacon, then a layer of sprouts, another layer of bacon, a layer of sprouts. Top with the slices of ham.
2. Set the oven at 195°C (375°F; gas mark 5). Dissolve the stock cube in hot water and pour into the dish. Add salt, pepper and nutmeg.
3. Dot with butter and put in the oven. Cook for about 30 minutes until the sprouts are tender and the liquid has completely evaporated. Serve hot.

Chou au Fromage
Cabbage with Cheese Sauce

Serves 4. Preparation and cooking: 50 min approx
★ ★

- ○ **1 cabbage or kale about 1kg (2¼ lb)**
- ○ **50g (2 oz) lard**
- ○ **½ litre (18 fl oz) cold water**
- ○ **salt**

For the sauce:
- ○ **125g (6 oz) smoked bacon**
- ○ **125g (6 oz) grated Gruyère cheese**
- ○ **40g (2 oz) flour**
- ○ **1 medium-sized onion**
- ○ **salt and pepper**
- ○ **pinch nutmeg**

1. Cut off the stalk, discarding any withered leaves, and quarter the cabbage. Wash and slice it. Melt the lard in a pan, put in the cabbage and cook for 5 minutes over a low heat, stirring frequently. Then pour in the cold water, add the salt, and cook covered for 25 minutes over a low heat.
2. Meanwhile, prepare the sauce. Peel the onion and chop it finely. Cut the bacon into thin sticks and put them into a saucepan without any fat. Brown the bacon over a low heat. Add the onion, and when it is transparent, drench with the flour. Stir constantly until the flour has changed colour; then remove from the heat.
3. Strain the cabbage, then pour the stock it has cooked in into the saucepan. Add salt, pepper and nutmeg. Cook for 5 minutes over a medium heat, stirring constantly, then add the cheese, making sure it blends in well. When the sauce has thickened, add the cabbage. Cook everything for 3 minutes, and serve.

Flan d'Épinards
Baked Spinach with Eggs and Cream

Serves 4. Preparation: 20 min Cooking: 30 min
★ ★

- ○ **1kg (2¼ lb) spinach**
- ○ **4 eggs**
- ○ **60ml (4 tbls) fresh cream**
- ○ **15ml (1 tbls) white breadcrumbs**
- ○ **2 peeled garlic cloves**
- ○ **60ml (4 tbls) olive oil**
- ○ **40g (1¾ oz) butter**
- ○ **salt and pepper**
- ○ **pinch nutmeg**

1. Trim the spinach stalks, and wash and drain the leaves in a colander. Cut into broad segments.
2. Heat some oil in a frying pan and brown the garlic lightly. Add the spinach and salt and cook for 5 minutes, then remove from the heat and discard the garlic.
3. Beat the eggs well in a bowl with the fresh cream. Add salt, pepper and nutmeg. Pour onto the spinach and mix together well.
4. Set the oven at 212°C (412°F; gas mark 6½).
5. Grease a soufflé dish or mould with half the butter. Pour in the contents of the frying pan, scatter with breadcrumbs and dot with the remaining butter.
6. Place in the oven for 20 minutes and serve from the dish.

Dôme de Courgettes (p116) ▶

Gâteau d'Épinards

Spinach Cake

Serves 4. Preparation and cooking: 1 hr 15 min

○ **1kg (2¼ lb) spinach**
○ **15ml (1 tbls) coarse salt**
○ **30ml (2 tbls) fresh cream**
○ **30g (1¼ oz) butter**

For the sauce:
○ **1 tin 400g (14 oz) peeled tomatoes**
○ **1 carrot**
○ **1 stick celery**
○ **1 onion**
○ **100g (4 oz) shelled fresh peas**
○ **20g (1 oz) butter**
○ **15ml (1 tbls) oil**
○ **salt and pepper**

For the omelettes:
○ **4 eggs**
○ **50g (2 oz) grated Gruyère cheese**
○ **45ml (3 tbls) fresh cream**
○ **45ml (3 tbls) oil**
○ **salt and pepper**
○ **pinch nutmeg**

1. Clean and wash the spinach but do not drain. Put the moist leaves in a large saucepan and add the coarse salt. Cover and cook for 10 minutes in their own juice over a low heat.
2. Meanwhile, peel and slice the carrot thinly. Peel and chop the celery and onion.
3. Prepare the sauce. Pour the oil into a heavy pan, adding the butter, then the carrot, celery and onion. Brown them lightly very slowly over a low heat. Open the tin of peeled tomatoes, reserving the juice. Cut the tomatoes in half and remove the seeds. Mash the tomatoes roughly with a fork and pour them into the pan with their juice. Add the peas, salt and pepper. Cook over a low heat for 15 minutes.
4. Strain the spinach in a colander. Put the butter into a heavy pan. Add the spinach, cook for 10 minutes turning continuously, then add the fresh cream and mix well. Cook for a further 5 minutes over a high heat.
5. In a bowl, mix together the eggs, fresh cream and Gruyère cheese. Add salt, pepper and nutmeg. Divide the mixture into 3 to make 3 omelettes. Heat 5ml (1 tsp) of oil in a frying pan. Pour in the first omelette, lower the heat and allow to cook gently for 5 minutes. Turn the omelette by slipping it onto a plate and then returning it to the pan to cook on the other side for a further 5 minutes. Do this twice more with the rest of the mixture.
6. Set the oven at 205°C (400°F; gas mark 6). See if the tomato sauce has cooked and check the seasoning. Butter an ovenproof dish large enough to hold the omelettes tightly. Put in one omelette, cover it with a layer of spinach and half the tomato sauce. Do this once again, then top with the third omelette and finish with a layer of spinach. Put the dish in the oven for 10 minutes. Serve hot.

This 'cake' may be decorated with slices of Gruyère cheese.

Gâteau Vert

Green Cake

Serves 4. Preparation and cooking: 50 min

★ ★

○ **1kg (2¼ lb) spinach**
○ **200g (7 oz) soft white cheese: Ricotta or goat's milk cheese.**
○ **100g (4 oz) grated Parmesan or Gruyère cheese**
○ **1 garlic clove, finely chopped**
○ **15ml (1 tbls) chopped parsley**
○ **30ml (2 tbls) breadcrumbs**
○ **60g (3½ oz) butter**
○ **1 egg**
○ **salt and pepper**

1. Clean and wash the spinach with plenty of water. Do not drain. Put the leaves in a large saucepan, add salt and cover. Soften the leaves by cooking them in their own juice over a medium heat for 10 minutes.
2. When the spinach is ready, strain in a colander, pressing on the leaves. Chop the leaves roughly and put them in a bowl. Add the parsley, garlic, Parmesan and Ricotta. Season. Mix well, mashing the cheese with a fork. Add the egg. Mix again.
3. Set the oven at 220°C (425°F; gas mark 7).
4. Butter a mould or soufflé dish 22cm (10 inches) in diameter. Fill with half the mixture. Sprinkle the top with breadcrumbs and dot with knobs of butter. Put the dish in the oven for 20 minutes.
5. Serve very hot or very cold.

Haricots Verts au Persil

Serves 4. Preparation: 10 min Cooking: 35 min approx

French Beans with Parsley

★

○ **750g (1 lb 10 oz) French beans**
○ **2 large onions cut into thin rounds**
○ **45ml (3 tbls) chopped parsley**
○ **2.5ml (½ tsp) thyme flowers**
○ **2.5ml (½ tsp) savory**
○ **juice of 1 lemon**
○ **60ml (4 tbls) oil**
○ **½ litre (18 fl oz; 1 pint) hot water**
○ **salt and pepper**

1. Top and tail, wash and drain the beans. Cook them in salted, boiling water for 10 minutes, then strain.
2. Heat the oil in a heavy pan and lightly brown the onion rounds. Put these on one side.
3. Put a layer of beans into the pan, then a layer of onions, sprinkle with parsley, thyme and savory. Continue in this fashion until the ingredients are used up. Sprinkle with lemon juice. Add salt and pepper and pour in the hot water. Cover the pan and cook for 15 minutes over a low heat, then remove the cover, raise the heat, and allow the liquid to reduce. Leave to cool before serving.

Purée de Haricots Verts

Serves 4. Preparation and cooking: 1 hr 50 min

Purée of French Beans

★★

○ **1kg (2¼ lb) large French beans**
○ **125g (5 oz) fresh cream**
○ **salt and pepper**

1. Top and tail, and wash the French beans. Cook in salted, boiling water for 25 minutes until they are tender.
2. When the beans are cooked strain them. Pass them through a sieve or blender to purée. Leave the purée to drain through a muslin cloth for at least 1 hour.
3. At the end of this time, put the cream in a saucepan and reduce it by half over a high heat. Then lower the flame and add the bean purée. Add salt and pepper. Mix well with a wooden spoon.
4. Serve the purée as soon as it is hot.

This purée, possibly served with croûtons browned in butter, goes well with all kinds of meat and also with grilled or poached fish.

Haricots Blancs à l'Étouffée

Serves 4. Preparation: 15 min Cooking: 1 hr 10 min

White Bean Stew

★★

○ **1kg (2¼ lb) white haricot beans (in pods)**
○ **1 small onion**
○ **1 leek**
○ **50g (2 oz) lean mild-cured bacon**
○ **1 garlic clove**
○ **15ml (1 tbls) chopped parsley**
○ **1 bay leaf**
○ **30ml (2 tbls) tomato concentrate**
○ **30g (1¼ oz) butter**
○ **30ml (2 tbls) oil**
○ **salt and pepper**

1. Shell the beans, wash and drain them. Peel and chop the onion. Clean the leek and cut into thin rounds 2mm (⅛ inch) thick. Peel and chop the garlic finely. Cut the bacon into thin sticks.
2. Heat the oil in a heavy pan, add the butter, onion, leek, bacon, garlic and parsley. Lightly brown everything, then add the beans and the bay leaf. Cover with cold water. Bring to the boil. Add salt and pepper. Cover the pan and simmer for 45 minutes over a low heat.
3. At the end of this time, dilute the tomato concentrate in 15ml (1 tbls) of water and pour it into the pan. Mix, leave to simmer for a further 15 minutes.

Serve hot to accompany braised or roast meat: duck, pork, or lamb.

Fenouils à la Mayonnaise

Fennel with Mayonnaise

Serves 6. Preparation and cooking: 35 min

★★

- ○ **6 medium-sized heads fennel**
- ○ **45ml (3 tbls) pickles**
- ○ **15ml (1 tbls) chopped parsley**

For the mayonnaise:
- ○ **1 egg yolk**
- ○ **5ml (1 tsp) mustard**
- ○ **100ml (3½ fl oz) oil**
- ○ **30ml (2 tbls) fresh cream**
- ○ **salt**

1. Remove the tough outer leaves of the fennel and cut off the stalks. Wash the rest and cook in salted boiling water for about 20 minutes until they are tender.
2. Prepare the mayonnaise. In a bowl put the egg yolk and the mustard. Beat quickly with a whisk. Put in the oil drop by drop, beating vigorously all the time. Add salt. When the mayonnaise is ready, fold in the fresh cream.
3. Strain the fennel and leave to cool. Cut each head into 4, but do not cut right through. Arrange them on a serving dish, sprinkle the dish with pickles and then cover all with cream mayonnaise. Sprinkle with parsley and serve cold.

Pickles are vegetables that have been grated, cubed or sliced and preserved in vinegar. They are salty, sweet and spicy all at the same time.

Fenouils aux Olives Noires

Fennel with Black Olives

Serves 4. Preparation and cooking: 30 min

★

- ○ **3 large heads fennel**
- ○ **2 anchovy fillets, canned**
- ○ **1 hard-boiled egg**
- ○ **30ml (2 tbls) vinegar**
- ○ **75ml (5 tbls) oil**
- ○ **50g (2 oz) pitted black olives**
- ○ **salt and pepper**

1. Remove the tough outer leaves of the fennel and cut off the stalks. Cut the heads into 4, wash and drain. Cook in salted boiling water for about 20 minutes until they are tender.
2. Meanwhile, mash the egg yolk with a fork in a bowl. Chop the anchovies, add them to the egg, and mix in the vinegar. Add a little salt and pepper. Blend in the oil little by little, beating with a fork.
3. When the fennel is cooked, strain and leave to cool. Arrange the fennel on a serving dish. Coat with the sauce. Chop the egg white and the olives, and sprinkle the fennel with this mixture. Serve.

Salade de Fenouils au Roquefort

Fennel Salad with Roquefort Cheese

Serves 4. Preparation: 15 min

★

- ○ **2 large heads fennel**

For the sauce:
- ○ **50g (2 oz) Roquefort cheese**
- ○ **50g (2 oz) fresh cream**
- ○ **15ml (1 tbls) vinegar**
- ○ **30ml (2 tbls) oil**
- ○ **15ml (1 tbls) chopped walnuts**
- ○ **salt and pepper**

1. Cut off the stalks of the fennel. Remove the tough outer leaves. Cut the heads into 4 and wash them. Chop finely and put into a salad bowl.
2. In a bowl, crumble the Roquefort with a fork. Add the vinegar and the fresh cream, the oil and walnuts. Add very little salt, and some pepper. Mix well.
3. Pour this sauce over the fennel. Mix again.

Serve immediately, adding if desired chopped herbs or chives.

Do not hesitate to scrunch raw young spinach leaves! As a salad they can be eaten with a vinaigrette made with oil or cream, with walnuts or grated nuts added, or a crushed garlic clove or a shallot, or slices of Roquefort. It is delicious!

Chou-Fleur au Gratin (p120)

Purée de Navets

Puré of Turnip

Serves 4. Preparation and cooking: 50 min

★

○ **1kg (2¼ lb) turnips**
○ **300g (11 oz) potatoes**
○ **150g (6 oz) fresh double cream**
○ **salt and pepper**

1. Peel the turnips, wash them and cut into 4. Peel the potatoes, wash them and dice. Cook the turnips and potatoes in salted, boiling water for about 30 minutes until they are very tender.
2. When the vegetables are cooked, strain them and put them through a fine sieve or blender.
3. Put the purée and the cream into a saucepan and heat through, stirring with a wooden spoon to prevent the bottom from scorching. Add salt and pepper. Allow the purée to reduce for several minutes if it is too liquid, and serve immediately or keep hot until serving.

This purée is delicious with pork, duck and goose.

Navets Glacés

Glazed Turnips

Serves 4. Preparation: 10 min Cooking: 45 min

★

○ **1kg (2¼ lb) small turnips**
○ **100g (4 oz) butter**
○ **15ml (1 tbls) granulated sugar**
○ **150ml (5 fl oz) hot water**
○ **salt**

1. Peel the turnips and trim them to a walnut shape. Wash, drain and wipe them.
2. Melt the butter in a saucepan which is large enough to hold the turnips without any overlapping and brown them lightly. Add salt, then sprinkle with sugar. Leave them to caramelize; then pour in hot water and leave to cook for 35 minutes over a low heat, shaking the saucepan to ensure that the turnips cook uniformly without turning them, since they are very fragile.
3. At the end of the cooking time, there should be no liquid left in the saucepan apart from a honey-like juice.

Serve these turnips very hot to accompany braised or roast pork, goose or duck.

Navets Farcis

Stuffed Turnips

Serves 4. Preparation: 30 min Cooking: 1 hr 30 min

★★★

○ **8 large round turnips**
○ **100g (4 oz) cooked ham**
○ **100g (4 oz) veal**
○ **100g (4 oz) sausagemeat**
○ **30ml (2 tbls) chopped parsley**
○ **50g (2 oz) grated Gruyère cheese**
○ **1 egg**
○ **50g (2 oz) butter**
○ **15ml (1 tbls) port**
○ **1 stock cube**
○ **250ml (9 fl oz) hot water**
○ **salt and pepper**

1. Peel and wash the turnips. Cut across the top 1cm (½ inch) deep to make a cap. Hollow out the centre with a small pointed knife without breaking the turnips.
2. Chop the ham and the veal, mash the sausagemeat. Mix everything together in a bowl, add the Gruyère cheese, parsley and port. Season. Add the egg. Mix again.
3. Stuff the turnips and put their 'caps' back on.
4. Set the oven at 195°C (375°F; gas mark 5). Prepare the stock by dissolving the cube in hot water.
5. Butter a gratin dish, arrange the turnips on it and pour over half the stock. Cook for 1 hour 30 minutes adding a little stock to the dish as the liquid reduces.

The ham and sausagemeat may be replaced by fresh pork and chicken.

Tourte aux Oignons

Egg and Onion Pie

Serves 4. Preparation and cooking: 1 hr 15 min

★ ★ ★

○ **600g (1 lb 5 oz) onions**
○ **100g (4 oz) smoked bacon**
○ **2 whole eggs**
○ **2 egg yolks**
○ **20g (1 oz) butter**
○ **30ml (2 tbls) oil**
○ **salt and pepper**
○ **pinch nutmeg**

For the shortcrust pastry:
○ **250g (9 oz) flour**
○ **180g (7¼ oz) soft butter**
○ **60ml (4 tbls) water**
○ **salt**

For the glaze:
○ **1 egg yolk**
○ **15ml (1 tbls) water**

1. Peel the onions and chop well. Dice the bacon as small as possible.
2. Put the oil in a frying pan and cook the onions and the bacon over a very low heat until the onions are transparent but not brown.
3. Prepare the shortcrust pastry. Make a well in the centre of the flour and add the salt, water and butter. Progressively work the butter into the flour until it is thoroughly incorporated. Knead the pastry until it comes away from the fingers to make one large ball.
4. Set the oven at 220°C (425°F; gas mark 7). Grease a pie dish 30cm (10 inches) in diameter.
5. Divide the pastry into two. Roll out one half to cover the base and sides of the pie dish.
6. Beat two eggs, plus the yolks from two more, in a bowl and add the onions and bacon. Season with salt, pepper and nutmeg. Pour the mixture into the pastry.
7. Roll out the other half of the pastry to make a lid. Trim off the extra pastry; press the edges together well and scallop. Make a glaze by mixing the egg yolk with a little water and brush the top of the pastry with it.
8. Place the pie in the oven and cook for about 40 minutes.
9. This pie can be eaten hot, warm or cold. Serve it at the start of the meal, or as a main course with a salad in season.

Soufflé d'Oignons aux Asperges

Onion and Asparagus Soufflé

Serves 4. Preparation and cooking: 1 hr

★ ★ ★

○ **500g (1 lb 2 oz) onions**
○ **500g (1 lb 2 oz) asparagus**
○ **3 eggs, separated**
○ **100ml (3½ fl oz) oil**
○ **50g (2 oz) grated Parmesan or Gruyère cheese**
○ **20g (¾ oz) butter**
○ **15ml (1 tbls) flour**
○ **salt and pepper**
○ **pinch nutmeg**

1. Peel the onions and chop them well. Scrape or peel the asparagus and cut into segments 2cm (¾ inch) long, using the top two-third of the stalk only.
2. Cook the asparagus gently in boiling salted water for 20 minutes.
3. Meanwhile, add the oil to a frying pan and sauté the onions over a low heat, turning constantly. When they are golden, leave them to cool, then put them through a sieve or blender. Add the egg yolks and cheese to this purée and season with salt, pepper and nutmeg.
4. Set the oven at 205°C (400°F; gas mark 6).
5. Strain the asparagus in a colander. Dip each stalk in flour before adding it to the onion purée.
6. Fold the stiffly-whipped egg whites carefully into the mixture.
7. Butter a soufflé dish double the volume of the mixture. Pour in the mixture and cook in the oven for 25 minutes.
8. Serve immediately.

If a sauce or mixture is too thick you should thin it by diluting it with an appropriate liquid. For instance, potato purée is diluted with milk, which you should pour in gradually, stirring all the time to make sure no lumps form until you achieve the consistency you want.

Oignons Farcis au Saumon

Serves 4. Preparation: 30 min Cooking: 50 min

Onions Stuffed with Salmon

★★★

- ○ **8 large onions**
- ○ **40g (1¾ oz) smoked salmon**
- ○ **250g (9 oz) cooked white chicken**
- ○ **1 egg**
- ○ **40g (1¾ oz) bread, without crusts**
- ○ **30ml (2 tbls) milk**
- ○ **15ml (1 tbls) chopped parsley**
- ○ **30g (1¼ oz) butter**
- ○ **100g (4 oz) fresh cream**
- ○ **1 chicken stock cube**
- ○ **250ml (9 fl oz) hot water**
- ○ **salt and pepper**
- ○ **pinch nutmeg**

1. Peel the onions and slice off the top quarter to hollow out the centre. Discard one-quarter of the cut-off section, finely chop the rest and put on one side. Grease a gratin dish with half the butter and arrange the onions on it.
2. Prepare the stuffing. Break the bread into pieces and soak in the milk; then mash it with a fork. Put the rest of the butter into a frying pan and lightly brown the chopped onion. Chop the salmon and the chicken very small. Mix the onions, salmon, chicken and bread together in a bowl. Add the parsley and blend in the egg. Add salt, pepper and nutmeg.
3. Set the oven to 205°C (400°F; gas mark 6). Fill the hollowed-out onions with the stuffing. Place on a gratin dish and dot with butter.
4. Dissolve the stock cube in boiling water and pour into the gratin dish. Cook for 50 minutes; 5 minutes before the end pour in the fresh cream. Serve very hot.

Oignons Farcis au Thon

Serves 4. Preparation: 20 min Cooking: 40 min

Onions Stuffed with Tuna

★★

- ○ **4 very large onions**
- ○ **1 tin 125g (5 oz) tuna fish**
- ○ **2 eggs**
- ○ **3 ripe tomatoes**
- ○ **15ml (1 tbls) chopped parsley**
- ○ **30ml (2 tbls) oil**
- ○ **10ml (2 tsp) breadcrumbs**
- ○ **250ml (9 fl oz) water**
- ○ **salt and pepper**

1. Peel the onions and cut them in half across. Hollow out the centres. Discard half the flesh and finely chop the remainder. Leave on one side.
2. Pour the oil into the bottom of a gratin dish. Arrange the onions in it.
3. Prepare the stuffing. Pour off the liquid from the tin of tuna, and mash the fish. Plunge the tomatoes into boiling water for 30 seconds, then drain them and cool them under the tap. Peel and cut in half to remove the seeds. Mash with a fork. Mix the tuna, tomatoes, eggs, chopped onion and chopped parsley together in a bowl. Add salt and pepper.
4. Set the oven at 205°C (400°F; gas mark 6).
5. Stuff the onions with the filling and scatter the tops with breadcrumbs. Pour the water into the dish.
6. Cook for 40 minutes, adding a little water to the dish if necessary, and serve immediately.

Cooking vegetables in a covered casserole can give marvellous results. Keep this method for new vegetables which have a delicate flavour, like carrots, turnips, peas, French beans, onions, lettuce hearts and chicory. Clean and wash them, then drain and arrange in a thick-based casserole that has been greased generously with butter. Add salt to accelerate the loss of the vegetables' natural juices – no other liquid, in fact, is used in the process. Cover the pan very tightly so that the steam condenses and falls back on to the vegetables; cook over a moderate heat throughout. If the heat is too low, the vegetables may disintegrate; if too high they may become caramelized and stick to the bottom of the pan. This method of cooking is slightly tricky so a certain amount of practice is needed. To minimize the risks the beginner can add 100ml (3½ fl oz) water to the bottom of the pan before starting.

Fenouils à la Mayonnaise (p126) ▶

Poivrons comme à Sorrente

Serves 4. Preparation and cooking: 1 hr 15 min

Peppers Stuffed with Mozzarella

★ ★ ★

○ **4 plump red peppers**
○ **200g (8 oz) Mozzarella cheese**
○ **25g (1 oz) butter**
○ **3 ripe tomatoes**
○ **1 egg**
○ **30ml (2 tbls) white breadcrumbs**
○ **salt and pepper**
○ **oil for frying**

1. Wash and wipe the peppers, and place under a very hot grill. Cook for about 20 minutes, turning them often, until the skin is completely black. Then put them in a saucepan with a tight cover, and leave to cool. This makes them easy to peel.
2. When they are cool, strip off their skins, cut in half and remove the seeds. Divide the Mozzarella into 8 pieces, adding salt and pepper to each. Put one piece into each pepper half; roll the edges over and secure with a cocktail stick.
3. Beat the egg well and add salt. Put the breadcrumbs on a plate. Dip each rolled-up pepper into the egg, and then into the breadcrumbs.
4. Heat the oil in a frying pan, brown the peppers lightly and drain on kitchen paper.
5. Wash and quarter the tomatoes, put through a sieve or blender. Melt the butter in a pan and add the tomato pulp. Season, and cook for 5 minutes.
6. Add the peppers to the tomato sauce and leave to simmer for 10 minutes over a very low heat. Serve immediately.

Poivrons Grillés

Serves 4. Preparation and cooking: 50 min approx

Grilled Peppers

★

○ **6 plump red peppers**
○ **3 garlic cloves**
○ **150ml (5 fl oz) olive oil**
○ **salt**

1. Set the grill at its highest.
2. Wash the peppers, and cook under the grill for about 20 minutes, turning frequently until the skin is completely black. Then put in a tightly sealed saucepan and leave to cool.
3. When the peppers are cool, peel off their skins, cut them open to remove their seeds, then cut them lengthways into strips about 2cm (¾ inch) wide.
4. Peel and finely slice the garlic. Layer the peppers in a bowl, placing several slices of garlic between each layer. Add salt and sprinkle with oil.
5. Serve these peppers warm or very cold.

You can use green or yellow peppers, or mix the colours. If they are served cold, garnish with anchovies and parsley.

Some vegetables are delicious grilled. Grill tomatoes, mushrooms, aubergines, peppers and onions over charcoal with meat and poultry cooked in the same way. Grilling is the oldest method of cooking known to man. Once cooked, the vegetables may be seasoned with a sprinkling of olive oil and lemon juice, and with salt and pepper.

Poireaux au Vin Rouge ou Blanc

*Serves 4. Preparation: 10 min
Cooking: 1 hr 45 min approx*

★

Leeks with Red or White Wine

○ **2kg (4½ lb) leeks**
○ **1 bottle red or white Bordeaux**
○ **80g (3¼ oz) butter**
○ **1 sprig thyme**
○ **½ bay leaf**
○ **salt and pepper**
○ **pinch nutmeg**

1. Clean the leeks, discarding three-quarters of the green part, and cut into pieces about 10cm (4 inches) long. Wash and drain in a colander.
2. Melt the butter in a heavy pan and cook the leeks over a low heat without browning them. Pour in wine. Add salt, pepper, thyme and the ½ bay leaf. Bring to the boil and cover. Cook for about 1 hour 30 minutes over a very low heat.

Serve the leeks very hot, with croûtons and poached eggs if you like.

Potiron Farci

Serves 4-6. Preparation and cooking: 1 hr 30 min

★★★

Stuffed Pumpkin

○ **1 good-sized pumpkin**
○ **800g (1¾ lb) veal**
○ **300g (11 oz) potatoes**
○ **1 stick celery**
○ **1 carrot**
○ **1 small onion**
○ **1 tin 400g (14 oz) peeled tomatoes**
○ **100ml (3½ fl oz) dry white wine**
○ **150g (6 oz) butter**
○ **30ml (2 tbls) flour**
○ **2 cloves**
○ **salt and pepper**

1. Cut a 'cap' off the pumpkin 3cm (1 inch) thick. Remove the seeds and scoop out the flesh with a spoon, leaving 1.5cm (½ inch) inside the skin. Put the flesh on one side.
2. Bring some salted water to the boil in a saucepan large enough to hold the pumpkin. Allow the pumpkin to simmer gently for about 30 minutes. Test by pricking with a fork to see if it is ready. When the pumpkin is tender, remove from the heat and drain upside down in a colander.
3. Meanwhile, peel and finely chop the onion. String the celery and peel the carrot, and slice finely. Cut the meat into cubes 4cm (1½ inches) square and sprinkle with flour.
4. Melt the butter in a heavy pan and brown the vegetables lightly. Add the meat and seal for about 5 minutes, turning with a wooden spoon to ensure that it browns equally all over. Then pour in the wine and allow it to evaporate over a high heat. Drain and reserve the juice from the tinned tomatoes; purée the tomatoes in a sieve or blender. Add all to the pan and season with salt, pepper and cloves. Cook over a low heat for 30 minutes stirring from time to time.
5. Meanwhile, peel and dice the potatoes. Cut the pumpkin flesh into cubes 2cm (¾ inch) square. Add these to the pan and cook, covered, for a further 30 minutes over a low heat.
6. 10 minutes before the end of this time, set the oven at 230°C (450°F; gas mark 8). Place the pumpkin on a dish and put in the oven for 5 minutes to allow it to dry out completely. Then arrange on a serving dish, fill it with the stuffing, and serve immediately.

Beef marrow lends an incomparable flavour to braised vegetables. Cook it with the vegetables, or poach it for 10 minutes in lightly simmering, salted water; then cut into fine rounds and arrange over the vegetables before serving. If the marrow is added directly to the vegetables, prepare it some hours beforehand by cutting into fine rounds 2cm (¾ inch) thick which you should plunge into iced, salted water and place in the refrigerator for at least 4 hours. Then drain, add to the blanched vegetables and continue braising them according to the recipe.

Pommes de Terre Farcies au Thon
Potatoes Stuffed with Tuna

Serves 4.
Preparation and cooking: 45 min
★★

- ○ **4 large potatoes**
- ○ **1 tin 200g (8 oz) tuna**
- ○ **100g (4 oz) pitted green olives**
- ○ **8 anchovy fillets, canned**
- ○ **30ml (2 tbls) tomato ketchup**
- ○ **yolks of 2 hard-boiled eggs**
- ○ **salt and pepper**

1. Wash the potatoes and peel them. Place in a large saucepan, cover with cold water and bring to the boil. Add salt. Simmer gently for about 20 minutes until the potatoes are cooked.
2. Meanwhile, mash the tuna fish with a fork and roughly chop the olives and 4 of the anchovy fillets. Keep back 4 olives and 4 anchovies for garnishing. Put the egg yolks in a bowl and mash them. Mix in the tuna, olives, ketchup and chopped anchovies. Add very little salt, and pepper.
3. When the potatoes are cooked, strain them and leave to cool. Hollow out their centres. Discard half the flesh and purée the rest. Add this purée to the mixture and check the seasoning.
4. Set the oven at 230°C (450°F; gas mark 8). Grease a gratin dish.
5. Stuff the potatoes with the mixture and garnish each one with a green olive wrapped in an anchovy fillet. Arrange the potatoes on the dish and put it in the oven for 5 minutes to heat them through.

Gâteau de Pommes de Terre
Potato Gâteau

Serves 4-6. Preparation: 20 min Cooking: 45 min
★★★

- ○ **1kg (2¼ lb) potatoes**
- ○ **125g (5 oz) butter**
- ○ **salt and pepper**

1. Choose long potatoes that remain firm during cooking. Peel and wash them, and slice across very finely into rounds 1mm (⅛ inch) thick (use an electric slicer if possible). Wash again until the water runs clear, so that all the starch is removed, then drain and wipe. Put in a bowl and sprinkle with salt and pepper. Mix well to distribute the seasoning evenly.
2. Put 25g (1 oz) butter on one side and melt the rest in a small saucepan. Pour over the potatoes and mix quickly making sure that every slice is coated.
3. Set the oven at 220°C (425°F; gas mark 7). With the 25g (1 oz) butter remaining, grease the base and sides of a mould or soufflé dish large enough to hold all the potatoes. Cover the bottom with a layer of potatoes arranged in overlapping circles, then line the sides in the same fashion. Continue like this until all the potatoes have been used up, but do not make more than six layers.
4. Put the cake into the oven for about 45 minutes. Check with the point of a knife to see if ready: it should pierce the potatoes easily. If it does not, continue cooking for a few minutes more.
5. Turn the cake out on to a serving dish. It should have a golden crust. Serve immediately.

This potato gâteau is a feast for the eyes and for the palate. It goes very well with all kinds of meat, but would be absolutely perfect with a large roast such as leg of lamb or rib of beef. For a really special occasion intersperse slices of truffle between the layers of potato. The butter in the recipe may be replaced by goose or duck fat.

Soufflé de Potiron

Pumpkin Soufflé

Serves 4. Preparation and cooking: 1 hr 10 min

★ ★ ★

- ○ 1 800g (1¾ lb) slice of pumpkin
- ○ 50g (2 oz) grated Gruyère cheese
- ○ 3 eggs, separated
- ○ 70g (3 oz) butter
- ○ salt and sugar
- ○ pinch nutmeg
- ○ 15ml (1 tbls) sieved flour

1. Skin the pumpkin slice and remove the seeds. Dice the flesh into cubes 4cm (1½ inches) square.
2. Put the pumpkin cubes in a saucepan, add 2ml (½ tsp) of salt and the same amount of sugar. Barely cover with water. Bring to the boil, then lower the heat and leave to cook for 10 minutes, simmering gently.
3. At the end of this time, drain the pumpkin in a colander and purée it in a sieve or blender. Put this purée in a saucepan with 50g (2 oz) butter, add the flour, and cook over a gentle heat for 10 minutes, stirring all the time to prevent the bottom from scorching.
4. When the purée is well-blended and of an even consistency, remove from the heat and add the grated cheese, a little more salt, and a little grated nutmeg. Beat in the egg yolks one by one, incorporating them well.
5. Beat the egg whites stiffly and fold carefully into the mixture. Set the oven at 187°C (350°F; gas mark 4½).
6. With the remaining butter, grease a soufflé dish large enough to hold one and a half times the quantity of the soufflé mixture. Pour into the dish; the dish should be only three-quarters full.
7. Cook the soufflé for 25 minutes in the oven, and serve immediately.

Flan de Potiron

Baked Pumpkin

Serves 4. Preparation and cooking: 1 hr 10 min

★ ★

- ○ 1 1kg (2¼ lb) slice of pumpkin
- ○ 125g (5 oz) butter
- ○ 250ml (9 fl oz) milk
- ○ 4 eggs
- ○ 100g (4 oz) grated Gruyère cheese
- ○ salt and pepper
- ○ pinch nutmeg

1. Skin the pumpkin and remove the seeds. Cut into cubes 3cm (1 inch) square.
2. Melt 50g (2 oz) butter in a pan and lightly brown the pumpkin. Add the milk and cook over a low heat until the pumpkin is tender, for about 15 minutes.
3. When the pumpkin is tender, pass through a sieve or blender to purée. Add 50g (2 oz) butter and the grated cheese to the purée in a bowl, and season with salt, pepper and nutmeg. Mix all together well.
4. Set the oven at 180°C (350°F; gas mark 4). Beat the eggs well and fold into the mixture carefully. With the remaining butter grease a soufflé mould and pour in the mixture. Place in the oven for 40 minutes.
5. Serve hot, warm or cold.

A mirepoix *is a mixture of vegetables invented in the nineteenth century by a nobleman who gave it his name. It usually includes carrots, celery, mushrooms, shallots and onions, cut into very small cubes and seasoned with aromatic herbs, all lightly sealed in butter. Sometimes small cubes of raw ham are added. It is used to thicken the gravy of braised meat or vegetables, and of roast meat.*

A mirepoix *should not be confused with* julienne *vegetables. These very fine sticks – between 1mm (⅛ inch) and 1.5cm (½ inch) thick and 4cm (1½ inches) long – are of ham, cooked chicken, orange and lemon peel, and all kinds of vegetables, such as carrots, celery, leeks, mushrooms. A special slicer called a* mouli julienne *facilitates their preparation.*

Crème Anglaise

Egg Custard

Serves 6. Preparation and cooking: 20 min

★ ★

○ **1 litre (1¾ pints) milk**
○ **8 egg yolks**
○ **150g (6 oz) caster sugar**
○ **1 vanilla pod**

1. With a sharp knife, split the vanilla pod lengthways. Put in a saucepan with the milk and bring to the boil; then turn the heat off and leave to infuse for 5 minutes.
2. Meanwhile, put the egg yolks in a heavy bottomed enamelled or stainless steel saucepan (aluminium will taint the cream and give it an unpleasant taste). Sprinkle in the sugar slowly, folding it into the egg yolks with a wooden spoon or spatula. If you pour all the sugar in at once over the egg yolks, it will literally 'cook' them and make them hard. Beat the mixture well with a spatula or whisk until it becomes lighter in colour, thick and frothy, and has doubled in volume. Then pour in the warm milk, drop by drop at first so that it blends perfectly with the egg mixture, then more rapidly.
3. Place the saucepan over a low heat – the mixture must not boil. Stir continuously with a wooden spoon or spatula in a circular movement, making sure that your spoon reaches right round the bottom and sides of the pan. In 5 to 10 minutes the mixture will have thickened. While it is cooking the froth on the surface will disappear, starting at the centre and moving outwards to the edge of the pan, as the custard gradually thickens. When the froth has completely vanished, the custard is ready: it should coat the spoon smoothly and evenly, and if you draw a line across it, it should stay there. Now remove the saucepan from the heat and quickly strain the custard through a fine sieve into a cold basin, which should preferably be standing in a larger one filled with cold water. It must be done quickly so that the custard stops cooking; otherwise the eggs will curdle. If this happens, do not despair: place the saucepan in cold water to stop any further cooking and beat the custard vigorously with a whisk or electric beater. It should soon become light, smooth and creamy. Leave to cool, stirring from time to time to make sure that a 'skin' does not appear on the surface.

You may need a little experience before you can be sure this egg custard will succeed every time; the first time you try it, you can add 5ml (1 tsp) of cornflour to the cold milk to make sure the custard does not curdle.

This custard makes a perfect sauce to serve with all kinds of biscuits and *brioches*, cream-filled cakes, charlottes, bavaroises, hot puddings, 'floating islands', and with stewed and puréed fruit.

The quantities given are variable. For a lighter custard, use only 6 egg yolks; or you may add as many as 12 egg yolks if you want it really rich and creamy. For extra richness, you may add 200ml (7 fl oz) of whipped cream or crème Chantilly once the custard has cooled.

For coffee custard, add 15ml (1 tbls) of instant coffee, or 30-45ml (2-3 tbls) of freshly ground coffee to the milk, and leave to infuse for a few minutes before pouring on to the egg yolks. Even better, flavour with chocolate by adding 30ml (2 tbls) of unsweetened cocoa to the milk, or 50 to 80g (2-3 oz) of plain bitter chocolate. More or less sugar may be added according to taste, whether the custard is flavoured, or what dessert it is to be served with.

Crème Suave à la Mandarine

Tangerine Cream Dessert

Serves 8. Preparation and cooking: 30 min
2 hr before serving
★★

○ **6 tangerines**
○ **½ litre (18 fl oz), milk**
○ **½ litre (18 fl oz) double cream**
○ **2 eggs**
○ **6 egg yolks**
○ **100g (4 oz) caster sugar**
○ **100g (4 oz) sugar lumps**
○ **100ml (3½ fl oz) tangerine liqueur**
○ **200g (7 oz) sponge cake or fingers, or macaroons**

1. Wipe the outsides of the tangerines and rub the sugar lumps over them.
2. Bring the milk to the boil, then leave to cool. When lukewarm, add the flavoured sugar lumps and let them dissolve.
3. Break the 2 eggs into a saucepan, and add the 6 egg yolks; sprinkle in the sugar and beat until the mixture has turned pale and frothy. Pour in the lukewarm milk, beating continuously; then beat in the cream. Place the saucepan over a low heat and cook until the custard thickens just enough to coat a spoon or spatula smoothly – but do not let it boil! Remove from the heat and strain through a fine sieve into a bowl. To cool the custard quickly, place the bowl in a larger dish filled with cold water.
4. While the custard is cooling, squeeze the tangerines, and strain the juice through a fine sieve into a bowl. Add 30ml (2 tbls) of the tangerine liqueur. Stir well.
5. When it is cold, add the rest of the tangerine liqueur to the cream, stirring well, and pour one-third of the mixture into a glass serving dish or bowl. Soak the sponge cake or fingers, or the macaroons, in the tangerine juice and liqueur and lay half of them on top of the cream. Pour in another third of the tangerine cream and place the rest of the biscuits on top. Slowly pour the remaining third of the cream over to finish, and refrigerate for at least 2 hours before serving.

If you decide to serve this dessert in individual glasses, first place a piece of sponge finger or macaroon at the bottom of each before pouring in the tangerine cream.

Crème Soufflée au Café

Coffee Cream Soufflé

Serves 4-5. Preparation and cooking: 15 min
1 hr before serving
★

○ **4 eggs**
○ **100g (4 oz) sugar**
○ **15ml (1 tbls) instant coffee**
○ **250ml (9 fl oz) milk**
○ **200ml (7 fl oz) double cream**

1. Bring the milk to the boil. Separate the eggs putting the whites in a large basin and the yolks in a saucepan. Sprinkle the sugar over the yolks and beat in until the mixture has turned pale and frothy.
2. Beat the egg whites until stiff. When the milk starts to boil, turn the heat off and sprinkle in the coffee; stir well and pour the milk a little at a time into the egg yolks and sugar. Then beat in the cream. Place the saucepan over a low heat and cook, stirring continuously, until it coats the back of a spoon smoothly. Remove from the heat and add the beaten egg whites all at once. Fold in quickly with a spatula and pour the soufflé into a bowl. Leave to cool.
3. When cool, you may leave the soufflé in the refrigerator for one hour, but do not serve it too cold.

Serve with *petits-fours*. You may add 50g (2 oz) of freshly ground coffee to the milk, and leave to infuse, to give this dessert a more delicate flavour.

The bark of the cinnamon tree is most easily bought as a finely ground powder. You can also find thin pieces of the peeled bark that have been dried to form curled-up 'quills'; or you can buy it as sticks. The essence of the spice can be extracted as a transparent liquid; in this form its flavour is extremely concentrated, and it must be used very sparingly.

Potiron Farci (p133) ▶

Petits Pots de Crème au Chocolat

Chocolate Ramekins

Serves 8. Preparation: 15 min
Cooking: 40 min 3 hr before serving
★

○ 1 litre (1¾ pints) milk
○ 150g (6 oz) plain bitter chocolate
○ 60ml (4 tbls) unsweetened cocoa
○ 1 vanilla pod
○ 1 egg
○ 6 egg yolks
○ 150g (6 oz) caster sugar

1. Set the oven at 195°C (375°F; gas mark 5). Split the vanilla pod in two lengthways. Place the cocoa and sugar in a saucepan and pour in the milk, a little at a time, stirring well to dissolve the cocoa and sugar; then add the vanilla, and break in the chocolate.
2. Cook over a low heat, stirring with a spoon or spatula until the chocolate melts, making sure it does not boil. Then turn the heat off and leave to cool for 5 minutes.
3. Beat the egg and 6 egg yolks together in a bowl and blend with 30ml (2 tbls) of the chocolate flavoured milk. Beat well once more, then add to the rest of the milk in the saucepan, beating continuously.
4. Fill 8 ovenproof ramekins with the custard, straining it through a fine sieve. Place the ramekins in a *bain-marie* and cook in the oven for 40 minutes. They are ready when the blade of a knife inserted in the centre of one of the ramekins comes out clean.
5. Remove the ramekins from the oven and leave to cool. Then refrigerate for at least 2 hours before serving.

Petits Pots de Crème au Porto

Ramekins of Cream with Port

Serves 6. Preparation: 15 min Cooking: 40 min
4 hr before serving
★

○ ½ litre (18 fl oz) milk
○ 300ml (10½ fl oz) single cream
○ 150g (6 oz) caster sugar
○ 6 egg yolks
○ 30ml (2 tbls) port

1. Set the oven at 195°C (375°F; gas mark 5). Put the sugar in a saucepan with 45ml (3 tbls) of water and cook over a medium heat until it has formed a light caramel.
2. Heat the milk and the cream together. When the caramel is ready, remove the saucepan from the heat and pour the warm milk/cream mixture over. Stir continuously until the caramel has completely dissolved.
3. Put the egg yolks and port in a bowl, and beat with a whisk until the mixture starts to froth. Then pour in the caramelized milk, a little at a time, beating continuously.
4. Fill 6 ramekins with the custard, straining it through a fine sieve. Place in a *bain-marie* and cook in the oven for 40 minutes. Check by inserting the blade of a knife to see if they are ready.
5. Remove the ramekins from the oven and leave to cook. Refrigerate for at least 4 hours before serving.

Flan de Chocolat à l'Orange

Baked Chocolate Custard with Orange

Serves 6-8. Preparation: 20 min Cooking: 45 min

★★

○ **125g (5 oz) fondant chocolate**
○ **100g (4 oz) caster sugar**
○ **65g (2¾ oz) butter**
○ **6 eggs**
○ **1 orange**
○ **15ml (1 tbls) flour**

For the icing:
○ **75g (3 oz) fondant chocolate**
○ **60g (2½ oz) butter**
○ **30ml (2 tbls) orange liqueur**

1. Separate the eggs; place the whites in a large bowl and reserve the yolks. Put the grated peel of the orange in a medium-sized saucepan, then add the squeezed juice. Add the sugar (reserving 30ml (2 tbls)) and cook over a very low heat, stirring with a spoon or spatula until the sugar has melted. Then break in the chocolate and cook until it melts, placing an asbestos sheet in between the saucepan and the heat.
2. Grease a mould or sandwich tin 24cm (9½ inches) in diameter with a little of the butter. Remove the saucepan with the chocolate mixture from the heat and add the rest of the butter, mixing well. Add the egg yolks, one by one, beating briskly; then sprinkle in the flour. Beat well.
3. Set the oven at 187°C (362°F; gas mark 4½). Beat the egg whites lightly and add the remaining 30ml (2 tbls) of sugar. Beat for another 10 seconds before folding quickly in to the custard, a third at a time, lifting the spoon from the bottom to the top. Pour in to the mould and cook in the oven for 45 minutes. Remove from the oven and leave to cool for 5 minutes. Turn out on to a serving dish.
4. Make an icing for the baked custard when it is cold. Break the chocolate into a small basin, add 15ml (1 tbls) of water and place over a saucepan of simmering water until it melts (make sure the water does not boil). Add the butter and orange liqueur, remove from the heat and blend together well, using a spatula. Pour this mixture over the custard and spread evenly with a palette knife.

Flan à l'Ananas

Baked Pineapple Custard

Serves 6-8. Preparation: 30 min Cooking: 1 hr 15 min
6 hr before serving
★★★

○ **1 pineapple, weighing about 1.2kg (2¾ lb)**
○ **300g (11 oz) caster sugar**
○ **6 eggs**
○ **50g (2 oz) flour**
○ **5ml (1 tsp) vanilla essence**
○ **30ml (2 tbls) white rum**
○ **juice of 1 lime**

1. Peel and dice the pineapple, making sure you cut out the woody core. Pass through a vegetable mill or blender; then through a sieve. Put this juice in to a saucepan with 200g (7 oz) of the sugar. Place over a low heat and bring to a gentle boil for 2 minutes. Remove from the heat.
2. Set the oven at 195°C (375°F; gas mark 5). Put the rest of the sugar in a small saucepan with 30ml (2 tbls) of water and cook gently until you have a golden syrup. Pour this into a mould or sandwich tin 22cm (8½ inches) in diameter, tilting it so that the syrup coats the bottom and sides evenly.
3. Break the eggs in a bowl, sprinkle in the flour, and beat well until the mixture starts to froth. Then add 30ml (2 tbls) of the pineapple juice and beat well; beat in the remaining juice.
4. Add the lime juice, vanilla essence and rum. Mix in well and pour into the mould. Cook in a *bain-marie* in the oven for 1 hour and 15 minutes until the surface of the custard is firm.
5. When it is cooked, leave to cool completely, and refrigerate for at least 6 hours before serving. If you first place the mould in hot water for 20 seconds, you will be able to unmould it easily, turning it out on to a serving dish.

Gâteau-Truffe au Chocolat Noir
Chocolate Truffle Cake

Serves 6-8. Preparation: 20 min
Cooking: 2 hr the day before serving
★★

○ **250g (9 oz) bitter chocolate, in pieces**
○ **250g (9 oz) softened butter**
○ **250g (9 oz) caster sugar**
○ **4 eggs**
○ **15ml (1 tbls) flour**

1. Put the chocolate in a bowl over a saucepan of water placed over a low heat. Leave it to melt; do not stir the chocolate, and make sure the water in the saucepan does not boil.
2. Meanwhile, preheat the oven to 195°C (375°F; gas mark 5). Break the eggs in to a bowl and sprinkle in the sugar; stir well, then sprinkle in the flour, and beat well until the mixture becomes light in colour. Reserve one knob of butter to grease the mould, and put the rest of the butter in a bowl; beat it well for 5 minutes.
3. Add the butter, a quarter at a time, to the melted chocolate, blending it in well with a spatula. Then add the egg mixture, stirring all the time.
4. Grease a non-stick charlotte mould 18cm (7 inches) in diameter with the knob of butter, or line an ordinary mould with greaseproof paper. Pour in the mixture, cover with a sheet of foil or a lid, and place the mould in a *bain-marie*. Cook in the oven for 2 hours. Make sure that the water in the *bain-marie* does not evaporate during cooking; if it does, add some boiling water.
5. After 2 hours, remove the cake from the oven and leave it to cool completely (for at least 3 hours) before unmoulding. Once removed from the mould, place the cake in the refrigerator. Serve the next day, or the day after – it is even better then!

This cake is a real delicacy for all who love chocolate and it should be soft and melting in the mouth. A complete dessert as it is, you may also serve it with an egg custard sauce flavoured with vanilla (if you like, you can stir some whipped cream into this).

You can also ice it. Melt 100g (4 oz) of plain chocolate with 30ml (2 tbls) of very strong coffee and 50g (2 oz) of butter; mix together well. Place the cake on a wire rack and spread the icing all over the top. Wait until it cools before serving.

Framboises en Clafoutis
Raspberry Pudding

Serves 6. Preparation: 10 min Cooking: 40 min
★

○ **400g (14 oz) raspberries**
○ **350g (12 oz) single cream**
○ **15ml (1 tbls) flour**
○ **2 eggs**
○ **2 egg yolks**
○ **130g (5¼ oz) sugar**
○ **25g (1 oz) vanilla sugar**
○ **25g (1 oz) butter**

1. Set the oven to 187°C (362°F; gas mark 4½). Mix the vanilla sugar with the sugar. Grease a fireproof porcelain mould or flan dish 22cm (8½ inches) in diameter with some butter and sprinkle in 30ml (2 tbls) of the sugar. Lay the raspberries on top.
2. Put the eggs and egg yolks in a bowl. Reserve 30ml (2 tbls) of the sugar and sprinkle the rest on to the eggs, beating thoroughly until the mixture turns pale. Then add the sifted flour. Mix well, and add the cream, beating for 1 minute. Pour the mixture into the mould over the raspberries and cook in the oven for 40 minutes.
3. At the end of this time, the *clafoutis* should be firm and have puffed up and turned slightly golden. Remove from the oven and leave to cool. Then sprinkle with the remaining 30ml (2 tbls) of sugar. Serve warm or cold.

Crème Suave à la Mandarine (p138) ▶

Île aux Pralines

Floating Island with Pralines

Serves 5-6. Preparation and cooking: 30 min
2 hr before serving
★ ★

○ **6 eggs**
○ **275g (10 oz) caster sugar**
○ **¾ litre (27 fl oz) milk**
○ **1 vanilla pod**
○ **2 pinches salt**
○ **24 pralines (candied almonds)**

1. With a sharp knife, split the vanilla pod in 2 lengthways. Put in a saucepan with the milk and bring to the boil. Turn the heat off and cover with a lid. Leave to infuse.
2. Separate the eggs, putting the whites in a bowl and sprinkling with salt. Put the yolks in a saucepan, sprinkle in 75g (3¼ oz) of sugar and stir well with a spatula until the mixture turns pale and frothy. Then pour in the milk, slowly at first to blend the ingredients, and then quickly. Place the saucepan over a low heat and cook until the custard thickens and coats the back of a spoon evenly. Do not let the custard boil. When cooked, strain it through a sieve into a bowl and leave to cool (place the bowl in cold water), stirring from time to time.
3. Put the rest of the sugar in a small saucepan with 45ml (3 tbls) of water over a medium heat. Beat the egg whites until they are just stiff. After the sugar has cooked gently for 5 minutes, check whether you obtained the right consistency of caramel by dropping a little of the syrup into cold water. If it sinks to the bottom and forms a small lump, it is cooked. By that time, the egg whites should be stiff. Slowly pour the syrup onto the meringue mixture, beating continuously, until the ingredients are cold. With an electric beater, beat for another 5 minutes. Meanwhile, crush the pralines, using a pestle and mortar.
4. Now add three-quarters of the crushed pralines (keep the rest for garnishing) to the egg whites, mixing them in with a spatula. Wet a mould or sandwich tin 20cm (8 inches) in diameter; shake off the excess water but do not dry it. Turn the mixture into the mould, flattening the surface with a spatula, and refrigerate for 1 hour. You should also refrigerate the custard, once it has cooled.
5. Just before serving, turn out the soufflé in a deep serving dish and pour the custard around. The soufflé should float like an island. Sprinkle with the remaining pralines and serve.

This dessert should not be served more than 4 hours after being made.

Île aux Ananas

Floating Island with Pineapple

Serves 4-5. Preparation and cooking: 30 min
1 hr before serving
★ ★

○ **5 pineapple slices (tinned in syrup)**
○ **4 egg whites**
○ **100g (4 oz) caster sugar**
○ **70g (3 oz) ground almonds**

For the custard:
○ **4 egg yolks**
○ **60g (2½ oz) sugar**
○ **25g (1 oz) vanilla sugar**
○ **½ litre (18 fl oz) milk**

1. Set the oven to 205°C (400°F; gas mark 6). Drain the pineapple on kitchen paper and cut each slice across in halves.
2. Beat the egg whites until just stiff, then add 100g (4 oz) caster sugar and the ground almonds, folding them in as lightly as possible with a spatula.
3. Arrange the pineapple slices on the bottom of a mould and pour over the meringue mixture. Cook in a *bain-marie* for 20 minutes in the oven. Meanwhile, prepare an egg custard sauce, following the recipe on page 9.
4. When cooked, remove the soufflé from the oven and turn out in to a deep dish. Surround with the custard and serve at once, or refrigerate for 1 hour.

Mousse au Chocolat au Whisky

Chocolate Mousse with Whisky

*Serves 6. Preparation: 15 min
3 hr before serving*
★

○ **250g (9 oz) fondant chocolate**
○ **6 eggs**
○ **30ml (2 tbls) scotch whisky**
○ **pinch salt**

1. Put 15ml (1 tbls) of water in a small saucepan and break in the chocolate. Put in a *bain-marie* (or use a double saucepan) and leave to melt over a gentle heat. The water should just shiver.
2. Meanwhile, separate the eggs. Keep the yolks on one side, and put the whites in to a large bowl. Sprinkle with salt, and whisk until just stiff.
3. When the chocolate has melted, remove the saucepan from the heat. Stir in the whisky, beating quickly with a spatula, then stir in the egg yolks. Beat until the mixture is smooth and well-blended. Then fold it into the beaten egg whites, lifting the mixture carefully so that the whites are not broken down.
4. Pour the mousse into a large serving dish, or into 6 ramekins, and put in the refrigerator for at least 3 hours before serving.

Serve with sponge fingers, *langues de chat*, wafers, *gaufrettes*, or brandy snaps.

You may use bourbon, cognac or rum instead of the whisky, or even an orange, tangerine or coffee-flavoured liqueur. The mousse can be made the day before.

Mousse Velours

Velvet Chocolate Mousse

*Serves 4. Preparation: 30 min
1 hr before serving*
★ ★ ★

○ **250g (9 oz) bitter chocolate**
○ **250g (9 oz) chilled double cream**
○ **3 eggs**
○ **80g (3¼ oz) caster sugar**
○ **pinch of salt**
○ **15ml (1 tbls) coffee essence**
○ **4 maraschino cherries**

1. If you own an electric beater, you will find that this recipe is extremely simple and quick to prepare. Put the cream into a large bowl and whisk with the beater until stiff. Put on one side.
2. Separate the eggs, keeping the yolks on one side. Put the whites in a large bowl, sprinkle with salt, and beat until stiff. Fold into the beaten cream, lifting the mixture from the bottom to the top.
3. Stir the coffee essence into the egg yolks. Put the sugar with 100ml (3½ fl oz) of water in a small saucepan and cook over a medium heat until it becomes syrupy. To check whether the caramel is the right consistency, drop a little into cold water: if it sinks to the bottom and forms a marble, the caramel is ready. Pour the warm caramel on to the egg yolks, a little at a time, beating as quickly as possible (preferably with an electric beater) until the mixture starts to froth and doubles in volume.
4. Meanwhile, break the chocolate into pieces and melt in a *bain-marie* (or use a double saucepan). Beat the melted chocolate into the egg yolk mixture; whisk until the mousse is nearly cold.
5. Stop beating and delicately fold in the meringue and cream mixture, using a spatula to lift the mixture carefully. Put in the refrigerator for 30 minutes.
6. Put the mousse in to an icing bag with a star-shaped nozzle. Pipe large dollops into 4 individual glass bowls, making sure that the mousse does not smear the edges. Decorate each one with a maraschino cherry, and refrigerate until serving.

Sabayon

Serves 4. Preparation and cooking: 15 min

Frothy Wine Sauce with Marsala

★★

○ **4 egg yolks**
○ **80g (3¼ oz) caster sugar**
○ **150ml (5 fl oz) marsala**

1. Place the egg yolks into a saucepan; sprinkle in the sugar and whisk until the mixture turns pale and frothy. Then whisk in the marsala.
2. Put the saucepan in a *bain-marie* (or use a double saucepan) and cook over a low heat (the water should hardly shiver). Beat until the mixture thickens, froths, and triples in volume. Then remove from heat.
3. Pour into cups and serve at once.

Serve with various *petits-fours* and garnish with a dab of crème Chantilly and a glacé cherry. This wine sauce may be served with charlottes, rice puddings or filled cakes. Leave it to cool completely and then pour it over a fresh fruit salad or fruit poached in syrup, such as strawberries, raspberries, peaches, or pears. Sabayon may be prepared with other wines such as port, madeira or sherry, a muscat or a sweet white wine – or even champagne. You can sweeten a dry white wine by adding a little more sugar to the egg yolks and 15ml (1 tbls) of rum, kirsch or maraschino liqueur.

If you want to serve the sabayon chilled in ramekins, you should add 2 sheets of gelatine (dissolved in cold water) or 30ml (2 tbls) of cornflour diluted with the cold wine to the mixture over the *bain-marie*, otherwise it will not set very well. At the end of the cooking you can add 2 stiffly beaten egg whites, to give extra lightness.

Mousse Moka au Pralin de Noix

*Serves 6. Preparation: 30 min
1 hr before serving*

Coffee Mousse with Walnut Praline

★★★

○ **6 egg yolks**
○ **200ml (7 fl oz) very strong coffee**
○ **120g (4¾ oz) caster sugar**
○ **200ml (7 fl oz) chilled double cream**
○ **2 gelatine sheets**

For the walnut praline:
○ **12 shelled walnuts**
○ **100g (4 oz) caster sugar**
○ **5ml (1 tsp) lemon juice**

1. Place the gelatine in cold water to soften it. Put the egg yolks in a saucepan together with the sugar and whisk, preferably using an electric beater, until the mixture turns pale and starts to froth. Then beat in the coffee, a little at a time. Still beating, place the saucepan in a *bain-marie* (or use a double saucepan) and cook over a low heat. When the mousse lifts into peaks when you take away the whisk or electric beater, add the squeezed gelatine. Remove from the heat and continue beating, but this time with the saucepan placed in cold water. Beat until the mousse has become lukewarm; then leave to cool entirely.
2. Whip the cream and fold gently into the mousse when it is cold. Turn into individual cups and refrigerate for at least one hour.
3. Prepare the walnut praline: put the sugar, 30ml (2 tbls) of water and the lemon juice into a small saucepan and cook over a low heat. Coarsely chop the walnuts. When the sugar has turned golden and is of a syrupy consistency, add the walnuts. Mix well, turning the saucepan over the heat. When the caramel is darker, pour the contents of the saucepan over a marble chopping board or metal tray. Spread with a thick knife and leave to cool. Then chop very finely with a knife.
4. Just before serving, sprinkle the mousse with the finely chopped walnut praline.

Bavaroise aux Fraises

Strawberry Bavaroise

Serves 6. Preparation: 20 min
4 hr before serving
★

○ **350g (12 oz) strawberries**
○ **250ml (9 fl oz) sirop de fraises + 30ml (2 tbls)**
○ **250ml (9 fl oz) chilled double cream**
○ **4 gelatine sheets**
○ **15ml (1 tbls) lemon juice**
○ **4 drops vanilla essence**

For the mould:
○ **15ml (1 tbls) caster sugar**

1. Place the gelatine in cold water and leave to soak. Whip the cream. Wash and hull the strawberries. Put 100g (4 oz) on one side for garnishing and pass the rest through a mill or blender. Add the lemon juice and vanilla essence, and mix well.
2. Heat 250ml (9 fl oz) of sirop in a saucepan, but do not let it boil. Add the drained gelatine, stir in well, and place the saucepan in very cold water.
3. When it has cooled, stir in the puréed strawberries. When the mixture starts to set, add three-quarters of the whipped cream, keeping the rest in the refrigerator for garnishing. Stir well.
4. Wet a mould, shake out the excess water but do not dry. Sprinkle the sugar over the bottom and sides, and pour in the bavaroise. Refrigerate for at least 4 hours before serving.
5. Just before serving, dip the mould in lukewarm water for 10 seconds – it should slide out easily. Pipe on the reserved cream to decorate. Decorate with strawberries and pour over the remaining sirop.

Bavaroise aux Framboises

Raspberry Bavaroise

Serves 6-8. Preparation: 45 min
4 hr before serving
★ ★ ★

For the white cream:
○ **400ml (14 fl oz) double cream**
○ **45ml (3 tbls) caster sugar**
○ **6 gelatine sheets**
○ **30ml (2 tbls) orange liqueur**

For the pink mousse:
○ **400g (14 oz) raspberries**
○ **150g (6 oz) caster sugar**
○ **30ml (2 tbls) lemon juice**
○ **30ml (2 tbls) kirsch or maraschino liqueur**
○ **4 gelatine sheets**
○ **200ml (7 fl oz) chilled double cream**

To decorate:
○ **200g (7 oz) raspberries**

For the mould:
○ **15ml (1 tbls) caster sugar**

1. Prepare the white cream. Put the gelatine in cold water to soak. Put the sugar with 30ml (2 tbls) of water in a saucepan over a low heat. When the sugar has melted, add the drained gelatine. Remove from heat, and stir in 30ml (2 tbls) of cream. Then add the rest of the cream and the orange liqueur, stirring briskly. Put the saucepan in cold water.
2. Sprinkle a wetted mould with sugar and place in a large bowl filled with cold water and ice cubes. As soon as the white cream starts to set, pour it into the mould and settle the mould in the bowl of iced water so that first the sides and then the bottom are coated with a layer of the cream. As soon as it is adhering firmly and evenly, put the mould in the freezer.
3. Prepare the pink mousse. Put the gelatine in cold water to soak. Melt the sugar in a saucepan over a low heat together with 15ml (1 tbls) of water. Add the gelatine and stir in well. Remove from the heat and leave to cool. Sieve the raspberries or pass through the fine mesh of a mill over the saucepan and briskly beat the purée in with a whisk. Then beat in the kirsch or maraschino liqueur, with the lemon juice. Whip the cream in a bowl and fold into the puréed raspberries. Mix together carefully.
4. Remove the mould from the freezer and pour in the pink mousse. Chill once more in the refrigerator for at least 4 hours.
5. Just before serving, turn the mousse out on to a dish and decorate with raspberries.

You can use strawberries for this bavaroise, or a mixture of both, or other red fruit such as redcurrants. To make it even more delicious, serve with an egg custard sauce flavoured with orange liqueur.

Bavaroise au Marrons
Bavaroise with Marrons

○ ⅓ litre (11 fl oz) milk
○ 4 egg yolks
○ 100g (4 oz) caster sugar
○ 200g (7 oz) tinned puréed or creamed marrons
○ 100g (4 oz) marrons glacés pieces
○ 300ml (10½ fl oz) double cream
○ 5 gelatine sheets
○ 30ml (2 tbls) rum or cognac

To decorate:
○ 7 or 8 whole marrons glacés
○ crystallized violets

1. Soak the gelatine in cold water. Bring the milk to the boil. Put the egg yolks in a saucepan, sprinkle in the sugar and beat until they turn pale and frothy. Then stir in the warm milk. Cook over a low heat until the custard thickens enough to coat the back of a spoon evenly. Then add the drained gelatine. Stir in well, then sieve the custard in to a bowl standing in cold water.
2. When it has cooled, stir in the rum or cognac and then the puréed marrons, mixing together well. Whip the cream.
3. When it starts to set, stir in the pieces of marrons glacés and the whipped cream.
4. Wet a mould and fill with the bavaroise. Chill for at least 4 hours.
5. Just before serving, dip the mould in warm water for 10 seconds and turn on to a serving dish. Decorate with the whole marrons glacés and with as many crystallized violets as you like.

A hot chocolate sauce goes very well with this dessert. For this you will need: 100g (4 oz) bitter chocolate and 20g (¾ oz) butter, melted together and mixed with 100ml (3½ fl oz) of milk or whipped cream, sweetened with a little vanilla sugar.

Bavaroise au Café
Coffee Bavaroise

○ ⅓ litre (11 fl oz) milk
○ 60g (2¼ oz) freshly ground coffee
○ 5 egg yolks
○ 180g (7¼ oz) caster sugar
○ 5 gelatine sheets
○ ½ litre (18 fl oz) chilled double cream
○ 15ml (1 tbls) coffee beans in liqueur

For the mould:
○ 15ml (1 tbls) caster sugar

1. Bring the milk to the boil in a small saucepan. Stir in the ground coffee, mixing well, then turn the heat off, cover the saucepan, and leave to brew for 10 minutes.
2. Meanwhile, soak the gelatine in cold water. Put the egg yolks in a saucepan, sprinkle in the sugar and beat until they turn pale and frothy. Then slowly pour in the coffee-flavoured milk through a strainer. Place the saucepan over a low heat and cook until the custard thickens enough to coat the back of a spoon evenly. Remove from the heat and add the drained gelatine. Stir in well and strain the custard through a fine sieve in to a bowl standing in cold water.
3. While it is cooling, whip the cream. Reserve about 30ml (2 tbls) for garnishing. As soon as the custard starts to set, gently fold in the whipped cream with a spatula.
4. Wet a mould and sprinkle in the sugar. Fill the mould, and chill for at least 4 hours.
5. Just before serving, dip the mould in warm water for 10 seconds and turn out on to a serving dish. Pipe on the reserved whipped cream to decorate attractively, and garnish with the liqueured coffee beans.

Cécilia
Rich Lemon Cream Charlotte

Serves 8-10. Preparation and cooking: 2 hr of which 1 hr 10 min the day before
★ ★

For the cake:
○ **5 eggs**
○ **1 lemon**
○ **150g (6 oz) icing sugar**
○ **60g (2½ oz) flour**
○ **60g (2½ oz) cornflour**
○ **20g (¾ oz) butter**
○ **100ml (3½ fl oz) white rum**

For the cream:
○ **4 egg yolks**
○ **100g (4 oz) butter**
○ **160g (6½ oz) caster sugar**
○ **3 lemons**

To decorate:
○ **100g (4 oz) cooking chocolate**
○ **4 egg whites**
○ **200g (7 oz) caster sugar**

1. Prepare the cake the day before. Finely grate the lemon peel and add to 15ml (1 tbls) of lemon juice. Separate the eggs, and add the lemon juice and peel to the yolks. Sprinkle in the sugar and briskly beat (preferably with an electric beater) until the mixture has increased three times in volume. Set the oven to 187°C (362°F; gas mark 4½). Sift the flour and cornflour together. Whisk the egg whites until stiff and add 15ml (1 tbls) at a time, alternating with 15ml (1 tbls) of flour/cornflour, to the egg yolks, beating continuously. Stop beating, and add the rest of the beaten egg white all at once; mix until entirely blended. Butter a mould or sandwich tin 20cm (8 inches) in diameter and fill with the mixture. Cook for 45 minutes. Turn out on to a wire rack and leave to cool until the next day.

2. The next day, prepare the lemon cream. Finely grate the lemon peel into a bowl. Squeeze the juice and add to the peel. This should give you about 75ml (5 tbls) of juice. Put the egg yolks in a saucepan with the lemon juice and peel and beat well. Then sprinkle in the sugar and one-third of the butter. Mix together well and place in a *bain-marie* over a gentle heat. Do not let the water boil. Beat the mixture well, using a whisk or electric beater, until the cream thickens: the track of the whisk or beater should remain on the surface of the cream for a few seconds. Remove from heat and strain through a fine sieve into a bowl. Then stir in the remaining butter and beat again, until the mixture is well-blended, for about 1 minute. Leave to cool.

3. Meanwhile, cut the cake into 3 slices across. Mix the rum with the same amount of water, place one slice of the cake on a serving dish and moisten with one-third of the rum/water mixture. Spread with half the lemon cream. Place the second slice on top; moisten it, and spread with the remaining lemon cream. Place the third slice on top and moisten with the remaining rum/water mixture. You may decorate the cake and serve it one hour later, but it is best to chill it for at least 3 or 4 hours before decorating and serving it.

4. To decorate, melt the chocolate, with 30ml (2 tbls) of water in a *bain-marie*. Pour the melted chocolate on to the centre of the cake and spread evenly over the top with a spatula. Beat the egg whites until very stiff. Put the sugar in a small saucepan with 45ml (3 tbls) of water and cook until the syrup is of the right consistency (check by dropping a teaspoon of syrup into cold water. If it hardens and forms a small marble, it is ready). Pour the syrup onto the beaten egg white and continue beating until the mixture is cold: this is an Italian meringue. Fill an icing bag with the mixture and, using a star-shaped nozzle, pipe a border of rosettes round the edge of the cake. The name 'Cecilia' can be piped in the centre of the cake: it is best to use a simple glacé icing for this. Chill until serving time.

Charlottes can be prepared in all sorts of shape of mould, apart from the cylindrical mould (like a deep cake tin) usually associated with them. You can use a simple pudding basin or a fluted mould – even a dome-shaped cheese cover; anything you can think of, in fact.

Bavaroise au Marrons (p149) ▶

Charlotte à l'Orange
Orange Charlotte

Serves 6-8. Preparation and cooking: 1 hr
4 hr before serving
★★★

○ **4 large oranges**
○ **½ litre (18 fl oz) milk**
○ **250g (9 oz) double cream**
○ **6 egg yolks**
○ **220g (8¾ oz) caster sugar**
○ **105ml (7 tbls) orange liqueur**
○ **15ml (1 tbls) cognac**
○ **45ml (3 tbls) sirop de grenadine**
○ **5 gelatine sheets**
○ **20 to 24 sponge fingers**

1. Soak the gelatine in cold water. Pour the milk into a small saucepan and grate the peel of one orange into it. Bring to the boil, then turn the heat off, and leave to infuse.

2. Put the egg yolks in another saucepan. Sprinkle in 150g (6 oz) of sugar and stir until the mixture turns pale and frothy. Slowly pour in the warm milk, place the saucepan over a low heat and cook, without letting it boil, until it is thick enough to coat the back of a spoon evenly. Then remove from heat and add the drained gelatine, stirring it in well. Strain through a fine sieve into a bowl standing in iced water. Stir in 30ml (2 tbls) of orange liqueur.

3. Whip the cream. Pour 45ml (3 tbls) of orange liqueur into a deep dish with 90ml (6 tbls) of water. Dip the sponge fingers quickly into the liquid, and line the bottom and sides of a charlotte mould 18cm (7 inches) in diameter with them.

4. When the orange custard is starting to set, gently fold in the whipped cream, lifting the mixture carefully. Fill the biscuit-lined mould, trimming off any protruding ends. Cover the mould and refrigerate for at least 4 hours.

5. Prepare the garnish. Cut the peel off the 3 remaining oranges in thin spirals and cut these into julienne strips like matches. Plunge into boiling water and blanch for 1 minute, remove and drain. Put the remaining 70g (3 oz) of sugar with 200ml (7 fl oz) of water in a saucepan and bring to the boil. Add the strips of peel and the sirop de grenadine. Stir, and cook slowly over a low heat for 10 minutes. Then remove from heat and leave to cool. When cold, add the cognac and the remaining 30ml (2 tbls) of orange liqueur. Stir and pour into a bowl. Chill. Place the 4 peeled oranges into a plastic bag in the refrigerator until serving time.

6. Just before serving, peel the white membrane off the oranges. Break into segments and carefully skin each one with a sharp knife. Turn the charlotte out on to a deep serving dish. Decorate with the orange segments. Strain the orange juice and pour over the charlotte. Serve at once.

There is no need always to stick to sponge fingers to line a charlotte: you can use all sorts of biscuits, as we suggest in some of the recipes in this book. And what about cutting a slightly stale sponge cake into thin slices . . . that can be a really delicious way of using it up!

Soufflé au Grand Marnier

Serves 3. Preparation: 15 min Cooking: 25 min

Grand Marnier Soufflé

★★★

○ **75ml (5 tbls) milk**
○ **15g (½ oz) cornflour**
○ **60g (2½ oz) caster sugar**
○ **20g (¾ oz) butter**
○ **45ml (3 tbls) grand marnier**
○ **2 eggs**
○ **1 egg white**
○ **pinch salt**

For the mould:
○ **15g (½ oz) butter**
○ **15ml (1 tbls) caster sugar**

1. Set the oven to 200°C (387°F; gas mark 5½). Separate the eggs, putting the yolks on one side. Put the egg whites, plus the extra egg white, in a large basin.
2. Butter the bottom and sides of a soufflé dish 16cm (6 inches) in diameter and 5cm (2 inches) high. Sprinkle in the sugar.
3. Put 30ml (2 tbls) of sugar, the cornflour and cold milk in a saucepan. Mix briskly, using a whisk, and place the saucepan over a medium heat. Bring to the boil, beating with a whisk all the time so that the mixture, which thickens quickly, remains smooth and no lumps appear. When the mixture has thickened sufficiently, and as soon as it starts to boil, remove from the heat. Still beating with a whisk, fold in the butter, then the grand marnier, and lastly the egg yolks. Do not stop beating as you add each ingredient; the mixture should blend together quite quickly.
4. Sprinkle the egg whites with salt and whisk until stiff. Then fold in the remaining 15ml (1 tbls) of sugar and beat for another minute – do not let it get too stiff. Add 15ml (1 tbls) of beaten egg whites to the contents of the saucepan and beat briskly till blended, then pour the contents of the saucepan into the egg whites at one go; fold in carefully.
5. Pour into the soufflé mould and cook for 25 minutes.

Soufflé au Noix Café

Serves 2. Preparation: 20 min Cooking: 22 min

Walnut-Coffee Soufflé

★★

○ **4 eggs**
○ **60ml (4 tbls) caster sugar**
○ **30ml (2 tbls) finely grated walnuts**
○ **15ml (1 tbls) instant coffee**

For the mould:
○ **15g (½ oz) butter**
○ **30ml (2 tbls) caster sugar**

1. Butter a soufflé dish 16cm (6 inches) in diameter, sprinkle in the sugar and shake out the excess.
2. Dissolve the coffee in 30ml (2 tbls) of warm water. Separate the eggs, putting the whites on one side. Sprinkle the sugar on the yolks in a small saucepan and beat briskly (preferably using an electric beater).
3. Set the oven to 205°C (400°F; gas mark 6). Place the saucepan in a *bain-marie* (or use a double saucepan). Stir the dissolved coffee into the egg yolks and sugar and beat (with an electric beater) until it has increased three times in volume. Then remove from heat and beat again until the mixture is nearly cold. Stir in the grated walnuts.
4. Whisk the egg whites until stiff. Add one-third to the saucepan, mix well, and then pour the contents of the saucepan over the rest of the beaten egg whites. Fold in gently, and turn the mixture into the soufflé mould. Cook in the oven for 22 minutes.
5. Remove from the oven and serve at once.

A few tips for cooking successful sweet soufflés. Do not open the oven door for at least 12 minutes; otherwise the soufflé may sink. Do not overcook a soufflé – this, too, will cause it to sink. Wait a few seconds after the soufflé has risen and turned golden and then take it out of the oven. But check first that it is cooked all through: a soufflé that is uncooked in the middle is a disaster as well! After the all-important first 12 minutes, it will be quite safe for you to open the oven door. At any time after this you can check if it is ready by inserting a skewer in the centre – it should come out quite clean and dry.

Soufflé à la Noix de Coco

Coconut Soufflé

Serves 3. Preparation: 15 min Cooking: 25 min

★★

○ **150ml (5 fl oz) unsweetened coconut milk**
○ **50g (2 oz) grated coconut**
○ **3 eggs**
○ **1 egg white**
○ **20g (¾ oz) butter**
○ **45ml (3 tbls) caster sugar**
○ **25g (1 oz) vanilla sugar**
○ **15g (½ oz) cornflour**
○ **15ml (1 tbls) white rum**

For the moulds:
○ **25g (1 oz) butter**
○ **30ml (2 tbls) caster sugar**

1. Set the oven to 205°C (400°F; gas mark 6). Put the coconut milk and cornflour in a saucepan with 15ml (1 tbls) of caster sugar and the vanilla sugar. Whisk briskly and place over a low heat, beating continuously with the whisk. When the mixture has thickened and forms peaks, remove from the heat. Fold the butter in with the whisk and leave to cool.
2. Meanwhile, butter the bottom and sides of 3 soufflé moulds or ramekins 11cm (4½ inches) in diameter and sprinkle in the sugar, tilting the moulds to line them evenly.
3. Separate the eggs and add the yolks, one by one, to the saucepan, when the contents have cooled, folding in with a whisk. Then add the grated coconut and rum; mix well.
4. Whisk the egg whites and the extra white until stiff, adding the remaining 30ml (2 tbls) of sugar while beating. Add 30ml (2 tbls) of the beaten egg whites to the contents of the saucepan and mix well. Pour all back on to the rest of the egg whites, and fold in carefully using a spatula to lift the mixture. Put the soufflé mixture into the moulds and cook in the oven for 25 minutes. Serve at once.

If you cannot get any unsweetened coconut milk, use instead 200ml (7 fl oz) of milk. Bring to the boil and add 50g (2 oz) of grated coconut. Leave to steep for 20 minutes then pour through a fine strainer, pressing the coconut to extract all the juice. This should give you about 150ml (5 fl oz) of coconut-flavoured milk.

Soufflés d'Abricots au Noyau

Liqueur and Apricot Soufflés

Serves 6. Preparation: 15 min Cooking: 15 min

★★★

○ **250g (9 oz) dried apricots**
○ **120g (4¾ oz) caster sugar**
○ **4 egg whites**
○ **3 small macaroons or 1 sponge finger cut into small squares**
○ **30ml (2 tbls) liqueur de Noyau (almond-flavoured liqueur)**
○ **50g (2 oz) butter**

1. Soak the apricots in cold water overnight.
2. The next day purée the apricots in a mill or blender – you should get about 400g (14 oz).
3. Preheat the oven to 205°C (400°F; gas mark 6). Butter 6 small ramekins or soufflé dishes 12cm (4¾ inches) in diameter and 5cm (2 inches) high. Sprinkle the bottom and sides of each with 5ml (1 tsp) of sugar.
4. Put the remaining sugar in a small saucepan with 30ml (2 tbls) of water. Cook over a low heat until it has formed a thick syrup. Check its readiness by dropping a little in cold water. It should fall to the bottom and form a small marble.
5. Whisk the egg whites until very stiff. Crumble the macaroons well using a pestle and mortar or a rolling pin. Moisten with the liqueur. When the syrup is ready, slowly pour on to the beaten egg whites, still beating to blend; then add the puréed apricots, folding in gently with a spatula. Add the moistened macaroons and mix again. Turn the soufflé mixture into the ramekins.
6. Cook in the oven for 15 minutes. Serve at once.

Charlotte Doigts de Fée au Caramel (p150) ▶

Crêpes Soufflées Citron-Framboises
Lemon Soufflé Pancakes with Raspberry Purée

Serves 6.
Preparation and cooking: 50 min
★★

For the batter:
- ○ 100g (4 oz) flour
- ○ 2 eggs
- ○ 50g (2 oz) melted butter
- ○ ¼ litre (9 fl oz) milk
- ○ 15ml (1 tbls) caster sugar

For the purée:
- ○ 400g (14 oz) raspberries
- ○ 100g (4 oz) icing sugar
- ○ juice of 1 lemon

For the soufflé:
- ○ 4 eggs
- ○ 2 egg whites
- ○ 90ml (6 tbls) caster sugar
- ○ 15ml (1 tbls) cornflour
- ○ grated peel of 3 lemons
- ○ 15ml (1 tbls) lemon juice

For cooking:
- ○ 30g (1¼ oz) butter

1. Prepare the batter and cook the pancakes following the recipe for a quick pancake batter on page 66. This quantity of batter should give you about 15 pancakes. Put the 12 nicest on one side to fill later with the lemon soufflé. Prepare the raspberry purée: mash the raspberries, using a fork. Stir in the lemon juice and sugar and mix together well until the sugar has dissolved. Keep in the refrigerator. The pancakes and raspberry purée may be prepared a few hours in advance.
2. 25 minutes before serving, prepare the soufflé. Set the oven to 230°C (450°F; gas mark 8). Separate the eggs. Put the yolks in a bowl and sprinkle in half the sugar; beat until the mixture turns pale and frothy. Then stir in the cornflour, lemon juice and grated peel. Beat for another 30 seconds. Whisk the egg whites until stiff, beat in the remaining sugar, and continue beating for another minute. Beat one-quarter of this meringue mixture into the egg yolks, then pour all back on to the rest of the beaten whites and fold in carefully with a spatula.
3. Lightly grease an ovenproof dish. Spread one pancake on a plate and place 2 large tablespoons of the soufflé in the centre. Fold the pancake over and place it in the dish. Repeat with the 11 remaining pancakes, arranging them tightly in the dish. Cook in the oven for 4 minutes, until the pancakes start to open as the soufflé swells up inside them. Bring to the table, and serve the raspberry purée separately.

Crêpes Fourrées Orange-Cassis
Orange Pancakes with Blackcurrant Sauce

Serves 8. Preparation and cooking: 1 hr
★★

For the batter:
- ○ 125g (5 oz) flour
- ○ 2 eggs
- ○ 1 egg yolk
- ○ ¼ litre (9 fl oz) milk
- ○ 15ml (1 tbls) caster sugar
- ○ 100g (4 oz) melted butter
- ○ grated peel of ½ orange

For the crème pâtissière:
- ○ 4 egg yolks
- ○ 125g (5 oz) sugar
- ○ 60g (2½ oz) flour
- ○ ½ litre (18 fl oz) warm milk
- ○ 30ml (2 tbls) orange liqueur
- ○ grated peel of 1 orange

For the sauce:
- ○ 400g (14 oz) blackcurrants
- ○ 100g (4 oz) caster sugar
- ○ 30ml (2 tbls) crème de cassis (blackcurrant liqueur)

1. You may prepare the blackcurrant sauce, pancakes and crème pâtissière a few hours in advance. Purée the blackcurrants to make the sauce, using a mill or blender. Stir in the sugar and the crème de cassis and mix well; chill in the refrigerator.
2. Prepare and cook the pancakes following the recipe for a quick pancake batter on page 66. This quantity of batter should give you about 18 pancakes. You will need 16 so choose the best looking.
3. Prepare the crème pâtissière following the recipe on page 8. Let it cool a little, then stir in the grated orange peel and the liqueur. Mix together well.
4. 10 minutes before serving, set the oven to 220°C (425°F; gas mark 7). Place a large spoonful of the orange-flavoured filling in the centre of each pancake, roll it up like a cigar and arrange in an ovenproof dish. Cook in the oven for 6 minutes.
5. Put 2 pancakes on each plate and pour a little of the blackcurrant sauce around them. Serve immediately.

Make this dessert really special by flaming the pancakes at the moment of serving. Heat 45ml (3 tbls) of orange liqueur and 30ml (2 tbls) of cognac or rum in a small saucepan. Bring hot to the table and set alight. Pour the flaming spirit over the pancakes. It will add a real touch of luxury!

Beignets de Pommes à la Cannelle
Apple Fritters with Cinnamon

*Serves 5-6. Preparation: 15 min
(2 hr before cooking) Cooking: 15 min*
★

- ○ 150g (6 oz) flour
- ○ 250ml (9 fl oz) beer
- ○ pinch salt
- ○ 4 medium-sized apples
- ○ juice of 1 lemon
- ○ 60ml (4 tbls) caster sugar
- ○ 15ml (1 tbls) powdered cinnamon
- ○ oil for deep frying

To serve:
- ○ icing sugar

1. Sift the flour into a bowl; make a well in the centre and add the salt. Slowly pour in the beer, working the flour into the liquid with a spatula from the centre out. When the batter is smooth, leave to stand for 2 hours in a warm place.
2. Put the lemon juice together with the same amount of water in a basin. Peel and core the apples, and cut into slices. Dip them in the lemon juice, then sprinkle on both sides with the mixed sugar and cinnamon. Put on one side.
3. Heat the oil in a deep fryer. When it is very hot, but not smoking, wipe the apples and dip each slice in the batter. Then fry in the oil. When golden, turn over and brown on the other side. Remove from the oil with a slotted spoon. Drain on kitchen paper and arrange on a serving dish. Sprinkle with icing sugar and keep in a warm oven while cooking the other fritters.

Beignets de Pommes au Sésame
Apple Fritters with Sesame Seeds

Serves 4. Preparation: 15 min Cooking: 15 min
★★★

- ○ 2 medium-sized apples
- ○ 150g (6 oz) flour
- ○ 1 egg
- ○ 250g (9 oz) sugar
- ○ 15ml (1 tbls) oil
- ○ 15ml (1 tbls) toasted sesame seeds
- ○ oil for deep frying

1. Beat the egg with 150ml (5 fl oz) of water; put the flour in a bowl and slowly pour in the egg and water mixture, stirring with a spatula until the batter is blended.
2. Grease a serving dish with 15ml (1 tbls) of oil. Put 1 litre (1¾ pints) of cold water in a basin together with a dozen ice cubes.
3. Heat the oil in a deep fryer: it should be at least 5cm (2 inches) high. Peel and core the apples, and cut each one into 8, making the pieces roughly square. Add to the batter.
4. Put 15ml (1 tbls) of oil, 100ml (3½ fl oz) of water and the sugar in a frying pan 24cm (9½ inches) in diameter and place over a medium heat until a golden syrup forms.
5. When the oil in the deep fryer is hot but not smoking, remove the apple pieces one by one from the batter with tongs and fry. They should be golden in about one minute. Remove from the oil with a slotted spoon and drain on kitchen paper.
6. Reduce the heat under the caramel as low as possible (place an asbestos sheet between the heat and the frying pan, if necessary), and throw in the sesame seeds, and then the fritters, four at a time. Use a spatula or slice to turn the fritters all over in the caramel; then plunge them in the iced water. Leave in the water for 6 to 8 seconds; remove and place in the serving dish.
7. When all the apple fritters are cooked, bring them immediately to the table. You will enjoy this Chinese delicacy!

Pavé de Marrons aux Noisettes

Marron and Hazelnut Brick

Serves 6. Preparation: 20 min
2 hr before serving
★★

○ **1 tin 400g (14 oz) unsweetened marron purée**
○ **200g (7 oz) softened butter**
○ **4 egg yolks**
○ **100g (4 oz) caster sugar**
○ **100g (4 oz) finely chopped hazelnuts**

1. Put the sugar with 60ml (4 tbls) water in a small saucepan and cook over a low heat. Check whether the syrup is ready by dipping the tip of a teaspoon into it. Remove it from the heat and grip between your fingers. Threads should pull away from the spoon when you lift your fingers.
2. Place the egg yolks into a bowl and beat well. When the syrup is ready, slowly pour it into the egg yolks, beating all the time until the mixture is nearly cold, light and frothy. Add the butter, a little at a time, beating more slowly now.
3. When the butter is well-blended, add the marron purée, spoonful by spoonful, mixing well; then the hazelnuts, and mix once more.
4. Wet a rectangular mould (an ice tray would do well) and shake out the excess water. Fill the mould, pressing the mixture down well and chill in the refrigerator for at least 2 hours before serving. To unmould the brick more easily, dip the mould in warm water for 20 seconds and turn out on to a serving dish.

You can make this dessert even richer by adding chopped crystallized fruit that has been soaked in rum, or raisins soaked in madeira. You can also add 100g (4 oz) of finely grated fondant chocolate. Use fresh chestnuts when they are in season, cooked in milk and puréed. Serve with an egg custard sauce flavoured with vanilla.

Délice de Noix

Walnut Cream Delight

Serves 8. Preparation and cooking: 30 min
4 hr before serving
★★

○ **300g (11 oz) shelled walnuts**
○ **⅓ litre (11 fl oz) milk**
○ **4 egg yolks**
○ **200g (7 oz) caster sugar**
○ **15ml (1 tbls) cornflour**
○ **250g (9 oz) softened butter**
○ **45ml (3 tbls) rum, crème de cacao or coffee liqueur**
○ **icing sugar**

For the sauce:
○ **200g (7 oz) fondant chocolate**
○ **150ml (5 fl oz) coffee**
○ **100ml (3½ fl oz) cream**
○ **25g (1 oz) butter**

1. Keep 9 shelled walnuts for decoration and coarsely chop the rest. Dilute the cornflour in the cold milk.
2. In a saucepan, beat the egg yolks with half the sugar until the mixture turns pale and frothy. Then sprinkle in the remaining sugar and slowly pour in the milk. Place the saucepan over a low heat and cook, stirring continuously until it starts to boil. Allow to boil for one minute, then remove from the heat and stand the saucepan in cold water. Stir until the mixture is lukewarm. Add the liqueur and the butter cut into pieces. Whisk well, then fold in the chopped walnuts.
3. Wet a mould or sandwich tin and fill with the mixture. Chill in the refrigerator for at least 4 hours.
4. 10 minutes before serving, break the chocolate in pieces and put in a saucepan with the coffee and cream. Cook slowly in a *bain-marie* until melted. Turn the gâteau out on to a serving dish. Sprinkle with icing sugar and decorate with the reserved walnuts. When the chocolate has melted, stir in the butter. Mix until smooth with a spatula.
5. Bring the dessert to the table and serve the warm chocolate sauce separately.

Wines: the Finishing Touch

Nowadays excellent quality table wines are within the reach of everyone, though you should expect to pay more for a good vintage wine from one of the famous vineyards, such as Nuits-St-Georges or Schloss Johannisberg Riesling. When buying French wine, look for the *Appellation Contrôlée* label, which is a guarantee of quality.

Below is a guide to the wines that go best with certain foods, but there are no absolute *rules* about which wine to serve with what food – in the end it is your palate that must decide. For a large, formal meal, certain wines traditionally follow each other through the menu and you could serve three or even four wines at one meal. In this case, it is usual to serve dry sherry with the soup, dry white wine with the fish course, claret or burgundy with the meat or game and a white dessert wine or medium sweet champagne with the dessert. For cheese, your guests would return to the claret or burgundy. Certain foods kill the flavour of wine and should therefore be avoided if you are planning to serve wine with the meal. Mint sauce, for example, or any salad with a strong vinaigrette dressing, will destroy the taste of the wine.

Remember that red wines are generally served *chambré*, or at room temperature, to bring out the flavour. Draw the cork at least three or four hours before you plan to drink the wine and let the bottle stand in the kitchen or a warm room. (Never be tempted into putting the bottle in hot water or in front of the fire – the flavour will be ruined.) The exception to the *chambré* rule is Beaujolais, which can be served cool – some people even serve it chilled. White or rosé wines are usually served chilled – the easiest way is to put them in the fridge an hour before serving, or plunge them into an ice bucket, if you have one. Champagne should also be served well chilled and is generally brought to the table in an ice bucket.

Wines to Serve with Food	
Oysters, shellfish	Chablis, dry Moselle, Champagne
Fried or grilled fish	Dry Graves, Moselle, Hock, Rosé, Blanc de Blanc
Fish with sauces	Riesling, Pouilly-Fuissé, Chablis
Veal, pork or chicken dishes (served simply)	Rosé, Riesling, a light red wine such as Beaujolais
Chicken or pork served with a rich sauce	Claret, Côte de Rhône, Médoc
Rich meat dishes, steaks, game	Red Burgundy, Rioja, Red Chianti
Lamb or duck	Claret, Beaujolais
Desserts and puddings	White Bordeaux, Sauternes, Entre Deux Mers
Cheese	Burgundy, Rioja, Cabernet Sauvignon